# AFTER THE WARS

Reconstruction in
Afghanistan, Indochina, Central America,
Southern Africa, and the Horn of Africa

# AFTER
# THE WARS

Anthony Lake
and contributors:

Selig S. Harrison
Nayan Chanda
Benjamin L. Crosby
Mark C. Chona and Jeffrey I. Herbst
Carol J. Lancaster

Series editors:
Valeriana Kallab
Richard E. Feinberg

**Transaction Publishers**
New Brunswick (USA) and Oxford (UK)

ISBN: 0-88738-392-0 (cloth)
ISBN: 0-88738-880-9 (paper)
Printed in the United States of America


Library of Congress **Cataloging-in-Publication Data**

Lake, Anthony.
  After the Wars: Reconstruction in Afghanistan, Indochina, Central America, Southern Africa, and the Horn of Africa.

(U.S.–Third World Policy Perspectives: No. 16)
  1. Economic conversion—Asia.  2. Economic assistance—Asia.  3. Economic conversion—Central America.  4. Economic assistance—Central America.  5. Economic conversion—Africa.  6. Economic assistance—Africa.  7. International cooperation.   I. Title.

HC415.D4L35 1990              338.9'1' 091724—dc20              90-19830
ISBN: 0-88738-392-0 (cloth)
ISBN: 0-88738-880-9 (paper)

*Photo Copyrights and Credits:*

Steve McCurry/Magnum, AFGHANISTAN (p. iv)
David Alan Harvey © National Geographic Society, CAMBODIA (p. xi)
L. Astroem/UNHCR Photo, NAMIBIA (p. 2)
Wendy Wallace/Panos Pictures, SUDAN (p. 30)
Steve Reymer © National Geographic Society, AFGHANISTAN (p. 43)
Wilbur E. Garrett © National Geographic Society, CAMBODIA (p. 75)
Steve Cagan, EL SALVADOR (p. 101)
Ron Giling/Panos Pictures, MOZAMBIQUE (p. 139)
Santha Faiia/CARE Photo, ETHIOPIA (p. 168)


*Design and Maps:*
John Kaljee

# AFTER THE WARS

# Acknowledgments

*After the Wars* Guest Editor and Project Director:
Anthony Lake

*Series Editors:*
Valeriana Kallab
Richard E. Feinberg

The Overseas Development Council gratefully acknowledges the support of the John D. and Catherine T. MacArthur Foundation for ODC's MacArthur Scholars in Residence, two of whom contributed to this study; a special grant toward the preparation of this study from the United States Institute of Peace; and the support of The Ford Foundation, The Rockefeller Foundation, and The William and Flora Hewlett Foundation for the Council's overall program, including the ODC U.S.-Third World Policy Perspectives series of which this book is part.

On behalf of the Council and all of the contributing authors, the editors wish to express thanks for valuable comments and criticisms on the various drafts to Larry Minear, Marianne A. Spiegel, Paul Kreisberg, Roy A. Stacy, Coralie Bryant, John W. Sewell, John P. Lewis, Vincent Ferraro, and the numerous other experts and policymakers who participated in a series of informal ODC workshops at which the draft chapters were discussed. Responsibility for the final content of the chapters of course rests with their authors.

Special thanks are also due to Cynthia R. Carlisle, particularly for her work as assistant project director on the *After the Wars* project during the manuscript development stage; to Jacqueline S. Edlund, ODC production editor; to Rosemarie Philips for assistance in the preparation of the summaries of recommendations and picture research; to Patrick W. Murphy for researching the data in the Overview chapter; to Catherine Bowen for library research assistance; to Danielle M. Currier for production assistance; and to Joycelyn V. Critchlow for processing the manuscript.

# Contents

AFTER THE WARS

# Overview
# and Summaries of
# Recommendations

# After the Wars— What *Kind* of Peace?

## Anthony Lake

For a decade and more, they have been the playing fields—the killing fields—of the Cold War: Afghanistan, where the British and the Russians played their own Great Game more than a century ago; Indochina; Central America; Southern Africa; and the Horn of the continent. Now, as the conclusions to the wars that have ravaged them may be in sight, it is time to be planning their reconstruction.

The roots of these wars were indigenous, deeply embedded in the history of these regions. In Afghanistan, the fighting was fundamentally the result of a conflict between modernizing and fundamentalist factions in Afghan society, complicated from the start by rivalries between the ruling Pushtuns and non-Pushtun ethnic groups (as well as among the Pushtuns themselves)—and then a war of independence against the Soviet invaders. The war in Cambodia has had more to do with the centuries-old hostility among the Vietnamese, Thai, and Khmer, and the still more ancient conflict between the Vietnamese and Chinese, than it has been about ideology and U.S.–Soviet rivalry. Similarly, whatever the policies of Washington and Moscow, ethnic conflicts in the Horn of Africa and the southern reaches of that continent (complicated by the legacy of colonialism and South African policies) would almost certainly have produced bloodshed. The point is perhaps less clear in Central America, but even there the civil wars in El Salvador and Nicaragua can be traced to fissures within those societies dating back to the nineteenth century.

Nonetheless, by superimposing their own ideological and strategic rivalries on these conflicts, the superpowers, and sometimes their allies, have done much to expand and intensify the bloodshed. Beyond the arguments as to whether or not the ideals and interests of one or the other of the two sides justified such policies, that fact is inarguable. For example, even after their military withdrawal from Afghanistan, the Soviets mounted 25-40 supply flights a day, conveying nearly $2 billion in military equipment by mid-October 1989—including MiG-21 jets and Scud-B missiles.[1]

The costs of the conflicts have been immense. To some degree, the bills have come due in the Soviet Union and Washington—not only in the dollars and rubles they spent on their favored factions and in the Soviet lives lost in Afghanistan, but also in the domestic political difficulties created by Afghanistan for the Soviet government and by Nicaragua for the American. But overwhelmingly, the price has been paid by the peoples of these areas, and especially by civilians. For in the Sudan and Ethiopia, in Angola and Afghanistan, and elsewhere—both through the nature of the conflicts and sometimes because of the conscious policies of the combatants—the lives of civilians have been sacrificed for military and political objectives to a degree seldom seen in the history of modern warfare. According to one estimate, 90 per cent of the casualties in the Third World wars of the last decade have been civilians.[2]

The statistics are appalling. As Selig Harrison notes in the first essay in this volume, "The devastation and disruption left by the Afghan war is staggering in its dimensions: nearly 1 million dead; 535,000 disabled veterans; 700,000 widows and orphans; one-third of all villages destroyed; two-thirds of all paved roads unusable; 26 types of deadly mines strewn over the countryside, largely unmapped; and a refugee exodus of 5.9 million people to Pakistan, Iran, and the West—including 1 million children born and brought up in camps who have never known their homeland." The toll has been terrible also in Indochina (some 70,000 dead in the current war in Cambodia); in the Horn of Africa (more than a million dead in Ethiopia and Sudan); in Central America (some 100,000 people killed since the late 1970s in El Salvador and Nicaragua); and in Southern Africa (where a United Nations estimate put the deaths in 1980–88 at some 1.5 million lives).[3]

One's eye tends to move quickly over such statistics, numbing as they are in their scope, and unpleasant as they are in their implication. But consider what the statistics mean for the people trapped in the reality they summarize, and the burdens now faced by the societies and governments of these regions, not only in finding peace but also in rebuilding their national lives after the wars. One of the many gloomy statistics about these challenges makes the point: In

## Table 1. Value of Arms Transfers to Governments,[a] Cumulative 1983–87 ($ millions, current)

| Recipient | Soviet Union | United States | Total[b] |
|---|---|---|---|
| Afghanistan | 4,000 | 0 | 4,070 |
| Angola | 5,800 | 0 | 6,350 |
| Cambodia | 1,100 | 0 | 1,110 |
| El Salvador | 0 | 310 | 340 |
| Ethiopia | 4,200 | 0 | 4,330 |
| Mozambique | 1,300 | 0 | 1,330 |
| Nicaragua | 1,800 | 0 | 1,970 |
| Somalia | 0 | 70 | 195 |
| Sudan | 0 | 110 | 350 |
| **Total** | 18,200 | 490 | 20,045 |

*Note:* Figures for Namibia are not included because they are still more fragmentary than the incomplete data available for the other areas.

[a]Does not include U.S. or Soviet arms transfers to rebel groups.
[b]Including other sources of arms.

Source: U.S. Arms Control and Disarmament Agency, *World Military Expenditures and Arms Transfers, 1988* (Washington, D.C.: U.S. Government Printing Office, 1989).

these five areas, more than 15 million people have left their homes to become internal or external refugees. Their resettlement will be a tremendous task for years to come. As Carol Lancaster writes of the Horn of Africa, the devastation includes not only the dead and displaced people, but also livestock lost, schools and clinics destroyed, and many missed years of economic production.[4]

Yet in all these areas, new hope is arising out of two of the startling changes in international politics during the past few years: the growing involvement of the United Nations in peace*making* as well as peace*keeping*, and more important, not only reduced hostility but also the evolution of new forms of diplomatic cooperation between the United States and Soviet Union in the Third World.

Too little popular attention has been drawn to the fact that in recent years the United Nations has become increasingly vigorous in promoting peace in Third World conflicts: in diplomatic efforts regarding the Afghanistan and Iran-Iraq conflicts, in sending elections-monitoring teams to Namibia and Nicaragua, and in managing a major aid program in Afghanistan. Most impressively, the United Nations is now contemplating not only the management

## Table 2.  The Human Costs of War

**REFUGEE STATUS, 1989**

| | Internally Displaced | Externally Displaced | Asylum for Refugees (of other countries) |
|---|---|---|---|
| Afghanistan | 2,000,000 | 5,934,500 | — |
| Angola | 638,000 - 1,178,000 | 438,000[a] | 26,500 |
| Cambodia | — | 334,166 | — |
| El Salvador | 147,000 - 397,000 | 61,100[a] | 500 |
| Ethiopia | 700,000 - 1,500,000 | 1,035,900 | 740,000 |
| Mozambique | — | 1,354,000[a] | 400 |
| Nicaragua | 390,000 | 89,700[a] | 7,400 |
| Somalia | 70,000 - 400,000 | 388,600[a] | 350,000[a] |
| Sudan | 2,000,000 - 3,200,000 | 694,300 | 694,300 |
| Total | 5,945,000 - 9,065,000 | 10,330,266 | 1,819,100 |

**APPROXIMATE WAR FATALITIES, 1980–1990**

| | Civilian Deaths | Military Deaths | Total Deaths |
|---|---|---|---|
| Afghanistan | 670,000 | 50,000 | 720,000 |
| Angola | 320,000 | 20,000 | 340,000 |
| Cambodia | 20,000 | 50,000 | 70,000 |
| El Salvador | 50,000 | 20,000 | 70,000 |
| Ethiopia | 500,000 | 40,000 | 540,000 |
| Mozambique | 370,000 | 50,000 | 420,000 |
| Nicaragua | 10,000 | 20,000 | 30,000 |
| Somalia | 5,000 | 5,000 | 10,000 |
| Sudan | 500,000 | 10,000 | 510,000 |
| Total | 2,445,000 | 265,000 | 2,710,000 |

*Note:* Figures for Namibia are not included because they are still more fragmentary than the incomplete data available for the other areas.

[a]*World Refugee Survey* indicates that the numbers reported to be externally displaced vary significantly in the available sources of information.

Source: Data on refugee status from *World Refugee Survey: 1989 in Review* (Washington, D.C.: U.S. Committee for Refugees, 1990); and data on war fatalities from Larry Minear, "Civil Strife and Humanitarian Aid: A Bruising Decade," in *World Refugee Survey, 1989* (Washington, D.C.: U.S. Committee for Refugees, 1990).

(rather than simply the monitoring) of elections in Cambodia, but also taking on partial responsibility for its governance and that of the Western Sahara if proposed peace plans are implemented. Some of the credit goes to the Secretary General and his staff. It is also due to a new period of cooperation within the Security Council, another happy result of the thaw in the Cold War.[5] (As this is written, continuing action by the Security Council in ordering and enforcing sanctions against Iraq after its invasion of Kuwait offers still more powerful evidence of a new era at the United Nations and the extraordinary U.S.–Soviet partnership there.)

Cooperation between the United States and Soviet Union on these issues goes beyond the corridors and council chambers of the United Nations. The Angolan-Cuban-South African Accords of 1988 that led to the peaceful independence of Namibia—and that offer some hope of peace in Angola—were brokered by American diplomats with the essential cooperation of the Soviets. In the late spring of 1990, Washington and Moscow made joint efforts to try to open the port of Massawa, the scene of heavy fighting between Ethiopian government and rebel forces, to humanitarian relief shipments. More impressive still, on July 18, 1990, when Secretary of State James A. Baker 3d announced an important shift in U.S. policy away from diplomatic support for the Cambodian coalition including the Khmer Rouge, he did so after consultations with and in the presence of the Soviet Foreign Minister.

And so, as the Cold War winds down, there are new openings, at least, for peace in areas of Third World conflict.

- In Afghanistan—the withdrawal of Soviet combat forces in 1989 and, during the first half of 1990, a narrowing of the differences between the United States and Moscow over the terms of a final settlement;

- In Central America—free elections and an end to the Civil War in Nicaragua, and talks, however sporadic, between the government and rebels in El Salvador;

- In Cambodia—the withdrawal of Vietnamese combat forces in 1989 and considerable diplomatic progress centered on an Australian plan for free elections under U.N. supervision (supported by the five permanent members of the Security Council);

- In Ethiopia, Sudan, and Somalia—much tougher diplomacy ahead, but preliminary talks, at least, among the Sudanese and Ethiopian parties; and

- In Southern Africa—the withdrawal of South African forces from Angola and the first stages of a planned Cuban military withdrawal, elections and independence in Namibia, diplomatic efforts to resolve the conflicts in Angola and Mozambique, and the historic openings within South Africa that followed the release from prison of Nelson Mandela.

In some areas, peace has come. In others, it may be in sight— although barely so in a few. The striking fact is that in all these regions, new possibilities for peace do exist.

## A Central Question

The hope that has come with the new pattern of U.S.–Soviet behavior in these regions is, however, tempered by a question: Once peace is achieved, will there be sighs of relief in Moscow, Washington, and other major capitals as attention shifts to other areas? Is the interest in resolving these regional disputes primarily driven by a desire to become disentangled? Or will the superpowers, including the Japanese and European economic superpowers, remain involved to help in the recovery process once peace is achieved? A more pessimistic version of the same questions would ask whether the American, Soviet, and other diplomats might at some point simply throw up their hands and walk away from efforts at achieving peace at all, in frustration at the intractability of the local rivalries that caused the conflicts in the first place.[6]

The answer to these questions is very much in doubt. The Cold War ended more because of domestic political pressures and economic necessity than by enlightened choice. The pragmatism of the Bush administration and the extraordinary ideological innovations and diplomatic initiatives of President Mikhail Gorbachev reflect not only personalities, but a fundamental shift in national priorities toward domestic economic concerns and those foreign areas of greatest economic relevance. To be sure, even without the Cold War, the Soviet Union has clear security interests in Afghanistan, as does the United States in the Caribbean. But the involvement of each side in places such as Cambodia, Ethiopia, and Mozambique was produced in much the largest measure by a reaction to the real or potential involvement of the other, and the ideological or strategic fears this engendered.

As one State Department official said in July 1990 to Thomas L. Friedman of the *New York Times*, "When you had a Stalinist in power in Moscow, everything in the world was dichotomized. Anyone who was with them was against us. Now when you have an ambiguous figure in Moscow, those who are with them may not be against us. They may be with us. And those who were with us, we may not want with us any more. For the first time in years, you really have to think about what your interests are."[7]

As Friedman's anonymous policymaker thinks about those interests, it is unlikely that he or she will conclude that they lie importantly in the future of, for example, Ethiopia or Afghanistan. To be sure, there are important reasons of self-interest for Washington to remain involved in the fate of these nations. A failure to help settle these conflicts, or their renewal in the future, could once again lead to the costly and destructive involvement of outsiders, including ourselves. An end to the Cold War does not presage an end to the rough and tumble of international relations as they have always been conducted. Continued or new conflicts there could also lead to needless drains on future aid programs, to deal with new, war-caused famines or refugee flows. It would be better to spend funds now on reconstruction than to spend them later on new relief programs. And in some of these areas, such as Angola and Mozambique, natural resources suggest economic interests to be served by American involvement. But compared to the stakes in the evolution of Eastern Europe, or the future of the Persian Gulf, these interests are merely "important." They are hardly likely to be judged "vital," as U.S. interests abroad are so often portrayed within and by our government.

On the Soviet side, the calculation of interests seems clear already. A process of financial withdrawal is under way in some regions even while diplomatic engagement remains. In Vietnam, reduced Soviet supplies of fertilizers and petroleum are hurting agricultural production. A report in *The Journal of Commerce* on July 10, 1990 stated that "Vietnam is being driven toward economic crisis" by such aid cuts.[8] Similar cuts have been reported in aid to Cambodia. Earlier, the Soviet Union reduced its aid, notably petroleum supplies, to the Sandinistas in Nicaragua. Thus there can be no easy expectation of lavish aid to former clients on either side in the future. Nor is such aid as central to the rebuilding of shattered economies as are the decisions made by present and future governments in the regions.

It would be a tragedy of very large proportions, however, if narrow calculations of interest by the larger powers were to lead to a loss of foreign concern about these lands once peace emerges. As the essays in this volume make clear, participation by the international community in the rebuilding of these nations will be crucial. And for the Soviet Union and United States, it is, quite simply, a question of moral obligation that these areas not become the detritus of the Cold War, left to fend for themselves as their former enemies and patrons turn their attention elsewhere. After so many billions of dollars and rubles were spent on these wars, should not some of the savings from peace in these areas be devoted to their repair? This is an issue of international responsibility that policymakers in Washington and Moscow should not evade.

This volume is written, therefore, in the hope that attention *now* to the particular problems of reconstruction in each of these regions will serve a useful purpose—that it will both help stimulate and assist local planners as they address the futures of their nations and encourage continued attention in the international community to their needs.

None of the authors pretends that these essays offer full plans for reconstruction. We hope, however, to suggest possible strategies and ways of thinking about recovery programs that might be of value—for example, in seeking to relate economic planning to the inevitable fragility of postwar political arrangements. We also write in the knowledge that a planning exercise is always about an uncertain future and must be modest in suggesting any certainties. We should be chastened by the recollection of one former official that in the immediate aftermath of World War II, there was a consensus among planners that Japan would never be able to attain sufficient export earnings to pay for the food imports it would need.[9]

# A New Marshall Plan?

Especially today, as a new Europe emerges in ways that even the most optimistic of planners in the late 1940s and 1950s would find exciting, there is a temptation for anyone concerned with the reconstruction of some war-torn area to call for a "new Marshall Plan." And it is a temptation few have resisted. The call goes forth, the old juices flow, and a few more votes may be gained in Congress for generous aid to, say, Central America. But while there is much to be learned from the success of American participation in European recovery after World War II, it is also instructive to consider the ways in which that experience does *not* apply with regard to most of the conflict-ridden areas of the Third World.

### Lessons That Do Apply Today . . .

The common image of the Marshall Plan is the one used by proponents of its replication in the Third World: massive amounts of American aid priming the local pumps of economic growth. In fact, this is the aspect of the Marshall Plan that least applies in the Third

World, as will be argued below. Nevertheless, important lessons can be derived from this earlier triumph in foreign assistance.

*Local planning* was emphasized in the effort of 1947. Certainly the Americans played an important role, but it was the Europeans who necessarily took the lead. In today's Third World, reconstruction efforts will fail if they are perceived as shaped rather than supported by outsiders.

Similarly, some argue that the framers of the Marshall Plan were willing to rely on *pragmatism* during the reconstruction period—to change plans when progress was not being made. By late 1946, piecemeal efforts at European reconstruction were failing, based as they were on a model of "balanced" recovery that would limit German growth. The new approach adopted in 1947 recognized that failure and shifted course to an emphasis on productivity (and thus the most productive areas, including Germany). There was also a concentration on the need to stabilize currencies, fix realistic exchange rates, and allow the freest possible flows of capital and goods. But the attention to productivity and getting the macroeconomic policies right did not bring with it a set of ideological straitjackets. As Michael J. Hogan points out, American Marshall Planners (who were themselves drawn from both government and the private sector), "tried to transform political problems into technical ones that were solvable."[10] The effort promoted neither socialism nor pure free enterprise.

Today, throughout the Third World, the ground for non-ideological approaches is expanding. As Richard Feinberg puts it, one of the benefits of the recent revolutions in Eastern Europe is that, "In many developing countries, the wide gap between 'progressives' and 'conservatives,' between statists and free marketeers, has precluded agreement on basic rules of the game. As 'progressives' now move toward a greater appreciation of the private sector, and 'conservatives' no longer fear that any activity of the state is but a prelude to a communist takeover, the prospects for more stable economic policies are brighter."[11]

It would be a shame if foreign advisers from Western governments or multilateral institutions were to attempt to impose a narrow, ideological version of the free market on Third World governments just when many of the latter are shaking loose from their own socialist orthodoxies.

The most important lesson the Marshall Plan has to offer today to those involved in planning reconstruction efforts in Third World areas of conflict today can be drawn from one of its greatest successes: the impetus it gave to *regional planning*, even regional integration. As Hogan emphasizes, the American focus on "fusing sepa-

rate economic sovereignties into an integrated market capped by
supranational institutions of economic planning and administration" helped overcome British objections to the postwar beginnings
of the Europe that is today emerging.[12]

Without such a regional perspective, most of the authors of the
essays in this volume argue, it is unlikely that enduring solutions
can be found to the economic and political problems of the individual
societies that they discuss. Mark Chona and Jeffrey Herbst emphasize the crucial role to be played by the Southern African Development Coordination Conference (SADCC) in planning the integration
of Namibian and Angolan transportation routes to the rest of the
region; in encouraging private enterprise; and in promoting innovative education and training programs in Angola, Mozambique, and
Namibia.[13] They argue that SADCC plays an important geopolitical
role in such activities—by helping to build the strength of economies that are today too easily dominated by that of South Africa and
could remain so even when South Africa is under majority rule.

Even where supranational planning institutions are unlikely
to be created, thinking in regional terms is important. As Carol
Lancaster writes of the Horn of Africa, it will be important in
designing transportation routes to bear in mind the desirability of
linking nations together in economic enterprises—and within
nations, to link regions that have achieved some form of autonomy,
as could be the case within Ethiopia and Sudan. Taking an even
longer view, Nayan Chanda argues that the regional stakes in the
reconstruction of Cambodia are truly historic: Without a strong
Khmer economy and society, the centuries-old rivalries between
Thailand and Vietnam, as well as China and Vietnam, will continue
to revolve around that unhappy country, with harsh consequences
for the region as a whole.

All of these features of the Marshall Plan—local planning and
initiative; pragmatic, relatively non-ideological approaches (as much
as any policy can be called non-ideological); an emphasis on productivity and sensible macroeconomic policies; and most of all, thinking
in regional terms—should commend themselves to the planners of
reconstruction after Third World wars. But while the lessons are
instructive, there are even larger *differences* between the challenge
of European recovery then and the plight of war-torn Third World
nations today.

### . . . and Lessons That Don't Apply

*Different Societies, Different Times.* Postwar Europe faced a far
less daunting road to recovery than the areas considered in this vol-

ume. Despite the devastation of World War II, European nations had the remnants of a strong physical infrastructure on which to build; the political and entrepreneurial traditions that would provide both growth and stability; cultural, ties that would facilitate regional cooperation; and economic, cultural, and intellectual links to almost every other region of the world.

Consider the contrast with the societies described in this volume: in addition to the economic problems faced by all Third World nations, these nations will inherit a legacy of bitterness from what are, in every case, savage civil wars. They have been flooded with weapons of all kinds that will enormously increase crime, violence, and long-term threats to political stability. And they cannot count on the continuing, sympathetic attention of the rest of the world once peace is achieved. It is an unhappy fact that television images of suffering in the far corners of the Third World do not invoke the same feelings in our own society that the plight of Europe did four and one half decades ago. This is not simply a matter of political, cultural, and ethnic ties. In charitable appeals and news reports, Americans have repeatedly seen the faces of the victims of starvation, wars, and natural disasters in the Third World. Most Americans still respond with sympathy, but they have also become accustomed to the images of suffering. In the late 1940s, a newly devastated Europe seemed an anomaly to be corrected, not a seemingly endless tragedy to be ameliorated.

*Making as Well as Maintaining Peace.* Europe (except Greece) was at peace at the time of the Marshall Plan. In most of the areas considered in this study, however, "peace" itself is an ambiguous concept. In some regions within these nations torn by civil war, a kind of peace may already have arrived, in advance of formal, nationwide settlements. It also may well be that after agreement at the peace table, certain areas of one or more of these nations may continue to experience significant violence.

The Marshall Plan was designed to reinforce an established peace. In contrast, the authors of these essays were asked to consider how the plans, promises, and processes of reconstruction could *contribute to the achievement* of peace. In the most general sense, attention to the prospects for recovery could encourage combatants to consider the benefits of settling their differences. A specific suggestion also flows from this line of thought. Foreign donors could use the promise of specific reconstruction assistance as an inducement to compromise at a crucial point in negotiations.

Some of the authors suggest reconstruction efforts that could begin even before a full "peace" has arrived. In Afghanistan, as

Selig Harrison notes, the U.N. coordinator, Prince Sadruddin Aga Khan, has promoted a policy of "humanitarian encirclement" under which reconstruction efforts can begin in relatively peaceful areas, or "zones of tranquility." Such efforts, Prince Sadruddin has said, offer "the best prospect of achieving the degree of socio-economic stability from which a political settlement . . . may yet emerge."[14] In effect, reconstruction has begun in relatively secure areas of Mozambique. Mark Chona and Jeffrey Herbst suggest reconstruction assistance—primarily through private voluntary agencies and in forms that cannot be diverted to military purposes—in certain areas of Angola as well. And while the security situation in Cambodia still precludes such an approach in most of the countryside, Nayan Chanda suggests that, "While waiting for a peace settlement, training of technical and administrative cadres, too, can begin in the [refugee] camps and inside the country."[15]

Any aid programs attempted in the course of a civil war, and especially training programs aimed at the future administration of a country, are certain to encounter political difficulties. Do the programs benefit one side more than another? Does the selection of the cadres to be trained imply a form of political endorsement? The answers will require exquisite political judgment. But the benefits of "peaceful encirclement" would seem to outweigh the diplomatic difficulties one might encounter, and the difficulties themselves can be diminished both by channeling such aid through multilateral or private volutary agencies and by attempting to be as inclusive as possible in the programs. Indeed, involving personnel from various factions to a conflict in the same training programs might open up channels of communication and contribute in some measure to the prospects for peace.

*International Funding.* A still more obvious dissimilarity between the Marshall Plan and reconstruction programs in these five regions is that, even under optimistic scenarios, the funds for new "Marshall Plans" in the Third World simply do not seem to be available. As Hogan notes, the American financial contribution in the late 1940s has been overstated; the Europeans themselves accounted for 80–90 per cent of the capital formation during the first two years of the Marshall Plan.[16] Nevertheless, the U.S. contribution was immense, amounting to some $110 billion in 1989 dollars. It is cruel to suggest to potential recipients today that aid on anything like that scale might be forthcoming. Neither foreign nor domestic priorities among potential donors will allow it. In the United States, the twin pillars of domestic support for programs such as the Marshall Plan—the fear of communism on which an administration could play in approaching the Congress, and the sense of relative American economic power that made a policy of true generosity seem affordable to American citizens—have crumbled. It is certainly true that the United States could, and indeed should, manage far larger and more foresighted aid programs than it now contemplates, but the fact remains that the political basis for such programs is far different from what it was in the late 1940s.

In both Western Europe and especially Japan, the public mood is more optimistic and the outlook better for generous new foreign assistance. While European concerns are focused largely on the needs and opportunities in Central and Eastern Europe, Tokyo's view is ever more global. Japanese planners are strongly interested in the futures of Indochina and Afghanistan, and Japanese involvement in the affairs of Southern Africa and Latin America is growing. But as the current crisis in the Persian Gulf demonstrates, there are numerous and competing claims on Japanese financial contributions abroad. And the Soviet Union, despite its involvement in the conflicts now winding, one hopes, to a close, is an unlikely source of significant aid. In July 1989, the Supreme Soviet assumed responsibility for aid appropriations—and according to Sergei I. Shatalov,

> In Moscow, as in Washington, the aid budget has become a target of the deficit-cutting effort. Many parliamentarians echo the growing 'aid fatigue' of their constituencies. It is hard to defend an aid budget which is 20 times as large as the health budget at a time when the Soviet infant mortality rate is among the highest in Europe and rising.[17]

It is ominous in this regard that the Russian President, Boris Yeltsin, is using an attack on the foreign aid budget in his appeals to populist Russian sentiment.

*Absorptive Capacity.* The capacity of these regions of the Third World to absorb such large quantities of aid is, in any case, sadly limited. Not only in postwar Europe, but in Japan and South Korea as well, the primary requirement was simply foreign capital. While investment is sorely needed in today's Third World cases, as Benjamin Crosby emphasizes in his essay on Central America, the challenge in most of the areas covered in this volume is far more complicated. Poor physical infrastructure, a lack of trained personnel stemming from a legacy of colonial neglect (as in Angola, Mozambique, and Namibia), and the massive loss of trained personnel due to the losses of war and the flight of refugees (as was the case most tragically in Cambodia) severely limit the ability of local governments and other institutions to make good use of the levels of foreign assistance that could begin to meet the needs of their socieites. For example, Chanda reports criticism of a U.N. Development Programme report calling for expenditures in Cambodia of $450 million over two to three years as being "beyond the absorptive capacity of the country."[18] Chona and Herbst suggest that the capacity of the SADCC nations in this regard is already strained.

With available international resources limited and the local capacity to use them also constrained, it is vital that careful attention be paid to priorities in reconstruction planning—that in every case there be a clear strategy rather than merely a summons to every possible task. As a number of private commissions and study groups have shown, when the needs are so great, it is tempting to call for a massive effort to resolve all the problems at once. But an effort to do everything quickly will inevitably lead to waste, confusion, and disillusion.

*Starting Over.* Shaping such strategies begins with the recognition that in many cases the issue is really one of *construction* rather than *reconstruction*, of building rather than rebuilding—politically as well as economically. After World War II, the challenge in Europe was to re-create, for the most part, the democratic and economic institutions that had at some point in the past served those nations well, even if the physical damage called for new factories, bridges, and the like. (In Japan, the task was largely one of economic reconstruction and political construction.)

Today, it may be hubristic to try to design new economic or political patterns in Third World nations, and even to try to apply new technologies, when there were important cultural and environmental reasons for the old. But in many of the areas we consider here, there may be no real choice. Politically, few have traditions that are inclusive enough to offer much hope of enduring reconciliation after "peace" is achieved. In Angola and Mozambique, for example, Chona and Herbst point out that the prewar past to which one could turn is that of Portuguese colonial rule—and one would hardly wish to re-create the habits of political behavior of that period. Economically, also, a colonial past—and often also the period immediately following independence—offers little on which to build. In Cambodia, as Naranhkiri Tith has argued, the statist economic policies pursued by Prince Norodom Sihanouk, after independence from the French had been achieved and before the civil war, contributed to underdevelopment. "It would be a pity," he wrote, "if after all the suffering incurred by the Cambodian people . . . since 1970, the Cambodian society would be rebuilt to the same one prevailing before (then)."[19]

When it comes to repairing the physical rather than the institutional destruction of the wars, the arguments for reconstruction rather than construction become stronger. But Nayan Chanda cites a number of sectors in Cambodia in which outmoded machinery, often of Soviet manufacture, should simply be scrapped and replaced. Crosby makes the same point about Nicaragua, noting that reliance on the Soviets for spare parts may not make sense in the light of current political realities.

## Strategies of Construction

Whether the need is for construction or for reconstruction, there are a number of common, central strands in the strategies suggested by the authors of these essays.

1. **Enhancing Absorptive Capacity.** In almost every case, the authors' strategies begin with *training programs*, initiated in advance of peace settlements, so that as little time and effort as possible is wasted once full-scale reconstruction begins. Some suggest ways to attract back home the personnel whose technical as well as managerial skills are needed in the country from which they had fled. In Cambodia, for example, in 1985 there were only two civil engineers in the whole Department of Hydrology. Chanda suggests offering exiled Cambodians with such skills contractual jobs under U.N. or other international agencies. This might help address the "reluctance of prospective returnees to endure the hardships of Cambodia after years of relatively comfortable life in the West."[20] Selig Harrison recommends special training programs in the refugee camps "in areas directly related to the use of aid inputs and equipment. Younger refugees should be emphasized in these programs to stop the continuing flow of talented Afghan youth to Europe and the West." A similar problem—and opportunity—exists with regard to the skilled refugees who left Nicaragua, El Salvador, and Ethiopia.

It will also be necessary to repair and create functioning *transportation systems* early in the recovery process. According to Chanda, a U.N. team sent to Cambodia to assess the facilities available to the U.N. personnel who might be sent there as part of a peacekeeping team came away shocked by the lack of such basic facilities.

The training of technical and management personnel for the private as well as public sectors, in conjunction with the repair of physical infrastructure, is necessary as an early step to recovery— not only because it enhances the capacity of these nations to absorb aid, but also because it attracts the investment that can help make economic progress self-sustaining. As Chona and Herbst emphasize, this also requires macroeconomic and legal policies to encourage new investment. For political as well as economic reasons, it will be important to combine measures to encourage foreign investment with provisions for the gradual expansion of local ownership.

**2. Refugee Resettlement.** The most pressing of human needs is the provision of social services—in both urban and rural areas—to the millions of homeless and hungry victims of the fighting, and the creation of conditions that permit, even encourage, the return of millions of internal as well as external refugees not only to their homes, but to productive lives in the countries they fled. Indeed, they will not return unless the countryside from which they fled is being restored. A difficult policy question lies in determining the point at which progress in reconstruction allows the subsidies at refugee camps to be reduced in order to sever dependency on relief programs that are no longer necessary.[21]

**3. Rural Reconstruction.** Since the refugee problem is internal as well as external, putting huge pressures on the urban services of these nations, all of the authors emphasize the importance of progress in rural areas, so that the relief phase can turn quickly to one of recovery. Most immediately, this means massive efforts at *mine removal*, especially in Angola, Cambodia, and Afghanistan. Foreign expertise will be vital. Since the Soviets and the Chinese have been major sources of these mines, there is every reason to press both Moscow and Beijing for the provision of such experts and for direct participation (where acceptable) in the mine-clearing operations.

Rural reconstruction also means a concentration of resources on *agricultural development and rural public health*. For Cambodia, Chanda suggests that the first effort should be in public health—in defeating an enervating malaria epidemic. For Afghanistan, Harrison believes that priority should be assigned to agriculture. The authors agree that since so many farmers are starting up from nothing at all, there should be an emphasis on *small scale technology*: on basic tools in Sudan and Ethiopia; on draft animals in Afghanistan, the Horn, and Cambodia. This is not to suggest, however, that larger-scale rural efforts will not be needed—in building roads for farmers' access to markets, in schools and communications networks, in repairing irrigation systems, and in the provision of farm machinery and other agricultural inputs where appropriate.

No author suggests state-run agricultural enterprises. But governments must play an active part in *land reform policies* that encourage an agricultural resurgence; in *extension activities*; in preserving the *environment* against short-sighted, destructive agricultural practices; and in encouraging the provision of *credit* to farmers. Here the issue is not only the availability of such credit, but how it is provided. Each country is likely to require a very different technique in getting the right amount of credit into the right hands in an equitable manner and in ways that encourage frugality and productivity. The importance of such credit is illustrated by the fact that in Afghanistan, if farmers do not see real hope down other roads and lack the funds to pursue them, they will all too easily turn to narcotics production. Another issue of particular importance is the *role of women in rural areas*. For example, in Afghanistan, where women traditionally have been excluded from much of the life of the nation, the future of women's education is a subject of deep controversy. Harrison suggests, as an initial step, focusing training programs on the fields of public health and agricultural extension that are most relevant to women's traditional activities: vegetable and fruit cultivation, and raising small livestock and poultry breeding. This could then lead to broader vocational training programs. In Cambodia, the need to incorporate women more fully into productive rural life is especially acute because the war has left the ratio of men to women in the general population at about 44 to 56.

**4. Political Implications**. Mention the deleterious political effects of a sound economic policy at a meeting of economic planners, and watch their fingers drum impatiently on the table. Talk about the economic details at a conference of diplomats working on a political settlement, and watch their eyes glaze. Tell a politician about the importance of painful economic sacrifice now for the sake of economic health later, and watch his or her eyes widen in alarm. But economists, diplomats, and political leaders must think in each others' terms, or reconstruction efforts will fail. Such thinking is necessary from the very beginning of the reconstruction process—as the diplomats fashion the political arrangements that could end the fighting, and as the economists plan the first stages of economic recovery. Will the former arrange peace by stitching together a political coalition so fragile that it cannot make the tough economic choices necessary for economic health? Will the latter recommend economic policies so draconian as to blow apart any compromise political arrangement? Will the modalities of a settlement encourage reconstruction? For example, Nayan Chanda suggests that one of the advantages of a strong United Nations role in a Cambodian peace process would be the encouragement this would provide for a continued role in the reconstruction process by the United Nations and its members. (In addition, some of the expense of an interim U.N. presence in Cambodia, likely to run in the billions of dollars, would go to rebuilding the badly damaged physical infrastructure in that nation.)

Difficult questions of economic priority must be answered in a political as well as economic context. In deciding whether to devote limited resources to investment in future productivity or in immediate social welfare, there must be careful consideration of the implications of the choice for the survival of a new coalition government, and thus, for peace.[22] Indeed, there may be more at stake than the prospects of a newly elected democratic regime. The institutions of democracy itself may depend on such economic choices. For it is almost certain that in all these societies, instability of all kinds will be a pervasive condition in the immediate postwar period. There will be continuing local rivalries and the settling of scores, with plenty of weapons available for such enterprises. Economic policies that exacerbate the instability may destroy the peace completely. Chanda points out the likelihood that the Khmer Rouge will oppose even a democratically elected government in Cambodia—and that economic policies that are not immediately seen to be promoting social justice will offer the rebels a popular cause. While supporting productivity as a central goal, Harrison suggests that, "Decisions concerning the allocation of reconstruction aid should not be made solely on the basis of whether a given area promises to be productive. Focusing myopically on economic criteria could aggravate ethnic, regional and tribal tensions. . ."[23] Or as Chona and Herbst argue regarding Southern Africa, "without progress toward economic justice, as well as economic growth, the mass of the people will soon perceive little stake in new democratic institutions. Colonialism left no legacy of democratic habits on which to draw, such as those in much of Eastern Europe. A new democracy cannot be built from the top down. It must be based on economic and social progress in society as a whole."[24]

This is a central point also in the essay on Central America. While agreeing that some degree of structural adjustment is needed in the economies of El Salvador and Nicaragua, Benjamin Crosby argues that neither the Christiani nor the Chamorro government has anything close to the amount of political capital required to carry out the kind of programs often insisted upon by the International Monetary Fund and World Bank as a condition for their loans. To attempt such programs would not only destroy those governments, but threaten the fragile institutions of democracy. Instead, Crosby supports a strategy of spending on agricultural and other infrastructure projects that will produce employment and enhance the demand for goods, thus helping to create a stable political as well as economic climate conducive to necessary investment in the economies of the two nations.

Certainly, concern for the survival of fragile democratic institutions and achievement of the political stability needed to preserve a newly won peace suggests that the World Bank and International Monetary Fund should be particularly careful about the policies upon which they insist as a condition of their participation in the reconstruction of all these war-torn regions. World Bank programs designed to cushion the impact on the poor of such anti-inflationary measures as an end to food subsidies are helpful. But there is a need also to examine the structural adjustment programs themselves more closely from this perspective—both in their shape and in the rapidity with which they expect painful reforms to be undertaken. As a paper prepared in the Bank's Strategic Planning and Review Department puts it:

> Relatively little attention has been given to introducing changes in the design of adjustment programs. Appropriate design changes can help mitigate the possible adverse impact on the poor, for example, by slowing price adjustments in cases where short-term supply elasticities are low and uncertain, or by targeting subsidies effectively to the poor. They can also help to foster pro-poor growth through generating demand for labor, for example, by removing biases that favor capital-intensive production or other impediments to employment-growth, or reallocating public expenditures towards programs that enable the poor to take advantage of the emerging economic opportunites.[25]

Where is it more important for the international financial institutions to pursue such politically aware and pro-poor policies than in nations just emerging from shattering wars?

National governments could also be encouraged to adopt policies that foster economic justice—for example, through:

(a) progressive taxation policies designed to leave more money in the hands of the poor, thus bringing more of the fruits of production to them;

(b) through measures to limit the ability of large economic enterprises to export their capital while encouraging the growth of small private enterprises that are less tempted to let their capital fly; and

(c) through credit policies targeted for small farmers and entrepreneurs.

# The Response of the International Community

Despite the limits on the absorptive capacity of these governments, there will be an enormous need for foreign assistance, bilateral as well as multilateral. It is impossible accurately to state the full dimensions of the requirement for all five regions, since no reliable survey has been made for a number of them. But it is safe to say that the needs of these societies—and even the ability of their governments to make use of foreign help—are very likely to outstrip the assistance available. This should not be so. As many have argued, enhanced foreign aid programs would take up only a very small percentage of expected "peace dividends" in the United States and other donor nations.[26] Moreover, foreign assistance funds now ticketed for military assistance could well be reprogrammed for reconstruction aid. It is ironic that in a period of some hope for peace in conflicted areas of the Third World and democratic progress in Eastern Europe, the FY1991 U.S. foreign assistance budget request remains heavily weighted toward security rather than development assistance— with 59 per cent for the former.[27] While security assistance programs managed by the Agency for International Development can be used for development purposes, the political and military goals such programs are meant to serve tend to focus them in a few nations and on short term objectives.

Nonetheless, at a time of economic difficulty—and with the maw of the savings and loan bailout ever widening—it would be very optimistic to believe that a significant increase in foreign aid will attract much support in Washington. This makes it all the more important for the United States to pursue diplomatic policies that can contribute as much as possible to early reconciliation and the beginnings of reconstruction.

While there has been startling progress in Soviet and American diplomacy toward these regions, more could be done. In his essay on Afghanistan, Selig Harrison supports policies of so-called "negative symmetry," under which both Moscow and Washington would cease the supply of military assistance to their clients in Afghanistan. It should now be clear that a military victory by the resistance groups is unlikely in the foreseeable future. And it makes no sense to continue to force large Soviet expenditures in Afghanistan while our allies in Europe consider large-scale aid programs to bail out the Soviet economy. Similarly, Chona and Herbst call for an end to arms supplies by Washington and Moscow for all the combatants in Angola; this would, of course, necessarily depend on the willingness of the Cubans and South Africans to observe such a ban. (There are reports of continuing assistance to UNITA from private South African sources.)

The limits on foreign assistance funds also should encourage thought about how to use the funds that are available in the most innovative and effective ways possible. To the degree feasible, multilateral agencies should be emphasized in the provision of reconstruction assistance—although not at the cost of a reduction in overall levels of assistance. By definition, societies emerging from internal military conflict are highly charged politically. Assistance from multilateral agencies is much less likely to run afoul of lingering resentments than is aid from the former patrons of one side or another. (Indeed, Selig Harrison recommends that *all* U.S. aid to Afghanistan be shifted to the United Nations program there.) For some of the same reasons, and because they are often the most cost-effective means available, private voluntary organizations should be used as a vehicle for local reconstruction projects whenever possible. The work of indigenous non-governmental organizations should be emphasized; they are especially effective in encouraging and drawing upon local initiative and effort.

## An International Fund for Reconstruction

In addition to existing programs, the time is ripe for the creation of a supplementary international fund for the reconstruction of war-torn areas in the Third World. A start along these lines already has been made. In 1989, the reports on foreign assistance legislation of both the Senate Foreign Relations Committee and the House Committee on Foreign Affairs included language encouraging the executive branch to give greater priority to efforts to meet human needs in post-conflict settings. The Foreign Affairs Committee stated its belief that "it is in keeping with U.S. humanitarian traditions and national interests for this nation to participate fully in international efforts to help build a brighter future for war-weary people in such settings."[28]

The attention of the committees to this issue flowed in part from a proposal by Interfaith Action for Economic Justice that the U.S. government create a $100-million Global Post-Conflict Reconstruction Fund. The Fund would be additional to already programmed levels of development assistance to the Third World areas emerging from conflicts, and most of these U.S. funds would be provided through multilateral channels. This was an idea worthy of attention. Now, it could and should be extended—both in its funding and in its structure. Why not combine the concept with the proposal made by Secretary of State James Baker 3d in early July 1990 that the twenty-four Western nations (the G-24) that have been coordinating their aid to Eastern Europe also establish an aid program for Central America? Why not create through this G-24 an International Fund for Reconstruction not only for Central America, but for the other conflict-ridden areas of the Third World as well? The fund could support reconstruction not only in the areas of conflict considered in these essays, where there has been significant superpower involvement, but also some day in nations such as Sri Lanka, Liberia, Lebanon, and Peru.

Alternatively, such a fund could be established through the U.N. Development Programme or the World Bank (thus restoring the "R" to IBRD). But the modalities of the fund's management should be established only after consultations not only among the donors but also with potential recipients—as Secretary Baker has suggested with regard to his Central American proposal. Certainly, the world does not lack for international funds and the attendant international bureaucracy. But the disadvantages of adding another instrument could be ameliorated if a fund such as this were used to solicit contributions and then to disburse them primarily through existing multilateral or special regional channels (such as the Japanese-proposed International Committee on the Reconstruction of Cambodia). Preferably, it would also be managed through an existing office in one of these multilateral institutions.

The advantages of such an International Fund for Reconstruction would be numerous:

- An initial proposal and contribution by the United States (or by any other government) could be used as a lever for further funding.
- A leadership role for Japan in the fund would provide Tokyo with another useful vehicle for expressing its increasingly positive global outlook.
- Once established, the fund could be used to encourage local planning for reconstruction at an earlier stage than now generally seems to be the case.
- The fund could bring international experts on the various regions together to share information and ideas on reconstruction planning.
- The fund could be used to solicit multi-year pledges—not only from governments but also from funds such as the OPEC Fund for International Development.

- Pledges for the fund could be solicited *now*, before peace is achieved, while the plight of these countries is still in the headlines from time to time and they have the best chance of receiving the sympathetic attention that they deserve in donor legislatures.

- Most important, the fund could be used to promote innovative answers to some of the particular problems of these nations. The fund could, for example, support special training programs not only for technical and management personnel to be employed by understaffed new governments, but also for private entrepreneurs (as recently carried out in England for Chinese businessmen by a U.N.-funded management development consortium.)[29] It could finance special investment insurance and loan guarantee programs to encourage investors in areas where they would normally fear to tread. It could assist governments in writing foreign investment regulations that would protect their own sovereignty while encouraging foreign involvement; and contribute to regional currency stabilization funds. It could support model projects assisting the reintegration of refugees into rural areas. The fund could also promote multiparty democracy through training programs and elections support. And it could encourage attention to the environment in reconstruction planning and through specific projects. It is not surprising that nations buffeted by war have paid little attention to environmental issues. It will take a special effort to make sure that such attention is paid at the time it matters most: when new economic recovery programs are being designed.

## Conditions for Assistance

This raises the question of conditionality. Should such a fund, and reconstruction assistance generally, not only be targeted in its programs on the reduction of poverty, respect for the environment and the promotion of democracy, but also be conditioned on certain areas of performance? Such conditions might include, for example, continued respect for whatever accords brought peace, the observance of human rights, and perhaps certain standards with regard to corruption. (In societies where there has been so little money and so little development, the likelihood of high levels of corruption when aid flows increase cannot be disregarded.) Most of the authors of the essays in this volume believe that donors should indeed link their aid to certain standards of performance and the adoption of effective domestic policies. As Chona and Herbst write: "This would not represent an effort to dictate future policies so much as a recognition that it would be a waste of precious resources to try to underwrite in the future the failed policies of the past."[30]

The European Commission, in consultation with the G-24 member states, has developed five criteria to determine eligibility for G-24 assistance in Eastern Europe. As summarized by Secretary Baker, these are: "adherence to the rule of law; respect for human rights; introduction of multi-party systems; the holding of free and fair elections; and the development of market-oriented economies."[31] Certainly, it would be wrong to hold Afghanistan or Angola to the same standards as Poland when it comes to conducting Western-style elections, for example, or the rapid development of a market-oriented economic system. The political traditions, rates of literacy, and limited development of an entrepreneurial sector in most Third World nations—even those not torn by war—make such an approach unfair and damaging. Nor should there be a narrow definition of a "market-oriented economic system"; it would be a mistake to force particular forms of capitalism on societies that should be developing their own solutions to the problems of equity and growth. And to deny desperately needed aid to the poor of a Third World nation because of the human rights abuses of its governing elite is simply wrong. But it would be condescending to suggest that these criteria need not be applied in reasonable ways to areas beyond Europe. And as public opinion polls confirm, the American public and its elected representatives are unlikely to be generous in supporting aid programs to nations pursuing policies that seem either self-defeating or philosophically repugnant.

## The Soviet Role

Few of the programs of international assistance thus far mentioned would provide the Soviet Union a role commensurate with the responsibilities for reconstruction assistance that it has accrued through involvement in the conflicts. For reasons suggested above, it is unlikely to contribute much in the way of development assistance. But the Soviet Union must be urged to make whatever contributions it is able to make. There is no reason why Moscow should be held to a lesser standard of international responsibility than Washington. Indeed, Soviet leadership in enhancing the role of the United Nations and the new Soviet policies that have promoted the prospects for an end to Third World conflicts have earned the Soviets the right to be taken seriously with regard to international efforts at reconstruction.

The Soviets should certainly provide what development assistance they can. And what better places, for symbolic as well as practical purposes, than these areas for launching the sorts of cooperative U.S.–Soviet development projects suggested by W. Donald Bowles and Elena B. Arefieva in the Overseas Development Council's recent *Tripartite Projects: Proposals for Joint U.S.–U.S.S.R Cooperation with Developing Countries?* An additional modest, immediate contribution by the Soviets might be to provide the international financial institutions with detailed information on their loans and economic transactions in these areas as an aid to reconstruction planning.

### Debt Relief

Perhaps the most substantial Soviet contribution to healing the wounds of these wars could be in leading, with the United States, an effort to gain promises of official debt relief from all bilateral creditors for these nations—once they achieve peaceful settlements of

## Table 3.  Debt Burdens
### (percentages and $ millions)

|  | Debt Service (TDS/XGS)[a] | Interest (INT/XGS)[b] | Long-Term Debt *($ millions)* |
| --- | --- | --- | --- |
| Afghanistan | 8.9% | 7.3% | 1,482[1] |
| Angola | 17.3 | 4.8 | 1,283[1] |
| Cambodia | 31.3 | 28.1 | 564[1] |
| El Salvador | 19.5 | 7.8 | 1,685[2] |
| Ethiopia | 38.6 | 13.5 | 2,790[2] |
| Mozambique | 21.6 | 9.2 | 4,039[2] |
| Nicaragua | 51.7 | 25.0 | 6,744[2] |
| Somalia | 5.7 | 4.3 | 1,754[2] |
| Sudan | 17.0 | 12.4 | 8,418 |
| Average | 23.5 | 12.5 | 3,195 |

[a] Ratio of debt service to exports of goods and services.
[b] Ratio of interest payments to exports of goods and services.

Sources: (1) The 1987 figures for the Non-Debt Reporting System Countries are from Central Intelligence Agency, *World Factbook 1989, 1990* (Washington, D.C.: U.S. Government Printing Office, 1989 and 1990); and *Financing and External Debt of Developing Countries: 1988 Survey* (Paris: OECD, 1989). (2) 1988 figures are from *World Debt Tables 1989–1990* (Washington, D.C.: World Bank, 1990).

their conflicts. (See also pp. 186–87 of Chapter 5, by Carol Lancaster, for an interesting suggestion on how the debts to multilateral institutions could be managed in a way that would reinforce peace accords.) The promise of debt relief could thus provide some inducement for diplomatic compromise. And fulfillment of the promises could be of tremendous importance to their reconstruction (see Table 3).

The debt-financing burden for Mozambique, for example, has been huge: in 1987, external debt servicing was $533 million.[32] In many cases, the Soviet share of the debt owed is very large. In some, Moscow has written off or rescheduled some of it—about one-third in the cases of Ethiopia and Angola.[33] It should now—with others if possible, or alone if necessary—offer to forgive them all once peace has arrived.

Peace *will* come, sooner in some regions and, in all likelihood, later in others. The question is: What kind of peace will it be? A peace of reconstruction or a peace of lost new hopes? A peace built with the help of other, larger nations, or one threatened by new great power rivalries? A peace based in the free institutions that economic progress can buttress, or a peace enforced by the military power of a government struggling to survive a time of economic distress?

The answers will be decided in much the greatest measure by the actions of local leaders and peoples. But the international community, too, will help determine them. The response of the United States, and others, should not be based only on a narrow definition of national interests. For the answer we give will also help to define our place in the histories of these peoples and offer judgment on our contemporary character.

## Notes

[1] Barnett R. Rubin, "The Fragmentation of Afghanistan," *Foreign Affairs,* (Winter 1989–90), pages 162–63.

[2] See Larry Minear, "Civil Strife and Humanitarian Aid: A Bruising Decade," *World Refugee Survey-1989 in Review* (Washington, D.C.: U.S. Committee for World Refugees, 1990). Pages 14–15 provide a description of these policies, including calculated policies of interference with international humanitarian relief efforts within Sudan and by the insurgents in Mozambique. Similar actions by combatants in Angola and Ethiopia have been all too frequent.

[3] Minear, "Civil Strife," op. cit., p. 14. The U.N. study is cited by Mark Chona and Jeffrey Herbst in Chapter of this volume, p. 142.

[4] Lancaster, Chapter 5 of this volume, p. 180.

[5] See George Sherry, *The United Nations Reborn: Conflict Control in the Post-Cold War World, Critical Issues 1990.2* (New York: Council on Foreign Relations, 1990) for a summary of these events; see also Paul Lewis, "The United Nations Comes of Age, Causing Some Anxiety," *The New York Times,* August 5, 1990, page E3.

[6] An irony in current American foreign policy debates is that many of those analysts who once saw regional conflicts primarily as the result of Soviet indirect aggression

are now among those most likely inclined to point out the likely persistence of those conflicts despite the lack of Soviet involvement, while many of those who have discounted the importance of the Soviet role now look for the biggest peace dividends from the new policies in Moscow.

[7] Thomas L. Friedman, "Us vs. Them Is No Longer Enough," *The New York Times*, July 22, 1990, p.2E.

[8] "Loss of Soviet Aid Worries Vietnam," *The Journal of Commerce*, July 10, 1990.

[9] Ambassador Edwin Martin, "Preparing to Cope with World Economic Stress," in *Adapting American Diplomacy to the Demands of the 1990's* (Washington, D.C.: The American Academy of Diplomacy, 1990), p. 100.

[10] Michael J. Hogan, *The Marshall Plan: America, Britain, and the Reconstruction of Western Europe, 1947–1952* (New York: Cambridge University Press, 1987), p. 19.

[11] Richard E. Feinberg, "Eastern Europe and the Third World" (Unpublished manuscript, Overseas Development Council, Washington, D.C, April 1990), p. 5.

[12] Hogan, *Marshall Plan* op. cit., p. 22–23.

[13] Chona and Herbst, Chapter 4 of this volume, pp. 160–61.

[14] Harrison, Chapter 1 of this volume, pp. 31-32, p. 63.

[15] Chanda, Chapter 2 of this volume, p. 26, p. 92.

[16] Hogan, *Marshall Plan* op. cit., p. 431, citing Charles Maier, "The Two Postwar Eras and the Conditions for Stability in Twentieth-Century Western Europe," *The American Historical Review*, Vol. 86 (April 1981), pp. 34–42.

[17] Sergei I. Shatalov, "Soviet Assistance to Africa: The New Realities," *CSIS Africa Notes*, No.112, May 22, 1990.

[18] Chanda, Chapter 2 of this volume, p. 99.

[19] Narankhiri Tith, "An Agenda for the Economic and Social Reconstruction of Cambodia," paper submitted at the International Symposium on Cambodia, California State University, Long Beach, February 17–19, 1989; draft dated April 7, 1989, pp. 6 and 10–14.

[20] Chanda, Chapter 2 of this volume, p. 68.

[21] See Harrison, Chapter 1 of this volume, on the current U.N. program to address this problem in Afghanistan.

[22] A central issue, for example, in *Reconstruction and Development in Nigeria: Proceedings of a National Conference,* edited by A.A. Ayida and H.M.A. Onitiri (Oxford: Oxford University Press, 1971).

[23] Harrison, Chapter 1 of this volume, p. 68.

[24] Chona and Herbst, Chapter 4 of this volume, p. 151.

[25] "How Adjustment Programs Can Help The Poor: The Experience in the World Bank," Strategic Planning and Review Department (Washington, D.C.: World Bank, November 9, 1989), p. 21.

[26] See, for example, "The Peace Dividend and Foreign Aid," Policy Consensus Report (Washington, D.C.: Johns Hopkins Foreign Policy Institute, August 1990), signed by David Abshire, John Brademas, Harold Brown, Alexander Haig, Barbara Jordan, Melvin Laird, Charles McC. Mathias, Edmund Muskie, Charles Percy, Peter Peterson, Elliot L. Richardson, Alice Rivlin, James Schlesinger, Cyrus Vance, and Paul Volker.

[27] See "U.S. Foreign Aid in a Changing World," ODC *Policy Focus* No.2 (Washington, D.C.: Overseas Development Council, 1990).

[28] Committee on Foreign Affairs, U.S. House of Representatives, *International Cooperation Act of 1989* (Report 101–23, Part 2), p. 2. See also Committee on Foreign Relations, U.S. Senate, *International Security and Development Cooperation Act of 1989* (Report 101–80), p. 19.

[29] See "Chinese Look West for Change," *Financial Times*, June 8, 1990.

[30] Chona and Herbst, Chapter 4 of this volume, p. 151.

[31] "Assistance and Reform: Eastern Europe and Central America," Remarks by Secretary of State Baker at the G–24 Ministerial Meeting, Palais D'Egremont, Brussels, Belgium, July 4, 1990.

[32] U.S. Agency for International Development figures, USAID, Washington, D.C.

[33] Shatalov, "Soviet Assistance to Africa," op. cit., p. 3.

# Summaries of Chapter Recommendations

## 1. Afghanistan
## (Selig S. Harrison)

The War in Afghanistan has not only left behind a legacy of physical destruction but also torn apart the fragile prewar social and political fabric. Soviet intervention and the resulting influx of economic and military aid from other external powers to contending Afghan resistance groups has intensified tribal, ethnic, and religious divisions. Thus the central reconstruction issue is how to carry out effective economic programs in ways that help rather than hinder what is likely to be a protracted process of social and political stabilization.

Prior to the war, agriculture provided one-half of Afghanistan's national income and four-fifths of its export earnings. But the war has crippled the country economically by removing vast areas from cultivation and reducing the level of production in those areas where farming has continued. Today, 25 per cent of the population—twice the prewar average—is concentrated in cities and towns. If not reversed, this artificial level of urbanization will greatly impede a balanced development effort.

The primary economic reconstruction challenge therefore lies in regenerating agricultural productivity while pursuing the broader, related task of restoring the overall social and economic infrastructure in the countryside in order to draw people back to rural areas.

The reconstruction effort is complicated by the fact that fighting continues in some areas, and a stable political settlement is unlikely to emerge for some time. Reconstruction can and should begin, however, in the many areas where fighting has stopped.

Focusing on what he calls "zones of tranquility," U.N. Coordinator Sadruddin Aga Khan has initiated such a selectively targeted program, in which aid "of a strictly non-political and neutral character" is administered on a multilateral basis by the United Nations. Support for this approach would help to promote political accommodation while also advancing economic reconstruction.

The United States and the international community can integrate their efforts in support of Afghanistan's social, political, and economic reconstruction by adhering to the following guidelines:

- Donors should use multilateral channels, especially the United Nations, for providing aid to Afghanistan. Resources now being allocated to existing, politically motivated bilateral aid programs, which reinforce social and political divisions, should gradually be transferred to the U.N. program as bilateral programs are phased out.
- Donors should increase their overall contributions to the reconstruction effort. The U.S. contribution, which cumulatively totaled $45.5 million in 1990, should be increased to $250 million annually for the next five years, incorporating existing bilateral aid contributions, which totaled $114.23 million in 1990. Since the Soviet contribution to date of $600 million is entirely in the form of commodities, not foreign exchange, it should also be increased.
- In implementing the U.N. effort, initial emphasis should be on resettling refugees rather than on long-term development projects.
- Priority should be given to increasing food production. In particular, irrigation systems should be repaired; livestock replaced; and seeds, fertilizers, and other agricultural inputs provided.
- Mine-clearance programs should be stepped up, especially in areas where fighting has been heavy.
- Training programs should be emphasized to help Afghanistan make effective use of aid and to stop the flow of talented youth to other countries.
- While most initial reconstruction efforts should be community-based, the basic infrastructure of bridges and roads should also be rebuilt and eventually extended.
- Projects with potential for export earnings—in particular mining and industrial projects and fruit and vegetable exports—should be encouraged.

- Special efforts should be made to prevent new opium cultivation by offering incentives such as irrigation canals and tubewells to get farmers to commit to cultivating other crops besides poppies.
- Since Pakistani drug lords are primarily responsible for organizing and marketing Afghan opium production, the international community, especially the United States, should press for meaningful Pakistani narcotics control efforts.
- All bilateral donors, including the U.S.S.R. and the United States, should write off Afghanistan's debts.
- Given the built-in tensions in Afghan society, reconstruction aid should not be allocated solely on the basis of economic criteria but should seek to promote development with equity to avoid aggravating economic disparities between contending social groups.
- Since the establishment of a broad-based interim government is necessary to facilitate a coordinated reconstruction effort, the superpowers should seek to promote such a government. Their first step should be a simultaneous termination of their military aid to create a climate conducive to political compromise. The task of promoting intra-Afghan dialogue leading to a new government should be entrusted to the United Nations Secretary General.
- Pending the establishment of a new government, the Kabul regime should be consulted concerning the location of U.N. reconstruction activities to establish stable "zones of tranquility" in areas where an uneasy peace now exists between resistance field commanders and pro-government local militias.

## 2. Indochina
## (Nayan Chanda)

The war in Cambodia has had more to do with centuries-old ethnic hostilities and paranoia than with an ideological struggle between superpowers. There is no promise yet of an end to the fighting, although the parties have accepted a United Nations peace plan. But even after the fighting is stopped, enduring peace can be achieved only if there is economic development. The task of reconstruction in Indochina is not just to heal the wounds of war but also to promote economic development in Cambodia, Vietnam, and Laos in a way that redresses serious economic disparities and reduces possible sources of future conflict.

Once peace is achieved, Cambodia will need to address two urgent priorities:

• Restoring normal life after wartime conditions, which includes repatriating refugees from Thailand, removing land mines, and fighting a burgeoning malaria epidemic; and

• Rapidly raising the living standards of a growing population to at least the pre–1970 level.

Cambodia's ability to carry out such reconstruction efforts successfully will be significantly affected by *how* the conflict is ended. A settlement in which the United Nations organizes elections and provides a peacekeeping force offers the best prospects to improve Cambodia's absorptive capacity. Just to do its work, the United Nations would need to undertake extensive infrastructural work. Rail and road systems, radio communications, navigational and air traffic control facilities, domestic and international communications systems, and ports and inland waterways will all require rehabilitation.

A U.N. presence would also help alleviate the country's acute need for skilled personnel. But additional measures would be needed to address the dramatic shortage of qualified workers and managers. One solution would be to encourage Cambodians living abroad—professionals as well as skilled workers—to return home. Another possibility would be for U.N. volunteer agencies to send personnel to Cambodia on long-term assignment. Finally, refugee camps could provide technical training while the refugees wait for a peace settlement; people so trained could in turn train others when they return home.

Over the long term, Cambodia should carefully plan and manage the use of its valuable natural resources, world-famous temples, and favorable geographic position for its developmental purposes. Its development strategy should have six major emphases: rice, rubber, fisheries, forestry, tourism, and trade.

When peace comes to Cambodia, the principal sources of funding will necessarily have to be Japan, the United States, Western Europe, and the international financial institutions. Although there is disagreement about how much external assistance Cambodia can absorb, it is clear that Cambodia will need a sustained flow of development aid for at least a decade. Coordinating this aid and preventing duplicated effort, competition, and waste will be a major task. An International Committee on the Reconstruction of Cambodia should be formed to provide a framework for cooperation.

A massive inflow of foreign aid poses the danger of an economic gap developing between the cities and the countryside, and between a newly emerging merchant class and the vast majority of poor Cambodians. Foreign aid therefore should be used to create jobs and generate income in the countryside. In addition, the unfavorable people/land ratio in Vietnam is likely to encourage emigration to Cambodia, creating potentially explosive ethnic conflicts. Long-term stability and peace thus require regional development plans that ensure balanced growth in both Vietnam and Cambodia.

## 3. Central America
   (Benjamin L. Crosby)

In the 1980s, civil war and economic crisis plagued both El Salvador and Nicaragua and stymied economic progress throughout the region. The United States and the U.S.S.R. together spent some $12 billion in the region between 1981 and 1990—bringing neither victory nor peace nor economic development.

The 1987 Arias Peace Plan has brought significant diplomatic progress. But after the devastation of the fighting, the achievement of growth and development will be difficult.

Successful implementation of economic reforms requires governments with the political will and the capacity to manage those reforms, the resources to carry them out, and sufficient support from non-governmental organizations. The governments of Nicaragua and El Salvador have none of these attributes. They are based on fragile political coalitions; the leaders have only marginal control of their governments; resources are limited; and powerful interests are waiting for the governments to stumble. The guiding principle for reconstruction in the years ahead must be the pursuit of policies that build political support and create confidence—even if this means exercising caution in applying necessary economic reforms.

On the political side, the region's governments—particularly El Salvador and Nicaragua—face three daunting tasks:

- They must end the conflicts, military and political, that are continuing to drain their economic resources;
- They must find a way to consolidate their power in order to execute the difficult political and economic tasks ahead; and
- They must strengthen their infant democratic institutions— even if this requires them to make important concessions of power.

On the economic side, the governments need to:

- Stabilize national finances by slowing inflation, reducing subsidies, tax reform, aligning foreign exchange, and other efforts to restore financial balance.
- Rehabilitate economic infrastructure to reverse the decline in productivity and provide work and income for the large pools of unemployed people.
- Stimulate demand through job creation programs, particularly for resource-poor small farmers (who will invest their earnings

in their farm production), and through the provision of credit to the agricultural sector.

- Take measures to attract the return of flight capital and stimulate new investment. Temporary tax incentives, expeditious bureaucatic treatment of licenses and permits, tax amnesty, and attractive interest rates can create a climate conducive to local, expatriate, and foreign investment. Working with businessmen's associations in exile might be particularly fruitful.

- Pursue joint approaches to reinvigorating the Central American Common Market (CACM) to promote common interests in the areas of debt reduction, investment promotion, the development of trade links, and the establishment of communications, energy, and transportation infrastructure.

Because of the geopolitical nature of much of the Central American conflict, bilateral donors have an obligation to play a major role in the reconstruction process. Their role as well as that of the international financial institutions (IFIs) should be one of support for the reconstruction process in both the political and economic spheres:

- El Salvador and Nicaragua are for some time likely to have major balance-of-payments deficits (projected at some $400 million and $600 million, respectively, for 1990-91); these gaps are of an order that only the major bilateral donors and the IFIs can help alleviate.

- The major donors and IFIs should help Nicaragua and El Salvador achieve more favorable trade status and help broker agreements with other sources of financing.

- The donors also need to be patient and politically sensitive. They should not suspend financing when, for managerial or political reasons, objectives are not achieved in the time limits prescribed.

## 4. Southern Africa
## (Mark C. Chona and Jeffrey I. Herbst)

Angola, Mozambique, and Namibia all face daunting challenges in their attempts to reconstruct their economies, political systems, and societies after the devastating wars they have experienced. Yet none of the three countries would wish to "reconstruct" the colonial structures in place before the wars. The real challenge facing them is one of political, economic, and social *construction*. Although the three countries are all poor, there are significant differences among them, making it impractical for the international community to adopt a uniform policy toward them.

The primary focus of recovery efforts should be on Angola and Mozambique. The needs of Namibia are great, but given its small population (one-ninth that of Angola and one-fifteenth that of Mozambique) and the international attention received by the long struggle of the South West Africa People's Organization (SWAPO), Africa's newest nation probably will not face a dearth of foreign aid—at least not from European donors—in the foreseeable future.

Although peace in all three countries will in the end depend largely on decisions made by the Namibians, Mozambicans, and Angolans themselves, the international community must take all possible steps to help end the war and to promote peace and political reconciliation. There should be an immediate end to external military support (overt and covert) for the warring factions in Angola, while humanitarian relief and economic assistance are increased to areas that are relatively secure. In the cases of all three nations, most forms of economic aid should be tied to continued observance of political settlements and basic human rights.

The needs of more than one million internal and external refugees must be met—now, in their camps, and, as soon as possible, by assisting their return to their homes through resettlement and rural reconstruction programs.

Addressing the critical shortage of skilled personnel must be given first priority by governments and in aid programs. Strengthening agriculture and rebuilding infrastructure systems should also be high priorities.

In all three countries, there should be emphasis immediately on developing and implementing economic policies that are free of state control and consequent economic distortions that have plagued these economies and others in Africa in the past. Instead of pursuing discredited, statist policies, governments in the region should concentrate on what they can do best to meet their citizens' needs: construct and rehabilitate infrastructure, provide education and other necessary social services, and foster an environment that supports private-sector growth.

The Southern African Development Coordination Conference (SADCC) can play an important role in the development of a regional system of transportation, in promoting a vibrant private sector throughout the area, and in encouraging training programs that can enhance the limited absorptive capacity of its members.

## 5. The Horn of Africa
## (Carol J. Lancaster)

The Horn of Africa is one of the poorest and most conflict-ridden regions of the world. Sudan, Ethiopia, and Somalia each have long-standing internal conflicts in which one or more disaffected groups are demanding greater political participation, autonomy, or independence. The governments of these countries in turn frequently support the challenges of the rebels in neighboring countries; and the superpowers as well as other countries in the region periodically provide support and arms to one side or another.

At the moment, neither military nor political solutions to any of the conflicts in the Horn appear imminent. But some of the elements encouraging continued fighting appear to be changing, and the possibility of political settlements cannot be ruled out.

As long as active fighting continues, beginning the critical tasks of reconstruction is a waste of effort and resources. What should be undertaken immediately, however, are special programs to enable large numbers of young people from the war-torn areas to obtain an education outside their countries. Whatever the shape of the final peace arrangement, educated nationals will be needed to manage economies and governments and to promote development.

Once peace arrives, relief for refugees and displaced persons must continue until they can return to their homes and feed themselves. As they return, they will need not only food but also seeds, agricultural and household implements, and in some cases livestock to enable them to reestablish themselves as farmers. In addition to this ongoing relief effort, two other immediate priorities to help move people from dependence to subsistence production should be the reopening of schools and the reestablishment of health and veterinary services.

Moving people beyond subsistence to recovery and development will require additional measures:

- Once governments begin economic recovery and reform programs, creditors—including governments and international financial institutions—should consider generous debt relief measures. Sudan's debt, since it is so large, will present particularly difficult challenges, especially to the International Monetary Fund.

- Infrastructure must be rebuilt and expanded with an eye to regional security as well as national and regional economic integration.

- In both Sudan and Ethiopia, macroeconomic policies will need to be reformed. Reforms must address the problems of overvalued exchange rates; overextended bureaucracies; wage, price, and credit controls; and agricultural and trade policies. However, adjustment in these countries may be particularly difficult in the aftermath of war.

- Reversing the decline in agricultural productivity is another major challenge. This will require improved agricultural extension services and an effective agricultural research system. More productive agricultural systems must also be environmentally sound.

- Policies are needed to slow and reverse the environmental degradation resulting from the pressure of humans and livestock on fragile land. Most urgent is the deforestation resulting from the search for wood by poor peasants. New sources of energy must be made available and conservation measures introduced.

Ethiopia and Sudan will each need substantial amounts of external assistance—perhaps several billion dollars a year for at least a decade—to meet the challenge of reconstruction and development effectively. This is much more than the aid provided in 1988, for example, when each country received approximately $1 billion, excluding emergency relief.

Relief assistance and aid for priority activities such as reopening schools and health facilities is best channeled through local private voluntary organizations. Foreign private voluntary agencies that have been active throughout the war-torn regions should also be used to channel reconstruction assistance.

Aid for major development projects and in support of economic reform, on the other hand, should be provided on a government-to-government basis or through the international financial institutions and should be conditioned on the maintenance of peace as well as effective economic management.

# AFTER THE WARS

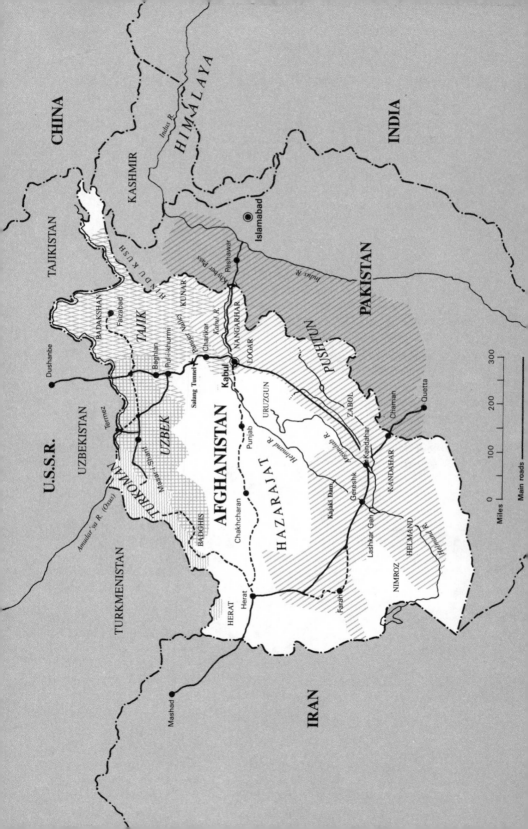

# Chapter 1

# Afghanistan

Selig S. Harrison

Even before the twin disasters of civil war and the Soviet occupation, Afghanistan was one of the poorest, least developed countries of the world. Economic impoverishment and political paralysis went hand in hand. Weak central governments, trapped in a web of endemic social conflicts, lacked the authority to mobilize resources and promote development. It was only at the turn of the century that Amir Abdur Rahman began to lay the first, frail foundations of an Afghan state, and it was only the rapid influx of superpower economic and military aid during the Cold War decades that gave Kabul the wherewithal to carry out significant development programs. By a tragic quirk of history, just when a national elite was emerging and the process of development was gaining momentum, eleven years of warfare intervened.

The devastation and disruption left by the Afghan war is staggering in its dimensions: nearly 1 million dead; 535,000 disabled veterans; 700,000 widows and orphans; one-third of all villages destroyed; two-thirds of all paved roads unusable; 26 types of deadly mines strewn over the countryside, largely unmapped; and a refugee exodus of 5.9 million people to Pakistan, Iran, and the West—including 1 million children born and brought up in camps who have never known their homeland. Out of 11.7 million people left in the country, some 25 percent—or twice the prewar average—are now in cities and towns. More than 2 million "internal refugees" have fled to urban centers for protection. With much of the countryside depopulated, agricultural production has plummeted. Annual production of wheat, the country's staple food crop, has declined by 54 per cent.[1]

Apart from the war's legacy of physical destruction and human suffering, the fragile Afghan social fabric has been torn apart, greatly complicating the task of economic reconstruction. More than 100,000 of the country's educated, technically trained elite have resettled abroad, while new, younger leaders schooled primarily in the arts of war are searching for ways to assert their authority in localities throughout the country, often in competition with the traditional leaders of tribal and ethnic groups. Land conflicts are emerging between refugees who left their land and new claimants to ownership who have been farming this abandoned land for a decade. Returning refugees are bringing with them new attitudes and a thirst for the modern life observed during their exile. The camps in Pakistan and Iran provided assured subsistence rations and, to a modest extent, access to health care and primary schools. In Afghanistan, by contrast, the returning refugees will have to struggle for survival and will find that even the limited health care and educational infrastructure of the prewar years has been largely swept away.

Perhaps the most debilitating legacy of the war has been the intensification of pre-existing divisions among rival political forces and contending tribal, ethnic, and religious groups. External powers seeking to advance their own perceived interests have consciously or inadvertently reinforced these divisions. The massive influx of some $5 billion in external military and economic aid has fostered an intense competition for the spoils among the Afghan recipients and has given them a common stake in perpetuating the conflict.

Pakistan, in particular, wary of irredentist Afghan claims on its territory, has played a divisive role, actively seeking to build up a narrowly based group of favored Afghan clients while working to undermine elements regarded as potentially hostile. Iran, Saudi Arabia, China, and a variety of Islamic fundamentalist factions in the Persian Gulf and the Middle East have also lavished aid on preferred Afghan groups. Above all, continuing U.S. and Soviet aid involvement has prolonged and deepened internecine conflict not only between the Communist regime and its opponents but also between warring resistance factions.

Against this background, it is clear that the social, political, and economic aspects of reconstruction in Afghanistan are inseparable challenges. The central issues involved in planning the reconstruction agenda concern how to carry out effective economic programs in ways that help rather than hinder what is likely to be a tortuous, protracted, and incremental process of political stabilization.

This essay will begin by examining the historical roots of Afghanistan's deep-seated historical divisions. It will then analyze the impact of the war on these divisions, focusing on the aid policies of the major foreign powers involved both before and after the completion of the Soviet combat force withdrawal in February 1988. In discussing the nature of the reconstruction problems that lie ahead, it will consider the debate already emerging over priorities. Finally, it will present detailed recommendations for meeting the multifaceted reconstruction challenge through modified bilateral and multilateral policies.

## A Divided Society: The Historical Setting

The Afghan state that Ahmad Shah Durrani founded in 1747 was unabashedly Pushtun in its ethnic character. It was a Pushtun tribal confederacy established for the express purpose of uniting the Pushtuns and defending their interests and integrity in the face of non-Pushtun rivals. To be sure, the peoples encompassed by the new state, even at its inception, were not entirely homogeneous ethnically, but Afghanistan had an overwhelming Pushtun majority in the early nineteenth century. This Pushtun-dominated Afghanistan stretched eastward as far as the Indus River into what is now Pakistan until 1823, when the British Raj annexed 40,000 square miles of Pushtun territory between the Indus and Khyber Pass containing half of the Pushtun population. It was adding insult to injury when the British imposed the Durand Line in 1893 to formalize their conquest and then proceeded to hand over their ill-gotten territorial gains to the new government of Pakistan in 1947.

By dividing the Pushtuns as they did, the British bequeathed an explosive irredentist issue that has perennially dominated the rhetoric of Pushtun-dominated Afghan regimes and has poisoned the relations between Afghanistan and Pakistan. At various times, Zahir Shah's monarchy, Mohammad Daoud's republic, and post–1978 Communist governments in Kabul have all challenged Pakistan's right to rule over its Pushtun areas, alternately espousing the goal of an autonomous Pushtun state to be created within Pakistan, an independent "Pushtunistan" to be carved out of Pakistan, or a "Greater Afghanistan" directly incorporating the lost territories.

The loss of the trans-Durand territories left a truncated Afghanistan with a complex ethnic makeup. As the "Great Game" between Britain and Russia progressed during the nineteenth century, the British encouraged successive Afghan rulers to push the borders of Afghanistan northward to the Oxus River. The British objective was to make Afghanistan a buffer state, and the Pushtun rulers in Kabul had imperialist ambitions of their own. Vast areas populated by Hazaras, Tajiks, Uzbeks, and other non-Pushtun ethnic groups were gradually subjugated by Kabul after bitter struggles. But in the new, multi-ethnic Afghanistan that resulted, the Pushtuns have been increasingly unable to assert the position of unchallengeable dominance to which they feel entitled as the "true" Afghans.

The ethnic composition of Afghanistan was hotly disputed prior to the war. Pushtuns generally claim that they were in a majority ranging from 55 to 65 per cent. Non-Pushtuns challenge this claim, however, with one estimate giving the Pushtuns only 39 per cent, the Tajiks 26 per cent, the Hazaras and Uzbeks 10 per cent each, and the remaining 15 per cent scattered among smaller groups. In any case, the relative position of the Tajiks has grown dramatically inside the country during the war, since 85 per cent of the 2.5 million refugees in Pakistan are Pushtuns.

A rough estimate of the Pushtun population in 1990 would be 20 million, consisting of some 10.99 million native to the Pakistan side of the Durand Line and 9 million—more than 2 million of whom are refugees—native to Afghanistan. Depending on how one categorizes them, there are from two to three dozen Pushtun tribes, and these are generally classified into four major groupings: the Durranis and the Ghilzais, both centered in Afghanistan; the so-called "independent" tribes straddling the Durand Line; and several tribes, including the Khattaks and Bannuchis, centered in the North-West Frontier Province of Pakistan. Several hundred thousand Pushtuns who have long been settled in urban or semi-urban areas have become de-tribalized, but the tribal hold is still powerful throughout Pushtun society.

Until King Zahir Shah was overthrown in 1973 by his jealous cousin, Mohammed Daoud, the Durrani Pushtun monarchy had provided the sole focus of political legitimacy and authority in Afghanistan for more than three centuries. The Afghan state was just barely a state, and separate ethnic and tribal communities paid obeisance to Kabul only as long as it accorded them substantial autonomy. In the 1920s, for example, King Amanullah was forced to abdicate in the face of opposition to his pioneering efforts to promote centrally directed modernization.

The number of politicized Afghans who wanted to create a centralized state before the war was minuscule in relation to the total population. During the period of political upheaval culminating in the establishment of the Daoud regime in 1973 and Communist rule in 1978, this politicized elite consisted of three distinct groups: Western-oriented intellectuals, who made up the largest segment; Soviet-oriented Communist factions; and Islamic fundamentalist elements with Moslem Brotherhood links in the Persian Gulf and the Middle East. None of these groups had substantial, independent organizational networks in the countryside. They were all equally dependent on alliances with the local tribal and ethnic leaders who held the real power then and who continue to hold the real power in Afghanistan today.

The concept of legitimacy has little relevance to the present struggle against the backdrop of recent Afghan political history. The overthrow of the monarchy in 1973 left a political vacuum in which no consensus existed concerning the future of the Afghan polity, and no single organized group could make a more clear-cut claim of greater legitimacy than another. Neither the Communists nor the Islamic fundamentalists claimed more than a few thousand members each when the monarchy fell. But even a few thousand disciplined, highly motivated members loomed large in such a limited political universe.

In addition to posing ideological challenges to the Western-oriented elite, the Communist and fundamentalist movements were vehicles of social protest for disadvantaged elements of the Afghan populace. The Parcham (Flag) Communist faction represented many of those in the de-tribalized Kabul intelligentsia and bureaucracy who felt shut out of power by the narrow Durrani in-group that dominated both the monarchy and the Daoud republic. The rival Khalq (Masses) faction had more of a Pushtun tribal base, especially among Ghilzai tribes. By contrast, the strongest fundamentalist cadres were organized in ethnic minority areas, notably the predominantly Tajik Pansjer Valley.

The fall of the monarchy opened the way for a polarization of Afghan political life between the Communists at one extreme and the Islamic fundamentalists at the other—with both of them opposed to Daoud's ineffectual, corrupt republic. When the fundamentalists fled to Pakistan to escape Daoud's repression, the Communists had a clear field to exploit popular dissatisfaction with the Daoud regime, which lacked the legitimacy of the monarchy but was nonetheless dominated by a pro-Daoud monarchist coterie.

Initially many Afghans adopted a wait-and-see attitude toward the Communist revolution of April 1978. They hailed the end of royal family dominance and hoped that the Communists, conscious of their narrow base, would work cooperatively with other groups in shaping their reform program. Communist leader Hafizullah Amin mixed his Marxism with a militant Pushtun nationalism that won applause in the tribal areas. But Amin gradually alienated many of the new regime's non-Communist sympathizers with his brutality, his overzealous reforms, and his attempts to centralize the country overnight. Most important, he was insensitive to Islamic sentiment and directly challenged the power and prerogatives of Islamic dignitaries, provoking the active intervention of fundamentalist groups throughout the Persian Gulf and the Middle East in support of the nascent anti-Communist insurgency.

Most Afghans today feel that the Communist leaders who succeeded Amin lost their patriotic credentials by collaborating with the Soviet occupation forces. At the same time, it was a mistake to think of the Afghan struggle in black-and-white terms as one between the Soviets on one side and all Afghans on the other. The Communist Party has a hard core of some 40,000 highly motivated activists who see themselves as nationalists and modernizers carrying forward the reform tradition identified with King Amanullah. The intractability of the continuing political stalemate in Afghanistan can only be understood if one recognizes that the Soviet occupation was superimposed on a civil war. Even during the occupation, a significant minority of Afghans either supported or tolerated the Communist regime, and this minority has grown since the Soviet withdrawal.

# A Divided Society: The Impact of External Intervention

To assess the reconstruction challenge accurately, it is necessary to understand why and how external intervention has exacerbated, and continues to exacerbate, the internecine divisions in Afghan society.

The devastating impact of Soviet intervention needs little elaboration. Moscow no longer even attempts to legitimize the introduction of Soviet combat forces in 1979 by claiming that Amin had asked for them. New evidence has conclusively proved that Soviet forces participated in his murder.[2] As the war proceeded, the disruptive impact of Soviet military operations on the Afghan physical infrastructure and social fabric intensified with each passing year. Moreover, in political terms, it was massive Soviet economic and military support that solidified the basic cleavage between a narrowly based Communist regime and its disparate opponents. Since the

Soviet withdrawal, it has been broadly accepted, even in Moscow, that in the absence of such support, the Communist regime in Kabul would have been unable to hold onto power.

As for the United States, Pakistan, and other powers that provided military and economic support to the Afghan resistance, historians are likely to take a generally benign view of their intervention. The resistance groups were, after all, struggling against a foreign occupation. Aid to their cause was a major factor contributing to the Soviet withdrawal, though it is increasingly clear that other factors, notably Mikhail Gorbachev's new foreign policy priorities, were no less critical.[3] What is often overlooked, however, is that foreign aid to the resistance has not been an unmixed blessing for Afghanistan. The United States and the six other major foreign patrons of the resistance groups were pursuing not only the lofty goal of Afghan self-determination but also a variety of more debatable geo-political and sectarian objectives of their own. As a consequence, the anti-Soviet cause has had an extremely divisive impact. Both weapons aid and cross-border economic aid have reinforced the endemic internecine conflicts between non-Communist Afghan factions.

## Pakistan and the Politics of Weapons Aid

Pakistan agreed to serve as a conduit for U.S. weapons aid on the condition that it would determine the allocation of aid to rival Afghan claimants. In accepting this condition, American officials were largely indifferent to the continuing importance of the centuries-old dispute over the Pushtun territories annexed by the British. Concerned primarily with raising the costs of the Soviet occupation, the United States let Islamabad use American aid leverage to settle old scores with Afghan nationalist adversaries and to pursue its own strategic objective of a Pakistan-dominated postwar Afghanistan.

Long before the war, Pakistani intelligence agencies had established contact with non-Pushtun, Islamic fundamentalist elements opposed to Daoud's Pushtun chauvinistic policies. Inspired by the Muslim Brotherhood, with its roots in Egypt, and by orthodox Wahabi groups in Saudi Arabia, the fundamentalists had a negligible organization in Afghanistan prior to the Communist takeover in 1978 and the Soviet occupation in December 1979. They were arrayed against the monarchy; against the entire traditional Moslem clergy, identified with the Hanafi school of Islamic law and various Sufi sects; and against Western-oriented and Communist modernizers alike. Above all, they had alienated the powerful tribal hierarchy among the Pushtuns by calling for the abolition of tribalism as incompatible with their conception of a centralized Islamic state. Despite harsh repression, the fundamentalists, who numbered perhaps 1,500, survived as an underground movement until 1973, when most of them fled to Pakistan. There they forged an alliance with Pakistani fundamentalist groups and Pakistani intelligence agencies that was to become increasingly important in the context of the Afghan conflict.

Although the advent of the Communist regime aroused widespread alarm throughout the Moslem world, it was the fundamentalist elements in the Gulf and the Middle East who reacted most purposefully and made the Afghan issue their own. The fundamentalists saw the war as a golden opportunity to build up organizational cadres among the Afghan refugees in Pakistan with an eye to eventually supplanting the entire pre-existing social and political hierarchy of the country. This meant that their enemies were not only Soviet troops and Afghan Communist infidels, but also most of the non-fundamentalist resistance elements.

Throughout the war, the late President of Pakistan, Mohammad Zia ul-Haq, consciously channeled most U.S. weapons aid to fundamentalist groups and other Afghan elements regarded as cooperative by Pakistan's Interservices Intelligence Directorate. Zia made no secret of his desire to install a postwar Pakistani satellite state in Afghanistan dominated by the fundamentalists. "We have earned the right to have a very friendly regime there," he told me in a conversation on June 29, 1988, shortly before his death in a mysterious plane crash. "We took risks as a front-line state, and we won't permit it to be like it was before, with Indian and Soviet influence there and claims on our territory. It will be a real Islamic state, part of a pan-Islamic revival that will one day win over the Muslims in the Soviet Union. You will see."

Zia consciously attempted to undermine the tribal leadership by building up non-Pushtuns and playing on intra-Pushtun rivalries, especially the conflict between the Ghilzais and the Durranis. Thus, the lion's share of American aid has been channeled to Burhanuddin Rabbani's Jamiat Islami, rooted primarily in the Tajiks, and Gulbuddin Hekmatyar's Hezbe Islami, embracing both Tajiks and detribalized Pushtuns from migrant families in northern Afghanistan, no longer attached to the tribal structure. Durranis in particular—as the most dedicated supporters of the former King—were anathema to Islamabad. Pakistan has given limited support to two Ghilzai tribes, the Jadrans and the Khogianis, who were linked to fundamentalist factions. However, by and large, Ghilzais and Durranis alike have been deliberately bypassed in aid allocations, and as a result, many Ghilzai tribes have collaborated with Ghilzai Pushtuns, such as Najibullah, who dominated the Kabul regime.

Islamabad's politically motivated aid allocation pattern explains why the seven Pakistan-based resistance groups have so few territorial strongholds inside the country and have been dependent on expedient alliances with some 350 locally based commanders rooted in the leadership structure of tribal and ethnic groups. Some of these commanders have formed liaisons with the Intelligence Directorate. More of them, however, function as free-wheeling warlords who resist domination by Islamabad and the Pakistan-based resistance factions. The Intelligence Directorate is widely perceived to be the hub of drug-trafficking and black-marketing in weaponry carried on in league with its network of cooperative commanders.

A 1987 poll in the refugee camps in Pakistan showed that 83 per cent of the refugees favored former King Zahir Shah as the leader of a postwar Afghan regime.[4] Yet Pakistan has consistently obstructed efforts by Zahir Shah's supporters among the Pushtun commanders and in the refugee camps to organize broad-based negotiations among Afghan factions that would pave the way for the peaceful replacement of the Communist regime. Since the start of the war, the former monarch and his closest advisers have consistently been denied visas to visit the camps. Instead, Pakistan has treated the seven-party resistance alliance as the sole voice of non-Communist Afghans.

The Intelligence Directorate played a conspicuous, heavy-handed role in arranging and manipulating the Islamabad *shura*, or council, that set up the Pakistan-based Afghan Interim Government (AIG) in February 1989. The exile government had never been able to escape the taint of Pakistani sponsorship. Kabul has skillfully appealed to nationalist emotions to discredit its opponents and to offset the stigma left by a decade of Communist collaboration with Soviet occupation forces.

The critical difference between the Communist Party and the Pakistan-based resistance groups is that the Communists have a strong political infrastructure in the limited areas under their jurisdiction while the resistance groups lack such an infrastructure. This is why the resistance was unable to follow up its military victories by consolidating territorial control. As for local commanders with ties to the traditional power structure, they, too, have made little effort to build local governmental machinery, with several exceptions, notably Ahmad Shah Massoud in the Pansjer Valley. "Only a handful of commanders," reported Edward Girardet, a perceptive journalistic observer of the war, "have established infrastructures comparable to those of UNITA in Angola or the EPLF in Eritrea by operating their own schools, literacy programs, medical dispensaries, and relief and agricultural facilities."[5]

## The United States and the Politics of Economic Aid

The United States has attempted to compensate for the political weaknesses of the Pakistan-based groups by providing them with massive cross-border "humanitarian aid" to be distributed in resistance strongholds inside the country. The objectives of this program, which totaled $380.7 million between 1985 and 1990, are frankly political as well as humanitarian. Reagan Administration officials unveiling the program "expressed the hope that it would unify the fragmented seven-party resistance alliance."[6] "By helping the Afghans to develop networks of resistance social services," said the U.S. Agency for International Development budget request to Congress in fiscal 1987, "our assistance will enable the mujahidin (freedom fighters) to protect and take care of the people who support them."[7] In a 1988 description of the program, the Agency was more explicit concerning its desire to transform the seven-party alliance into a government rivaling Kabul. "By working with the alliance," a USAID statement said, "we are able to develop an institutional capability among Afghans to perform the civil functions of government."[8] By 1989, the program emphasized the AIG as the principal vehicle through which cross-border aid would be channeled.[9]

In addition to providing "non-lethal" goods such as surplus U.S. military boots, sleeping bags, and a variety of equipment for schools and medical clinics in areas chosen by the seven parties, the Agency also makes cash payments for food purchases. According to the official figures, the cross-border program had trained 1,115 basic health workers by the end of 1988, plus 9,452 Afghans in first aid techniques; established 889 health facilities; opened 1,209 schools serving 120,000 students; supplied more than 1 million new elementary school textbooks; distributed foodpacks for 83 million meals; cleaned and repaired 549 irrigation schemes; provided 9,000 tons of fertilizer; and treated 800 wounded Afghans.[10]

Critics have questioned these statistics and have charged that the political purposes of the U.S. program detract from its humanitarian purposes. Peter Rees, director of Britain's Afghan Aid—one of some 58 private voluntary organizations carrying on cross-border aid from Pakistan—said that "the U.S. aid package is putting a lot of money into the political arena and away from direct humanitarian aid."[11] The most pervasive criticism of U.S. cross-border aid is that its multi-tiered distribution network invites corruption. Even if aid were given directly to field commanders, it is argued, USAID would be unable to monitor what happens to its money and supplies, and the problem is aggravated by a network of middlemen.[12] One official of a private voluntary organization pointed out that USAID relies on distribution receipts provided by the seven parties, "and the Americans don't know where these receipts come from."[13] A U.S. official privately told Girardet that only 15 to 25 per cent of the cross-border aid actually reaches the interior. The rest, he said, is skimmed off by Afghan and Pakistani middlemen.[14]

In some cases, U.S. cross-border aid has been administered through subcontracts with private voluntary organizations that have targeted their activities on selected areas where direct cooperation has been possible with politically accepted commanders and other local notables. These are the success stories of the U.S. reconstruction effort. More often, though, the United States has exerted heavy pressure on the private agencies and the United Nations to turn over all aid to the seven parties and, more recently, to the AIG.

Contributions by donor countries to the United Nations aid effort, received or pledged, totaled $991.5 million by September 1, 1989. Most of the aid received has been administered through United Nations agencies or private agencies working independently of the Pakistan-based parties. In keeping with the diversity of its donors, the United Nations has insisted on political neutrality. Prince Sadruddin Aga Khan, U.N. Coordinator for Humanitarian and Economic Assistance Programs Relating to Afghanistan, has declared that the United Nations will "determine its programs on the basis of a humanitarian consensus at the local level and will not be used as a political tool by any group."[15] This approach has included efforts to distribute aid in Communist-held areas despite active U.S. and Pakistani efforts to block such aid.[16] When the State Department argued that the seven-party alliance based in Pakistan should have a veto over any aid to Kabul, Prince Sadruddin, citing the effects of food shortages on women and children, responded that "at a time when everyone is focusing on political and military developments, we have to think of the humanitarian dimension of the problem."[17]

One of the more independent Afghan analysts of the war, Syed Naim Majrooh, director of the Afghan Information Center in Peshawar, wrote that by favoring particular Afghan parties and commanders, even the private agencies often aggravate intra-Afghan rivalries.[18] This view is reflected in the report of a German agency citing cases in which private organizations, caught in a tug-of-war between differing Afghan factions seeking to draw them into their areas, have in the end hardened the battle lines between these factions by choosing one over the other.[19] An American scholar who studied the aid effort concluded that the divisive impact of cross-border operations by both governmental and private agencies outweighed their benefits in the context of a continuing civil war.[20]

# The Challenge Ahead: Rebuilding the Rural Areas

Even if Afghanistan did not have such debilitating social and political divisions, the economic problems confronting postwar planners would be formidable. Beyond the issue of uniting for reconstruction lies the same underlying challenge that confronted prewar regimes: breaking the vicious circle of poverty.

Apart from the pervasive problems resulting from physical and social devastation, the complexity of this challenge has been magnified by one specific, war-induced structural change in Afghan society. This is the massive, continuing process of urbanization, mentioned earlier, that has concentrated 25 per cent of the population (twice the prewar average) in cities and towns. Primary attention, it is widely agreed, must be given to arresting this trend by revitalizing the agricultural economy. The "internal refugees" who fled to urban areas for protection are largely unemployed and would return to their home villages if meaningful reconstruction were under way. Moreover, in a country with such a limited industrial base, it is in the countryside that the reconstruction of economic life must necessarily begin. Agriculture provided one-half of the national income in prewar Afghanistan and four-fifths of national export earnings. The war has thus crippled the country economically by removing vast areas from cultivation and reducing the level of production in those areas where farming has continued. With normal access to seeds, fertilizer, and other inputs disrupted, and with irrigation systems damaged or neglected, yields have dropped dramatically. The loss of traditional marketing outlets has led many farmers to turn for survival to the cultivation of cash crops, including opium poppies, aggravating the dependence of Kabul and other urban centers on imported cereals.

The heart of the reconstruction challenge lies in regenerating agricultural productivity while pursuing the broader, related task of restoring the social and economic infrastructure in the countryside. The great majority of the refugees in Pakistan and Iran, as well as the "internal refugees" living in urban centers, were originally from rural areas. Will they go back in the foreseeable future to areas where fighting subsides? By October 1989, U.N. Coordinator Sadruddin Aga Khan reported that "despite continued fighting in many parts of the country, very large areas are now accessible, relatively peaceful and capable of absorbing whatever aid can be provided."[21] By May 1990, his estimate was that fighting was continuing in "basically four out of 29 provinces."[22] Officials of private voluntary organizations have offered similar assessments.[23]

Most evidence suggests that few of the refugees are likely to abandon their present access to U.S.- and Soviet-assured food and other assistance without reasonable hope of obtaining food, shelter, water supplies, agricultural inputs, and medical facilities in their former villages. Yet prolonging the status quo poses grave dangers for Afghanistan and its neighbors alike. For Afghanistan, the hardening of the present artificial level of urbanization would greatly impede a balanced development effort; and for its neighbors, a continued large-scale refugee presence would impose increasingly unbearable strains. The dilemma facing reconstruction planners is that preparatory programs are urgently needed to draw the refugees back, but foreign donors are reluctant to support reconstruction financially until the fighting ends, the future of the Kabul Communist regime is settled, and the bulk of the refugees actually return.

### Regenerating Agricultural Productivity

*Irrigation.* While it is difficult to single out any one overriding priority, the re-establishment and expansion of irrigation and other water systems is perhaps the most critical component of agricultural reconstruction. Given limited rainfall, there is no part of Afghanistan in which the rural population can live on rain-fed agriculture alone. Dry farming is always subsidiary to irrigated agriculture and must be combined with animal husbandry to make subsistence possible. Orchards, vegetable cultivation, and cash crops such as cotton, oilseeds, and tobacco are all dependent on irrigation.

Four types of water management systems existed before the war: canal networks in the North; underground irrigation channels (*karezes*); simple diversion channels from rivers and small streams (*juis*) south of the Hindu Kush; and the larger, foreign-assisted Helmand, Argandab, and Kunduz-Khanabad hydroelectric projects. Apart from direct war damage, lack of maintenance has left all of these systems in varying degrees of disrepair. Many *karezes* that have collapsed require desilting. Innumerable springs and wells also require rehabilitation. Afghan farmers are used to repairing *karezes* and *juis* periodically. But their effort would be greatly expedited with support in the form of cement, steel rods, and other construction materials, together with cash-for-work and food-for-work programs, and motor pumps would help to maximize the potential of the more developed irrigation networks. More substantial foreign assistance would be required to build the feeder canal networks in the North and the big hydroelectric projects.

*Seeds, Fertilizers, and Other Inputs.* As irrigation and water systems begin to function, the introduction of seeds, fertilizers, and other agricultural inputs should go hand in hand. Widespread evidence indicates that the wheat seed used in Afghanistan for the last fifteen years has lost part of its genetic potential and should be replaced. The United Nations has identified varieties of high-yielding, disease-resistant seeds suited to the varied climatic conditions of Afghanistan that can be obtained from Pakistan, Turkey, the Soviet Union, and international agencies.[24] Even with improved seeds, however, increased yields would be possible only with the appropriate application of manure and chemical fertilizers. The United Nations estimates that irrigated yields could be doubled through the systematic use of chemical fertilizers.[25] While adequate supplies of urea are produced in a fertilizer plant at Mazar-i-Sharif that has remained operative despite the war, other varieties would have to be provided through reconstruction aid. Many of the fertilizer warehouses and supply depots established before the war are reported to be in place and could be reactivated.

*Credit.* One of the built-in dilemmas of the agricultural reconstruction effort is that few credit facilities exist in the countryside to enable farmers to get loans for purchasing seeds and fertilizer. Before the war, the Agricultural Development Bank reached only 8 per cent of the rural population, and most farmers relied on private moneylenders. This is a basic argument cited by advocates of cash-for-food and food-for-work programs during the initial resettlement period.

*Replenishing the Livestock Population.* The damaging impact of the war on the population of oxen and other draft animals could jeopardize the success of the entire agricultural reconstruction effort. The shortage of farm labor resulting from the refugee exodus has been aggravated by the destruction of an estimated 150,000 pairs of oxen—together with an even larger movement of livestock, estimated to number 2.4 million animals, with the refugees. It would be prohibitively expensive to replace animal traction universally with mechanized tractors. Mechanized agriculture was limited in scope and inefficient before the war, and the necessary diesel fuel is not generally available. In most areas, the oxen population would have to be rebuilt to complement the return of farm labor, though a limited scope for the import of small tractors may exist in some productive areas where communal leasing was previously in use. Apart from cultivable farmland, it should be remembered that 65 per cent of Afghan territory is range land that has traditionally been used for sheep and goat herding. Often this herding has been carried out in conjunction with farming. However, much of the pastoral population is nomadic, and a healthy ecological balance would require providing herds to those pastoralists who lost all or most of their stock and have no farmland.

*Mine-Clearing.* For farmers and pastoralists alike, the problem of mine-clearing will be a nightmare, but the dimensions of this problem have been exaggerated. As a United Nations report points out, "the common perception of the Afghan countryside being littered with mines is not accurate." In areas where heavy fighting has occurred, mines have been sown indiscriminately, but more often "mines have been placed in predictable locations, e.g., the security perimeters of government garrisons and the lines of communications connecting these garrisons."[26]

The first mine fields to be cleared will logically be in populated areas, and only later, if ever, will mine clearance activities extend to the more remote steppes populated by only 2.4 persons per square mile. The most serious threat to civilians in rural areas is the plastic PMZ or "butterfly" mine designed to maim rather than to kill. This type was scattered on a large scale from the air by Soviet aircraft. Since it is plastic, it cannot be detected through existing equipment sensitive to metallic objects. With its green, brown, and yellow colors, the "butterfly" is often camouflaged in vegetation. "It will be a long and expensive process to clear those mines and other ordnance from Afghanistan," observed a 1989 United Nations report, "so that widespread reconstruction can be pursued."[27]

*Preventing Opium Production.* One of the built-in dilemmas in the reconstruction process is that, as the refugees return, there is a serious danger of an upsurge in opium poppy cultivation and illicit narcotics production and trafficking.

Even before the war, Afghanistan was one of the world's leading sources of illicit narcotics, with annual production of 200 to 400 tons of opium and up to 500 tons of cannabis. The United Nations reports a "substantial increase" in both poppy growing and drug trafficking during recent years, together with the conversion of large amounts of opium into heroin in covert laboratories in both Pakistan and Afghanistan. Farmers facing shortages of essential inputs and disrupted irrigation systems have resorted to drug production for survival, the United Nations said, "and the potential for a further acceleration of poppy production exists as the refugees go back to devastated villages."[28]

In the absence of other means of generating quick income, it will be difficult to prevent farmers from gravitating to the ready market for opium. Prices vary widely, but in some areas, top-grade "dry" opium sells for five times more than wheat. Poppy cultivation appears to be concentrated in Badakshan, Kunar, Nangarhar, Kandahar, Helmand, and Herat districts. Since many of these areas are likely to be focal points of reconstruction activity, one of the central concerns of reconstruction planners is how to encourage the substitution of other cash crops—especially wheat—for poppies.

## Restoring Social Infrastructure

*Health Services.* Among the more bitterly contested issues in the reconstruction debate is whether significant resources should be devoted to health and education programs, or whether the urgency of agricultural needs is such that major expenditures on health and education should come at a later stage. Initially, the United Nations adopted a firm "agriculture first" strategy. But it increased its allocations for health, in particular, in its Action Plan for 1990–91.

Apart from the limitations of the health services available in prewar Afghanistan, the population had only sporadic access to the services that did exist, given weather factors and poor transportation facilities. Infant mortality rates were among the highest in the world—190 per 1,000 live births—and have increased during the war to an estimated 220 per 1,000. Life expectancy at birth has dropped from 41 before the war to 38. Even in Kabul, where access to health services is much better than in rural areas, the maternal mortality rate in 1974 was more than 100 per 10,000 births, four and a half times higher than that of other developing countries.[29] In the case of some diseases, operational control programs existed before the war, but most of these programs are now virtually nonexistent. The spread of malaria has reached epidemic levels; tuberculosis is increasingly widespread. Among the other major target areas that would have to be addressed in new health programs are rampant gastrointestinal disorders, respiratory infections, neonatal tetanus, nutritional disorders related to a lack of iodine and other dietary insufficiencies, contaminated drinking water, and poor sanitation.

The case for giving a high priority to health care does not rest on humanitarian considerations alone. If the urbanization trend is to be reversed and people are to be drawn back to the countryside, the health infrastructure must be extended beyond its present urban-centered base. Of the 5,100 hospital beds reported in 1986–87, some 58 per cent were located in the Kabul area and most of the remainder in other urban centers. At least 80 per cent of the 2,400 doctors in the country were in urban areas—suggesting that a ratio of one doctor to 20,000 persons prevails in rural areas. While urban health centers grew slightly during the war years, according to the Kabul regime, the number of rural health centers dropped from 220 in 1978 to 90 in 1987. Most of the doctors and other medical personnel trained in Kabul during the war continue to be men despite the emphasis of the regime on the education of women. In recent years, a potentially important dimension of the health care environment has been the activities of private voluntary organizations operating cross-border humanitarian aid programs. One estimate suggests that some 290 local clinics with perhaps 40 qualified doctors have operated intermittently, primarily in areas near Pakistan, and have trained some 570 paramedical workers.

*Education.* The issue of how much priority education programs should receive is part of the larger issue of whether "reconstruction" should be addressed primarily to short-term relief and rehabilitation or to long-term development. Given Afghanistan's literacy rate of about 10 per cent, one of the lowest in the developing world, the importance of expanding educational facilities is incontestable. Technical and vocational education, in particular, would be particularly useful during the early stages of reconstruction, including university-level programs designed to provide a flow of engineers, doctors, and technicians in a variety of fields. Many other badly needed educational programs may lose out in the initial allocation of funds until the regeneration of agricultural production is well under way. One way to make the most of a difficult situation would be to concentrate new schools in areas where the refugee exodus has been relatively minimal. An estimated 30 per cent of the refugee children in Pakistan and Iran have received some schooling, and it is the United Nations hope that "the educational and vocational training programs established in refugee villages will move with the refugees as and when they return to their home areas."[30]

*The Role of Women.* It is in the areas of health and education that one sees most clearly both the importance of mobilizing the support of women in the reconstruction process and the sensitive problems involved in doing so. Afghan cultural mores require that women must receive care in clinics and hospitals from female doctors and medical technicians. Thus, with the shortage of trained female medical personnel even more acute than that of male personnel, health care for women will be severely impaired until medical training programs for women physicians and nurses gain momentum. Female medical technicians in the tradition of China's "barefoot doctors" are also urgently needed, especially in rural maternity hospitals and clinics.

In the case of education, serious controversy raged in Afghan society before the war over whether girls should be educated at all and, if so, in what types of schools and with what curriculum. During the war, this controversy grew sharper. The Communist regime actively promoted education for women in its urban strongholds and maintained the liberal policies on *purdah* (seclusion) and the wearing of the veil initiated by the monarchy and the Daoud regime. Islamic fundamentalist leaders, who had fought prewar reforms in the status of women, continued to make this opposition an article of faith.[31] Women were barred from the 1988 *shura* that chose the Pakistan-based interim government (AIG). One of the guidelines adopted by the exile regime called on Afghans "to develop moral virtues and combat corruption and denigration by observing the principles of *purdah* provided for in the Sharia." Nancy Hatch Dupree, an American woman who has strongly supported the resistance, observed that this document reflects "a disturbing collective thinking among the Peshawar leadership and projects a dim future for women. . . . Certainly the insinuation that corruption and denigration must necessarily arise from women's public presence is deplorable."[32] Most educated Afghan women, reports Dupree, spoke during the war "of waging two *jehads* [holy wars]: a *jehad* against foreign invaders, and a *jehad* against an undesirable [fundamentalist] ideology."[33]

Given the enormity of the reconstruction challenge, it would be tragic indeed if women were excluded from the life of the nation as in the past. Nevertheless, effective leadership in drawing women into the process can only be exercised by the present generation of educated Afghan women with professional experience in various fields. Some of those women are now working in Afghan urban centers but many are living in Pakistan and the West and would have to be encouraged to return. Initially, taking the sensitivity of this issue into account, efforts to promote education for women may have to be focused on training programs related to health services and to women's traditional activities (e.g., vegetable and fruit cultivation, raising small livestock, and poultry breeding) and training female agricultural extension workers competent in these areas. This can in turn lead to broader vocational training and special training for small business enterprises in fields where women are not likely to be resisted (e.g., dairy products, sericulture, and fruit and vegetable processing). Credit programs would be required to promote such small business ventures. Other areas where social acceptance would be relatively easy would be the training of women social workers and psychological counselors to help deal specifically with the problems of widows, orphans, and the disabled. Hopefully, depending on the political complexion of local leadership in different areas, expanded educational opportunities for girls in primary, secondary, and university education can be gradually expanded.

# Reconstruction Now, or a Settlement First?

Must large-scale, comprehensive reconstruction assistance await a political settlement and the establishment of a stable central government?

The United Nations program initiated on June 30, 1988, has been based from the start on the worst case assumption that a military and political stalemate is likely to continue for the foreseeable future. To be sure, U.N. Coordinator Sadruddin Aga Khan has strongly urged a political settlement and has specifically called for a mutual termination of military aid by the superpowers as the necessary prelude to an accommodation among Afghans.[34] At the same time, however, Prince Sadruddin has pressed for reconstruction efforts to begin while efforts to achieve a settlement continue. Advocating "a process of 'humanitarian encirclement' of Afghanistan," Sadruddin Aga Khan declared at the outset of his effort that "massive economic and humanitarian assistance administered on a multilateral basis by the United Nations system offers the best prospect of achieving the degree of socio-economic stability from which a political settlement and the large-scale return of refugee populations may yet emerge."[35] The 1989 and 1990 U.N. Action Plans outlined U.N. aid programs to be "determined on the basis of a humanitarian consensus at the local level"—aid "of a strictly non-political and neutral character" that "shall not be used as a political tool by any group."[36]

Prince Sadruddin did not attempt to implement this approach until March 1990, when he joined the U.N. High Commissioner for Refugees and the Director of the World Food Programme in announcing that United Nations reconstruction aid would initially be concentrated in selected "zones of tranquility" (ZOTs).[37] The precise location of the zones was not revealed to avoid making them a target for fundamentalist groups opposed to the concept. However, United Nations officials later indicated that the first ones would be located in areas within nine provinces: Kandahar, Kunar, Paktika, Herat, Nimroz, Hazarajat, Badakshan, Logar, and Badghis. The governing criteria for selection, these officials said, would be how long the locality has been at peace; whether local leaders are united in welcoming a United Nations presence; whether capable local leadership exists for carrying out aid projects; accessibility of the area to the delivery of supplies; and the absorptive capacity of the local economy. Inputs would follow a standard pattern, beginning with a mine-removal program and then proceeding to medical care, the establishment of food storage facilities, and the provision of seeds, other agricultural inputs, and building materials.

Despite confident United Nations assurances that both Kabul and many resistance leaders had agreed to respect the ZOTs, some critics among the 58 non-governmental organizations engaged in cross-border aid warned that recurring violence would threaten the safety of returning refugees. More basic controversy focused on the issue of whether existing aid to Afghan refugees in Pakistan should be phased out in tandem with the movement of refugees back to Afghanistan. If refugee aid in Pakistan is cut off, critics charged, the United Nations program would amount to forcible repatriation; but if aid is available on both sides of the border, others responded, many refugees would "double dip," keeping some family members in Pakistan to collect rations there in the name of the whole family while others return to Afghanistan.

In July 1990, the High Commissioner for Refugees launched a repatriation plan under which refugees are offered a sum equal to $137 and a three-month food supply if they turn in their ration cards and return to Afghanistan. However, fundamentalist factions and their Pakistani supporters, seeking to prolong the war until a fundamentalist regime is installed, are attempting to subvert the program. Fundamentalist hit squads, roving the refugee camps, are threatening violence against those cooperating with the United Nations.

In contrast to the U.N. approach, U.S. policy since the Soviet withdrawal has been based on the expectation that the Kabul regime will be replaced through military and political pressure with a more broadly based government. Until this takes place, the United States plans to emphasize bilateral cross-border aid designed to strengthen the resistance cause. While expressing perfunctory support for a United Nations role in Afghan reconstruction,[38] the United States has given relatively little financial support to the United Nations program in comparison with other donors. The target announced by Prince Sadruddin is $1.16 billion. Out of the $1.029 billion in contributions pledged as of September 1, 1990, the United States had given $45.5 million, while the Soviet Union had pledged $600 million and Japan $145 million. To put this comparison into perspective, it should be noted that Soviet contributions are in the form of commodities, not cash, and that in 1985–1990, the United States has contributed $387 million to U.N.-administered refugee support programs in Pakistan, including a projected $54 million in 1990, as well as $380.7 million to bilateral cross-border aid during the same five-year period. Reviewing the cross-border effort in January 1990, the U.S. Agency for International Development said that "the focus of the program has expanded beyond humanitarian assistance" to providing selected support for the interim government (AIG) through "close collaboration with functioning and capable ministries such as Health, Education, Agriculture and Finance" and through a new "Democratic Pluralism Initiative" linked with related programs in other countries designed to support democratic institutions.[39]

In my view, the United Nations has been realistic in proceeding on the assumption that a stable political settlement may not evolve for some time. By mid–1990, U.S. policymakers were beginning to have doubts about their earlier assumptions and were groping for ways to move toward a political settlement. Even if an early compromise is reached, however, the process of choosing and establishing a new government is likely to be protracted and fitful.

# Guidelines for International Action

Despite the prospect of continued military stalemate and political confusion, at least in the short run, the process of reconstruction can and should be accelerated. The following guidelines suggest how the United States and the international community can most effectively promote this process during the complex period of transition ahead:

**1. Channel assistance through the United Nations.** As Prince Sadruddin has suggested, a multilateral "humanitarian encirclement" effort can help to create the environment necessary for a political solution while efforts to achieve a more broad-based government proceed. Fighting has subsided in many areas of the country as Soviet and Afghan Communist forces have withdrawn and as local commanders have reached tacit "live and let live" understandings with Kabul. Bilateral aid in this environment directly reinforces political polarization, impeding moves toward accommodation at the local level. By the same token, to the extent that multilateral aid gradually replaces bilateral aid, traditional Afghan modes of conflict resolution are likely to operate more effectively. For the most part, since 1988, the United Nations has demonstrated both the administrative capability and planning know-how needed to lead an effective multilateral effort in Afghanistan.

**2. Phase out bilateral aid.** Both the United States and the Soviet Union should be encouraged to transfer their present bilateral economic aid spending to the United Nations. This de-politicization of economic aid should proceed even in the absence of movement toward a "negative symmetry" agreement providing for the mutual termination of military aid. In some cases, private voluntary agencies now carrying out cross-border aid under contracts with the United States should continue their projects under the aegis of the United Nations. However, where U.S.-funded cross-border aid has been politically motivated and has not reflected "a humanitarian consensus at the local level," it should not be continued.

**3. Increase support for the United Nations program.** Countries that have not yet given the United Nations program support commensurate with their capabilities should increase their contributions without delay. Out of the $1.029 billion pledged as of September 1, 1990, $693.6 million, primarily from the Soviet Union, represented contributions in kind. Cash contributions have totaled only $309 million. Implementation of the United Nations Second Action Plan for 1990–91, with projected expenditures totaling $410.34 million, will be stalled unless the United States and other countries capable of hard currency cash contributions upgrade their support. In the case of the United States, projected outlays ($114.23 million in 1990) of bilateral aid should be shifted to the United Nations and should be increased to at least $250 million annually for the next five years. Japan, the European Community, and Arab donors should provide a comparable level of support.

**4. Coordinate reconstruction with Kabul.** Consultation and cooperation with the Najibullah regime concerning the location of reconstruction activities will be imperative in the absence of a political settlement leading to its replacement. In large areas of Afghanistan, there is an uneasy peace between resistance field commanders and pro-government local militias. The United Nations will have to obtain the approval of both sides in order to establish stable "zones of tranquility." Kabul's cooperation will also be critical in securing safe passage through transit corridors necessary to reach many of the projected zones, especially in the face of growing harassment of United Nations and other reconstruction activities by fundamentalist resistance elements.

**5. Give priority to resettling refugees.** The initial focus of the reconstruction effort should be on resettling refugees rather than on long-gestating development projects. To begin the process, the United Nations repatriation plan and its "zones of tranquility" program should be actively supported and implemented without waiting for a political settlement leading to a new central government. The government of Pakistan should encourage the United Nations repatriation plan and take steps to prevent the fundamentalists from harassing cooperating refugees. Existing assistance levels to refugees in Pakistan and Iran should be reduced as a significant flow of refugees back to Afghanistan begins to get under way. Until then, the United Nations should tighten its aid distribution procedures to minimize "double-dipping" as much as possible.

A refugee-oriented approach would target 14 of Afghanistan's 28 provinces, where 90 per cent of the refugees originated. It would thus mean reallocating funds now devoted to cross-border programs in areas where fighting has been minimal and where the refugee exodus has been limited.

**6. Give priority to rural areas.** In its 14 target provinces, the United Nations should give priority to rural areas, emphasizing programs to increase food production. Two key aspects of the projected rural program deserve urgent attention: (a) support for the repair of irrigation systems, and (b) the introduction of fertilizers, crop protection chemicals, and other agricultural inputs. With respect to inputs, the ability to devise ways to channel credit where it is needed will be the key to a successful program; and until adequate credit facilities begin to take shape perhaps for the first two farming seasons, free fertilizer supplies should be made available.

The majority of Afghan farmers used oxen and other draught animals to plow their fields before the war. But some estimates indicate that at least 500,000 draught animals would have to be supplied to reach prewar levels. To the extent possible, oxen should be supplied, but threshers and tractors should also be made available on as wide a scale as possible to compensate for the expected shortage of draught animals.

Hired farm labor has been a traditional feature of the Afghan countryside. Given the exacerbation of rural poverty caused by the war, however, few returning refugees will be able to afford to hire labor. Food-for-work programs should thus be a central element of efforts to stimulate agricultural production.

**7. Include urban areas in reconstruction plans.** While focusing on the regeneration of food production in rural areas and on seeking to reverse the present trend to urbanization, the reconstruction program should not ignore urban areas under the control of the Kabul regime. Food aid and other humanitarian assistance is urgently needed for many urban "internal refugees" who have received much less help than the refugees in the Pakistani and Iranian camps. Other programs in the fields of education, health, and industrial development, in particular, should logically build on the foundations already laid by the Communist regime.

It would be a mistake to assume that the urbanization trend can be easily reversed. Even with an end to the fighting, many families who have found a livelihood in the cities are likely to remain there unless and until their villages are regenerated. Moreover, some refugees faced with discouraging prospects in their villages may migrate to the cities despite the best efforts of reconstruction planners.

**8. Include key infrastructure projects.** A sharp dichotomy is often drawn between top-down, supply-driven, large-scale programs on the one hand and bottom-up, demand-driven, community-based programs on the other. Most of the reconstruction effort should reflect the bottom-up approach. But this dichotomy tends to blur the fact that many of the large-scale projects needed to rebuild the basic infrastructure will be necessary even in a country where decentralization is the political norm.

The U.N. Action Plan for 1990–91 properly focuses on rebuilding bridges and repairing existing roads. As time passes, however, the construction of new roads, large irrigation systems, and other infrastructural projects may become necessary and could be implemented even in the absence of a stable central government. In planning road construction, geopolitical factors should be taken into account to avoid promoting an unbalanced dependence on any one of Afghanistan's neighbors.

**9. Promote development with equity.** In implementing the U.N. Action Plan for 1990–91, special attention should be given to balancing what are often the contradictory claims of growth and equity. Decisions concerning the allocation of reconstruction aid should not be made solely on the basis of whether a given area promises to be productive. Focusing myopically on economic criteria could aggravate ethnic, regional, and tribal tensions if too much aid is monopolized by the more aggressive and politically well connected groups or localities.

On the key question of how to select the areas receiving agricultural inputs, the United Nations has been vague in its public pronouncements, stating that "agricultural inputs will be utilized where needs are greatest and the potential for increasing production is highest."[40] This ambiguity may well have been deliberate, since needs will often be greatest in areas where the short-term potential for increasing production is the least promising. Aid planners will be under pressure to seek higher yields from lands currently under production rather than to restore lands abandoned during the war. In tenant farming areas, however, care should be taken to avoid exacerbating landlord-tenant frictions through allocations of inputs that aggravate local power inequities.

In addition to the competition between Pushtuns and non-Pushtuns, especially newly assertive Tajiks, reconstruction planners should be especially sensitive to Ghilzai-Durrani tensions within Pushtun ranks as well as to developing power struggles between older establishment leaders in the tribal and ethnic power structure and younger commanders with roots in this structure who are now seeking to enlarge their authority.

**10. Help to build long-term export potential.** Afghanistan cannot pursue an export-led growth strategy—given what will be a limited industrial base for many years. Nevertheless, over time, export earnings could help to stimulate growth. While focusing on the priority objective of agricultural regeneration, the reconstruction program should, to the extent that funds permit, include mining and industrial projects designed both to relieve unemployment and to build the potential for export earnings. The iron ore at Hajigak is only one example of unexploited mineral deposits located before the war that would have a ready market in more industrialized neighboring countries. Exports of fresh fruits and vegetables and food products should also be increased as the country regains agricultural self-sufficiency.

**11. Emphasize the training of administrative and technical personnel.** One of the most significant constraints on the capacity of Afghan society to absorb aid and use it effectively is the lack of trained administrative and technical personnel in all fields. This long-standing problem, intensified by the war, makes special training programs urgently necessary, especially in areas directly related to the use of aid inputs and equipment. Younger refugees should be emphasized in these programs to stop the continuing flow of talented Afghan youths to Europe and the West.

**12. Focus on preventing new opium cultivation.** Two differing approaches have been advocated for dealing with the problem of opium production: reducing existing production in areas of traditional poppy cultivation and forestalling the extension of cultivation to new areas by returning refugees.

U.S. aid planners, anxious to show dramatic results to Congressional committees, have favored direct assaults on traditional areas of opium cultivation, e.g., the Kama and Goshta areas of Kandahar and the Musa Qala and Kakajay regions of the Helmand Valley. In areas such as these, however, long accustomed to poppy cultivation as a way of life, costly crash programs will face deep-rooted local opposition and are likely to yield only transitory results. A case in point was the assassination of Nasim Akhunzada, a resistance warlord in Helmand, who negotiated a crop conversion plan with U.S. aid officials in 1989.

Where stable local arrangements appear possible, crash programs for converting traditional production areas may in some cases merit the risks involved. In general, however, a realistic approach would focus limited funds on preventing the extension of cultivation to new areas by returning refugees. This would mean giving priority to areas where poppy cultivation has been non-existent, or to mixed areas (e.g., Uruzgun and Zabol) where cultivation has started recently and opium is not yet the dominant crop. In such areas, a wide array of incentives, including irrigation canals and tubewells, should be offered to get farmers to commit themselves to the cultivation of other crops in place of poppies. Special attention should be given to those mixed areas, such as Nangarhar province, where the differential between the profitability of opium and other crops is not as dramatic as in the Helmand Valley example cited earlier.

**13. Press Pakistan to control narcotics traffic.** No meaningful approach to controlling Afghan opium production can ignore the fact that Pakistani drug lords are directly involved in organizing integrated networks reaching from the farmer to the processing laboratory to the smuggler. While hard public evidence is still fragmentary, it is widely assumed in Pakistan that important political and military figures are in league with the drug mafia. Regrettably, the United States, fearful of jeopardizing its security ties with Pakistan, has made relatively half-hearted efforts to press for Pakistani narcotics control efforts. Now that Soviet forces have left Afghanistan, however, the U.S. security relationship with Pakistan is no longer critical. The United States should exercise its maximum leverage in Islamabad to bring about the exposure and prosecution of the drug lords. Pakistan is not the only outlet for Afghan opium production, but crippling the Pakistan-based syndicates would lead to a significant reduction in production levels in Afghanistan.

**14. Increase mine-clearance programs.** The United Nations initially emphasized a "mine-awareness" program designed to educate refugees concerning the hazards posed by mines and how to remove them. The premise of this program was that the refugees concerned would conduct mine-clearance operations in their own areas when they went back to Afghanistan. After 20,000 Afghans had received two weeks of instruction, however, critics complained that the program was merely spreading fear among refugees who would be more hesitant than ever to return. In late 1989, the United Nations set up both mechanized mine-clearance units and ten professional manual mine-clearance teams, including both Afghan and non-Afghan employees, to conduct direct mine-eradication operations. These mine-clearance activities should be stepped up, especially in areas where fighting has been heavy and mines have been sown indiscriminately.

**15. Write off past debt.** The Soviet Union and the United States should both agree to write off Afghan debts to them totaling $2.1 billion and $80 million, respectively. In the case of Moscow, this could be treated as reparations. U.S. and Soviet debt forgiveness could be part of an international agreement embracing all bilateral donor countries.

**16. Pursue a "negative symmetry" agreement.** While supporting reconstruction assistance on a politically neutral basis, the superpowers should negotiate an agreement providing for the mutual termination of military aid to their Afghan clients in accordance with an agreed timeframe. The Bush Administration argues that such an agreement would serve the interests of Kabul because Moscow has provided the Communist regime with military equipment on a scale far surpassing that provided by the United States to the resistance. But the reverse may be true, for the Soviet-American military aid competition in Afghanistan is steadily multiplying the imbalance between Kabul and its opponents. Given its proximity to Afghanistan, the Soviet Union has a much greater stake there than the United States does, and it is likely to outbid whatever the United States provides in military aid. Unrest in its Central Asian republics has also heightened the Soviet desire to prevent the emergence of a hostile regime in Kabul. Moreover, the U.S. Administration's argument is based on the implicit assumption that Kabul can be defeated militarily in some foreseeable timeframe—an assumption that has been increasingly called into question by events.[41]

A mutual termination of military aid would shift the struggle against the Najibullah regime from the military arena, where the non-Communists have been ineffectual, to the political arena, where their strength is inherently greater than that of the Communists. The Afghan antagonists would no longer have a vested interest in perpetuating the conflict in order to keep the aid gravy train flowing. With no new supplies of military equipment in sight, internecine differences within the ruling People's Democratic Party (renamed the Homeland Party in June 1990) would be intensified. Advocates of political compromise would gain at the expense of hardliners. Processes of realignment between kindred ethnic and tribal elements in the regime and in the resistance would gain momentum.

The battle lines between Kabul and its opponents would gradually be blurred, opening the way for arrangements that in time could lead to a more broad-based central government.

**17. Encourage an interim government.** A "negative symmetry" agreement would create a climate conducive to U.N.–sponsored intervention to promote a political settlement. Since June 1989, U.N. Secretary-General Javier Pérez De Cuellar has been seeking the support of the powers concerned for a United Nations role.

The purpose of United Nations intervention would be to bring about a structured transfer of power from the Communist regime to a more broad-based interim government. Internationalizing the process of Afghan self-determination leading to a new regime is necessary in the context of the troubled history of Pakistan-Afghanistan relations. No scenario for elections or a traditional tribal assembly carried out under the direct or indirect auspices of Pakistan—or perceived to be—would be regarded as legitimate in the eyes of most Afghans.

With the country awash in arms, continued fighting and political instability are likely to undermine the effectiveness of any central government. But the establishment of a new government supported by substantial *multilateral* economic aid from the superpowers and others would reduce the level of violence and would greatly improve the prospects for a well-coordinated program of reconstruction.

All reconstruction assistance should then be channeled through Kabul. As the sole recipient of external aid, and the sole arbiter of where aid monies are spent, the new government would be greatly strengthened in reaching accommodations with tribal and ethnic warlords. Channeling aid through the central government, however, need not and should not mean that reconstruction aid should be centrally administered. On the contrary, while some infrastructure projects would have to be carried out by Kabul, most aid should be implemented under the control of local leaders. Given the heightened sense of group identity resulting from the war years, any postwar government is likely to face more powerful pressures than ever before for local political and economic autonomy.

It would be disastrous if Kabul were to overreach itself, repeating the abortive earlier efforts to over-centralize that are still fresh in the minds of all Afghans. But this is not the most likely scenario during the years immediately ahead. Rather, the clear and present danger facing Afghanistan is balkanization and a level of continuing, externally supported fratricide that would make it increasingly difficult to sustain an effective program of "humanitarian encirclement."

# Notes

[1] Office of the U.N. Coordinator for Humanitarian and Economic Assistance Programs Relating to Afghanistan, *First Consolidated Report,* Geneva, September, 1988; *Second Consolidated Report,* Geneva, October, 1989; *United Nations Plan of Action, 1989;* and *United Nations Plan of Action, 1990,* Office of the U.N. Coordinator for Humanitarian and Economic Assistance Programs relating to Afghanistan, Geneva.

[2] "Afghan War, A Lesson for the Future," *Izvestia,* May 4, 1989, cited in Novosti Press Agency's *Daily Review,* Moscow, May 5, 1989, p. 4.

[3] Selig S. Harrison, "Inside the Afghan Talks," *Foreign Policy,* No. 72 (Fall 1988).

[4] "What Do The Afghan Refugees Think? An Opinion Survey in the Camps," *Afghan Information Center Monthly Bulletin* (Peshawar, Pakistan: Afghan Information Center, July 1987), pp. 2–8.

[5] Edward L. Girardet, *Afghanistan: The Soviet War* (New York: St. Martin's Press, 1985), p. 183.

[6] "Administration Aids Afghan Rebels," *The Washington Post,* October 14, 1986, p. 32.

[7] U.S. Agency for International Development, Annual Budget Submission, FY 18 1988, *Afghanistan* (June 1986), pp. 38–39.

[8] U.S. Agency for International Development, "Cross-Border Humanitarian Assistance for Afghanistan," June 1, 1988, p. 2.

[9] U.S. Agency for International Development, "Afghanistan: Cross-Border Humanitarian Assistance Program," June 1, 1989, p. 2.

[10] U.S. Agency for International Development, "Cross-Border Humanitarian Assistance Program," January 1990, p. 3. See also Richard M. Weintraub, "U.S. Details Aid Project to Afghans," *The Washington Post,* February 17, 1989, p. 24.

[11] Edward L. Girardet, "U.S. Humanitarian Aid Under Fire," *Christian Science Monitor,* Dec. 8, 1987, p. 2. For a review of NGO programs published by a group representing NGO interests, see *Overview of NGO Assistance to the People of Afghanistan* (Peshawar, Pakistan: Agency Coordinating Body for Afghan Relief, March 1990).

[12] James Rupert, "U.S. Aid to Rebels Stirs Fear of Hurting Cause," *The Washington Post,* October 14, 1986, p. 26.

[13] Weintraub, "U.S. Details Aid Project to Afghans," op. cit.

[14] Girardet, "U.S. Humanitarian Aid Under Fire," op. cit.

[15] *United Nations Plan of Action 1989,* op. cit., pp. 3–4.

[16] See the Federal News Service account of State Department spokesman Charles Redman's daily news briefing on February 7, 1989, and Barbara Crossette, "Food Shortages Reported In Kabul," *The New York Times,* February 8, 1989, p. 3.

[17] Crossette, "Food Shortages Reported in Kabul," op. cit.

[18] "The Future of Humanitarian Aid in Afghanistan," *Afghan Information Centre Monthly Bulletin* (Peshawar, Pakistan: Afghan Information Centre, December 1988), p. 38.

[19] Deutsche Afghanistan Komitee, 1988 report, Bonn, cited in Helga Baitenmann, "NGO's and the Afghan War: The Politicisation of Humanitarian Aid," *Third World Quarterly* (London: January 1990), p. 84.

[20] J.H. Lorentz, "Afghan Aid: The Role of Private Voluntary Organizations," *Journal of South Asian and Middle Eastern Studies,* Winter 1987.

[21] *Second Consolidated Report,* op. cit., p. 6.

[22] Transcript of Extemporaneous Remarks by Prince Sadruddin Aga Khan, "Statesmen's Forum" (Washington, D.C.: Center for Strategic and International Studies, May 16, 1990), p. 3.

[23] For example, see Anders Fenge, "Aid In Afghanistan: Limitations and Possibilities" (Peshawar, Pakistan: Swedish Relief Committee, August 1989), p. 9. Fenge is director of the Swedish Relief Committee program in Afghanistan.

[24] *United Nations Plan of Action, 1989,* op. cit., p. 17.

[25] First Consolidated Report, op. cit., p. 99.

[26] Richard English, *Interim Report on Repatriation Planning for Afghan Refugees* (Geneva: United Nations High Commissioner for Refugees, September 31, 1989), p. 9.

[27] *Second Consolidated Report,* op. cit., p. 99.

[28] *United Nations Plan of Action, 1989,* pp. 22, 32.

[29] *First Consolidated Report,* op. cit., p. 116.

[30] Ibid., p. 136.

[31] Nancy Hatch Dupree, "Seclusion or Service: Will Women have a Role in the Future of Afghanistan?" Occasional Paper 29 (New York: Afghanistan Forum, December 1989), pp. 3–4.

[32] Ibid., p. 5.

[33] Ibid., p. 9.

[34] Transcript of Extemporaneous Remarks by Prince Sadruddin Aga Khan, op. cit.

[35] Second Consolidated Report, op. cit. p. 7.

[36] United Nations Plan of Action, 1989, op. cit., p. 3–4.

[37] USAID, "Cross-Border Humanitarian Assistance Program," January 1990, p. 3.

[38] Ibid., p. 2.

[39] Ibid., p. 2.

[40] United Nations Plan of Action, 1989, op. cit., pp. 16, 15.

[41] Selig S. Harrison, "What Next in Afghanistan?" The Washington Post, April 17, 1988; "Who Will Win the Bloody Battle for Kabul?" The Washington Post, January 29, 1989; "Fighting to the Last Afghan," Peace and Security (Ottawa: Canadian Institute of International Peace and Security, Autumn 1989); "Comment grantir une transition pacifique a Kabul?" Le Monde Diplomatique, November 1989.

# AFTER THE WARS

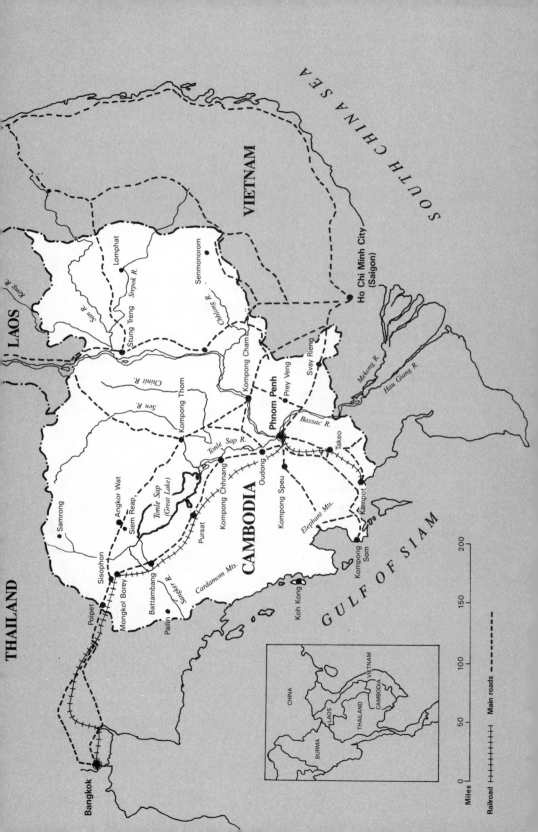

# Chapter 2

# Indochina

## Nayan Chanda

The one region in Asia that has become synonymous with war and destruction is Indochina. Nearly fifty years after the first shots were fired in what came to be known as the Indochina War, the region has yet to find peace. What began as a communist-led struggle for national independence for Vietnam, Laos, and Cambodia was soon viewed as a confrontation between two world political-ideological systems. In the course of this epochal battle, the more enduring nationalist roots of the conflict were overlooked. It was only after the Americans left Indochina to the victorious communists and the latter fell out among themselves that the forces of nationalism—Chinese, Vietnamese, and Khmer—came into sharper focus.

Ironically, one of the original objectives of the U.S. intervention in Vietnam was to halt the advance of the Communist Party of Vietnam, which was widely perceived as an agent of Chinese expansionism as well as the main force behind the Cambodian Communist Party. The events following the U.S. withdrawal from Vietnam and Cambodia turned these perceptions on their heads. The border skirmishes between Cambodia and Vietnam that began just as the Americans left led to a full-scale Vietnamese invasion of Cambodia in 1978. Soon after, Sino-Vietnamese border tensions gave way to a devastating Chinese punitive raid against Vietnam, which in turn led to growing friction between Laos and China. Even after the Chinese troops withdrew from Vietnam, the Vietnamese occupation of Cambodia continued for eleven years. And even now, after the withdrawal of Vietnamese troops, the conflict in Cambodia persists.

If the American intervention—with its massive fire power and injection of money—wrought terrible human and physical destruction and distorted the Cambodian economy, the bloody revolution and intra-communist conflict that followed have also resulted in enormous loss of life and damage to the economies of both Vietnam and Cambodia. Of even longer-term significance is the fact that the present and continuing Third Indochina Conflict (after those with France and the United States) has reinforced centuries-old ethnic hostilities and acute distrust among the peoples of the region.

Although the parties to the Cambodian conflict have agreed to form a Supreme National Council, as recommended by the five permanent (Perm Five) members of the United Nations and have accepted their framework for peace, the nationalist ambition and fears that led to the Third Indochina Conflict remain a potent force in the equation. Even after the fighting does stop in Cambodia, an enduring peace can be achieved only if economic development plans help redress the deep socio-economic gap *within* Cambodia and the glaring economic imbalance between Cambodia and its neighbors, especially Vietnam. Thus, reconstruction in Indochina is needed not only to heal the wounds of war but also to promote economic development in Vietnam, Cambodia, and Laos in a way that will help to redress serious economic disparities and reduce the possible sources of future conflict.

Clearly, the first priority is to bring about an end to the fighting. The specific manner in which the war is ended will to a large extent determine the *kind* of reconstruction and economic planning that emerges in Indochina. This essay will explore the likely shape of a political settlement and its impact on reconstruction efforts. It will then assess the economic and social consequences of the war in Indochina and their implications for short- and long-term reconstruction and development plans. The analysis will focus particularly on the crux of the difficulty: Cambodia.

## Ending the Conflict

The dramatic end to the Second Indochina War came on April 30, 1975, when the last American personnel were airlifted from the roof of the U.S. embassy in Saigon. Thirteen days earlier, the Americans had also pulled out of Phnom Penh, and the Khmer Rouge had marched in to order a brutal evacuation of the capital. Laos, too, fell into Pathet Lao hands as the coalition government collapsed and the demoralized U.S.-backed royalist forces fled the country. By the summer of 1975, all of Indochina was perceived to be in the hands of

Hanoi-dominated communists but (supposedly) at least "at peace." The reality turned out to be very different; for the past decade and a half, news headlines have continued to report one conflict after another among the Cambodians as well as between Vietnam and its neighbors.

In September 1989, after an eleven-year occupation, Vietnamese combat troops finally withdrew from Cambodia, leaving the Hanoi-installed Heng Samrin regime essentially to fend for itself. Vietnamese skirmishes with China along their common border have stopped, and Sino-Vietnamese trade and diplomatic ties have improved. But Vietnam cannot yet claim the fruits of peace, because it is being held hostage to the resolution of the conflict in Cambodia. Since 1979, the United States has expanded its trade embargo on Vietnam to block any loans to that country by the World Bank, the Asian Development Bank, or the International Monetary Fund—requiring that it cooperate with Washington on reaching a comprehensive settlement in Cambodia before any such funding is provided. In practical terms, that cooperation means that Hanoi would have to force its allies in Phnom Penh to accept a peace plan agreed to by the United States, China, and the Khmer Rouge.

Thus the key to peace and reconstruction in the entire Indochina region is Cambodia. And the difficulties of resolving the Cambodia conflict lie in the complex origin of the war: a deep-rooted social and political conflict among the Khmer overlaid with age-old racial enmities as well as regional rivalries and ambitions.

The Cambodian conflict can best be understood through a grasp of its three layers: its domestic roots, regional rivalries, and superpower involvement. What is today viewed as the "Cambodian problem" began twenty years ago with a coup that overthrew Prince Norodom Sihanouk. The coup, carried out by pro-American politicians and army officers, failed miserably in its promise to solve Cambodia's security and economic problems and deliver democracy. Instead, it created the conditions for the success of its leftist opponents—the Khmer Rouge—who sought to create an exploitation-free egalitarian society. Three years before the right-wing coup, the Khmer Rouge had mobilized poor peasants to launch an unsuccessful armed insurgency against the royal government. In a dramatic reversal, after the coup, Prince Sihanouk threw his support behind the Khmer Rouge–led resistance against the coup plotters. His charismatic appeal, along with Chinese and Vietnamese support, helped the Khmer Rouge to seize power in 1975. Their victory soon brought to the surface the deep divergences between the Khmer Rouge and the Vietnamese Communists and among the Khmer Rouge leadership itself, divided along pro-Vietnamese and anti-

Vietnamese lines. The differences led not only to a split in the Cambodian Communist Party and bloody purges, but eventually also to an anti-Vietnamese pogrom in Cambodia and generalized attacks on Vietnamese territory. The Khmer Rouge hatred for the Vietnamese was further intensified by Hanoi's invasion and the installation of a government of pro-Vietnamese Khmers and Khmer Rouge defectors. Despite the 1989 withdrawal of Vietnamese combat units from Cambodia, the Khmer Rouge are still carrying on their "holy war" against the Vietnamese—charging that Hanoi continues to maintain more than a million disguised soldiers and civilian settlers in Cambodia.

In the fall of 1990, as this book goes to press, Cambodia is still a country at war. The big powers have agreed on a framework of peace, and the Cambodian parties have formed a provisional body and have smiled for the camera—but the fighting continues.

## The Likely Shape of a Settlement

Hope for peace in Cambodia has been on a roller coaster ever since November 1987, when Prince Sihanouk, leader of the resistance coalition, and Phnom Penh Premier Hun Sen met for the first time in Fère-en-Tardenois, France. That encounter was followed by a series of bilateral meetings, the Jakarta Informal Meetings (JIM) among the Cambodian parties and the ASEAN countries, and the International Conference on Cambodia in July–August 1989. As of August 1990, however, they had all failed to produce any agreement to end the fighting. The Khmer Rouge and the non-communist resistance insisted on the dismantling of the Hun Sen regime and its replacement by a four-party coalition of equals. Prospects for peace seemed to brighten momentarily in early June, when Prince Sihanouk, at the urging of Thailand and Japan, met Hun Sen in Tokyo and signed a "voluntary self-restraint" agreement. But the accord proved to be stillborn as Sihanouk's partners, China and the Khmer Rouge, rejected such a bipartite arrangement.

While the regional attempt to find a solution has continued, a parallel effort was mounted in January 1990 by the Perm Five members of the U.N. Security Council. Since the Five included the Soviet Union and China—the two key supporters of the parties to the Cambodian civil war—it was hoped that the 'patrons' would be able to persuade their 'clients' to compromise. On August 28, after a series of meetings of the senior officials of the Perm Five in Paris and New York, the group adopted a "Framework for a Comprehensive Political Settlement of the Cambodia Conflict." This document, the first agreement among the big-power backers of the Cambodia conflict, provided an outline for transitional arrangements regarding the administration of Cambodia, military arrangements during the transitional period, elections under United Nations auspices, human rights protection, and international guarantees.

The Perm Five agreement was achieved principally because the Soviet Union—beset by troubles at home and eager to cooperate with the United States in resolving regional conflicts as well as to improve its relations with China—was willing to pressure its allies in Phnom Penh to make concessions. China, too, was keen to improve its image, sullied by the Tiananmen massacre, and to make some concessions at the expense of its Khmer Rouge protegés. The signs of a shift in U.S. policy toward Indochina, as evidenced by Secretary of State James Baker's July 18 announcement, also pressured China. After a meeting with U.S.S.R. Foreign Minister Eduard Shevardnadze in Paris, Secretary Baker stated the the United States would (a) begin a dialogue with Vietnam on Cambodia, (b) establish contact with Phnom Penh, and (c) withdraw recognition of the resistance coalition at the U.N. if it included the Khmer Rouge organization. The United States at the same time promised to facilitate humanitarian aid to Vietnam and Cambodia.

Despite strong Western opposition to the Khmer Rouge, however, the compromise between China and the West essentially involved the role the group would play as junior partner in a symbolic coalition. While the United States, Britain, France, and the Soviet Union gave in to the Chinese demand that there be no effort to castigate the Khmer Rouge by recalling their genocidal rule—or even to make indirect allusions such as that there be no return to the "universally condemned practices of a recent past"—China stopped insisting on an equal share for the Khmer Rouge in the interim administration or on a total dismantling of the Hun Sen regime.

The strong framework adopted by the Five sidestepped the issue of whether there should be a quadripartite or bipartite government in Cambodia by setting up a symbolic entity and handing over real authority over key ministries to the United Nations. The plan called on "Cambodian parties" to set up a Supreme National Council (SNC) consisting of "representative individuals with authority among the Cambodian people." The Perm Five implicitly rejected the Phnom Penh demand that notorious Khmer Rouge figures be excluded from all authority by stipulating that the representatives "should be acceptable to each other." If Hun Sen insisted on excluding a particular Khmer Rouge leader, then he himself might be declared unacceptable and kept out by the Khmer Rouge. This condition later forced the Phnom Penh regime to agree to include Son Sen—the notorious Khmer Rouge defense minister listed by Phnom Penh as one of the nine leaders responsible for genocide—as one of the Khmer Rouge members of the SNC.

Under intense pressure from their respective big-power backers, the Cambodian factions met in Jakarta on September 9–10, 1990 to endorse the U.N. framework and form the SNC. A delegation representing the SNC was to occupy Cambodia's seat at the United Nations.

Although the Khmer Rouge and the non-communist resistance agree with the broad outline of the Perm Five framework, considerable differences remain over crucial details. All sides agree that an international verification of the withdrawal of Vietnamese forces from Cambodia would be followed by a cease-fire among the Cambodian parties and that foreign military supply to the combatants would cease. There is also agreement that a free and fair election should elect a constituent assembly, leading to the formation of a new government, and that there has to be an interim authority representing the country's sovereignty while the United Nations organizes and monitors the election.

The 12 member SNC that was formed in Jakarta, with six from the Phnom Penh government and six from the resistance side, immediately ran into an organizational hurdle: the members could not agree on the chairmanship of the body. The issue at stake was whether Prince Sihanouk, preferred for chairman of the SNC by China and the West, was a balancing figure above the two factions or (as seen by Phnom Penh) himself a member of the resistance. The Hun Sen regime rejected the resistance and Chinese demand that Prince Sihanouk be appointed the 13th member and chairman of the SNC. Hun Sen proposed that Sihanouk could be made the chairman either by replacing one of the six representing the resistance or by an expansion of the SNC membership, with Sihanouk as the thirteenth member and a Phnom Penh government official the fourteenth member. That would give both sides equal representation. Failure to resolve this difference meant that the SNC could not meet to select a delegation to attend the U.N. General Assembly and take Cambodia's seat.

The reason behind the deadlock was the mutual suspicion of intentions during the twilight zone of the interim administration—a suspicion only enhanced by the ambiguity of the U.N. framework on the issue of power in Cambodia. While the Perm Five plan did not explicitly call for dismantling the Hun Sen regime, its standing nevertheless was weakened by the Perm Five's description of the SNC as the "unique legitimate body and source of authority."

The Perm Five did, however, state that to ensure a neutral environment for free and fair elections, administrative agencies that could influence the outcome of the elections should be placed "under direct U.N. supervision *or* control." While agencies dealing with foreign affairs, defense, finance, public security, and information would get special attention, the United Nations, in consultation with the SNC, would identify "which agencies, bodies and offices could continue to operate in order to ensure normal day-to-life in the country." The United Nations would also investigate complaints regarding action by "existing administrative structures in Cambodia."

This ambiguity as to the nature of power in Cambodia opened the way to conflicting interpretations of the United Nations framework and an impasse over its implementation. The Hun Sen regime interpreted the plan to mean that its administration would continue to exercise control over the country until the formation of an elected government. It would only hand over to the U.N. Transitional Authority in Cambodia (UNTAC) powers to organize, conduct, and monitor a free election. The resistance argues that continuation of Phnom Penh authority in any form would be prejudicial to a free and fair election and thus the United Nations should take over running the country.

Apart from its strenuous objection to a dissolution of its authority, the Phnom Penh regime was also opposed to the idea of disarming and cantonment of the troops of both sides, as proposed by the Perm Five. It argued that while the standing army of the regime could easily be disarmed and put in cantonments, the guerilla army of the resistance could hide their arms and men in the jungle. These and other issues concerning electoral procedures—most importantly, the nature of U.N. involvement in the administration of the country—remain to be resolved among the Cambodian parties before the planned international conference can take place to codify the accords and give international guarantee. Until then, the grisly war in Cambodia will continue.

In view of the deadlock over such key issues in a negotiated settlement, Cambodia faces three possibilities. First, a combination of military and economic pressure from both the Western world and the Soviet Union could force Hun Sen to compromise and fully accept the formula offered by the Perm Five. Second, a de facto solution could take shape if some Western countries—tiring of the unending conflict and worrying about a Khmer Rouge return—moved to recognize a coalition between the non-communist resistance and Hun Sen. There is considerable sympathy for the Hun Sen regime in Western Europe, and Japan, too, is eager to deal with Phnom Penh. Since the formation of the SNC, a French vice ministerial level delegation—the first such visit by a Western government—has visited Phnom Penh. Third, a low-level guerrilla war could continue indefinitely until one of the parties, short of men, materiel, and the will to fight surrendered. In such a scenario, the Khmer Rouge would be likely to persevere and emerge the victor.

## The Wounds of War

The task of rebuilding Indochina would have been daunting even had the Indochina War ended in 1975, but the devastation that has followed in the "post-Vietnam war" period has rendered the job infinitely harder. During the war, 7 million tons of bombs were dropped on Vietnam, and a similar tonnage of shells was fired from naval vessels—or six times the total tonnage of bombs dropped by the United States in the European and Pacific theatres in World War II. In northern Vietnam, industry and infrastructure were left in shambles; in the south, some two-thirds of the villages and 5 million hectares of forest were destroyed—and some 10 million people became refugees. At the end of the war, 1 million women were widows, 800,000 children were orphans, and 3 million people were left jobless. Four years later, the Chinese incursion destroyed many of the buildings, bridges, railway lines, and factories that still stood in Vietnam's border region.

In the immediate postwar years, Vietnam launched an ambitious economic plan designed to simultaneously develop agriculture and light industry and to lay the foundations for a heavy-industry sector. However, the Vietnamese failure to normalize relations with the United States and Hanoi's growing conflict with China—coupled with heavy-handed central planning, corruption, and a stultifying bureaucracy—sapped the reconstruction effort. It was abandoned in all but name during the economic crisis that ensued after the Vietnamese (beset by China and beleaguered by U.S. sanctions) became bogged down in Cambodia.

Neighboring Laos, which had become the target of an American "secret war," was devastated by bombing. A country with a population of only 3 million, Laos earned the dubious distinction of being the most heavily bombed nation on earth in per capita terms. Thousands of civilians were killed and maimed, some 350,000 people were rendered homeless, and parts of the country were turned into lunar landscapes.

Although the war lasted a much shorter time in Cambodia than in Vietnam or Laos, the devastation there was also staggering. In 1973 alone, Cambodia suffered heavier bombing than Japan dur-

ing all of World War II. In the five years after the 1970 coup, an estimated 600,000 people were killed, and most schools, hospitals,
roads, bridges, telecommunication installations, and motorized
means of transport were destroyed. The Khmer Rouge's forced march
toward a socialist utopia nearly extinguished the battered country.
Cambodia was hermetically sealed off by Pol Pot and his comrades
as they set out to build a powerful nation-state and return it to its
former glory through a policy of forced labor and ideological purifica-
tion. Money, the banking system, and the market economy were
abolished. One of the regime's slogans summed up its economic strategy: "With water we'll have rice, and with rice we'll have everything." Virtually the entire population was harnessed to the task of
digging canals, building embankments, and growing rice. Each
administrative unit was required to dig a certain length of canals
whether the conditions of the area called for it or not. Individual
members of village units in turn were assigned specific tasks to that
end. Rigid quotas were also handed down to individuals to plow the
fields and plant and harvest rice. By the end of 1978, a third of Cambodia was said to be under irrigation, but at a horrendous cost: Hundreds of thousands of people had been executed for failing to meet
their obligations, and an even greater number had died of exhaus-
tion and lack of medical attention. As for the value of the irrigation
system itself—many of the badly planned embankments collapsed,
and canals dug without regard for topography remained bone dry.

In Democratic Kampuchea, industry was to serve the peasantry and to train a new proletarian class from the peasantry. In
reality, a very small number of people were employed in factories
producing cement, textiles, footwear, cigarettes, utensils, fish paste,
and other necessities. With the exception of a few factories refur-
bished with Chinese aid, such as the Kompong Cham textile mill,
most lacked maintenance and spare parts and ran at a fraction of
capacity.

Cambodia's transportation and communication infrastructure,
already damaged by years of warfare, deteriorated further under the
Khmer Rouge and in the battle with the invading Vietnamese army
in 1978. Along with trade and other services, the education system
was eliminated. And the best trained men, women, and young people
suffered the heaviest toll among a million or more Cambodians who
perished during the Khmer Rouge rule. Casualties included 82 per
cent of the physicians, 65 per cent of the teachers, and half of the
high school students. Those staggering losses of skilled personnel
are compounded by a massive loss of the male population (leaving
the woman–man ratio at 56–44) in a country with a sharp traditional differentiation between male and female work roles. The mag-

nitude of Cambodia's destruction provides an idea of the country's postwar needs. "For practical purposes," notes a Cambodian economist, "the Cambodian economy was moved backward to the stone age."[1]

The worldwide sympathy and support for Cambodia's plight would have gone a long way in producing the economic support needed to restore the country's economy had the country not been caught in bitter regional and superpower rivalry. Cambodia has found its path to recovery blocked by political obstacles. After the initial spurt of sympathy, aid was reduced to a trickle, and reconstruction became hostage to Western and Chinese attempts to isolate and pressure the Phnom Penh government. At the same time, rapid population growth since 1979 brought the total population to an estimated 8.2 million by 1988—some 13 per cent higher than in 1968—while the nation's estimated GDP in 1988 was half that of 1968. With $190 per capita GDP, Cambodia is one of the world's ten poorest countries.

# An Indochina Development Strategy: Short–Term Measures

Differences in the level of economic development, as well as the availability of human and natural resources, dictate different courses for Vietnam, Laos, and Cambodia.

### Laos

Although closely allied with Hanoi, Laos nonetheless succeeded in maintaining not only tenuous relations with the United States but also an ongoing association with international financial institutions such as the Asian Development Bank, the World Bank, and the International Monetary Fund. With the help of those institutions and Western non-governmental organizations (NGOs)—as well as Soviet bloc aid that covered 80 per cent of its annual revenue in the immediate postwar years—Laos embarked on a modest reconstruction program after the war.[2] Nearly a third of the population that had been uprooted by U.S. bombing was resettled, some roads and bridges were repaired, and abandoned farmland was brought back under plough. However, a campaign to collectivize agriculture and a rigid system of socialist planning and state control brought the economy close to ruin, and thousands of citizens fled to neighboring Thailand.

A "new economic policy," initiated in 1979 and fully implemented since 1985, has restored private farming and trade, market pricing, and decentralized planning—and opened up the country for private foreign investment. Partly as a result of this policy switch and partly due to favorable weather, Laos has now achieved self-sufficiency in food. Yet certain areas of the country still suffer from food shortage, and a poor transportation network makes meeting their needs difficult. Laos also needs increased investment in construction for better exploitation of its significant forestry resources (45 per cent of the total surface) and mineral deposits, as well as in saw mills and modern mineral extraction. However, in view of a sharply rising debt burden (27 per cent of the 1987 export earnings, and 37 per cent of convertible currency borrowing)—and the possible release of funds for new borrowers like Vietnam and Cambodia—Laos would have difficulty in obtaining further large-scale loans.[3]

### Vietnam

Vietnam's economic reforms since 1979, its liberal investment code, its immediately exploitable resources, and its relatively sound infrastructure are likely to make it more attractive than Cambodia or Laos to foreign investors.[4] While Vietnam badly needs massive amounts of aid from international and bilateral donors for rebuilding and upgrading its damaged and decaying infrastructure, it can improve its economy through private investment and joint ventures in off-shore oil exploration, fishing, agri-processing, light industry, and tourism. A small amount of foreign investment, totaling $800 million, has already come in. The lifting of the U.S. trade embargo on Vietnam and the restoration of its eligibility for IMF and the World Bank loans (blocked to date by Washington) could pave the way for increased investment flows.

### Cambodia

The planning tasks in Cambodia are more basic than in Vietnam. Before adopting any program, Cambodia first needs to address the huge challenge of restoring normalcy of life. This challenge includes repatriating refugees from Thailand, removing land mines, and fighting a malaria epidemic.

Malaria, especially the dangerous Plasmodium Falciparum strain, accounts for a significant share of the deaths in Cambodia and has made certain zones virtually uninhabitable. The number of reported cases of malaria has gone up from 11,800 in 1981 to 168,000 in 1989.[5] Since malaria is a non-immunizable disease, its spread can be reduced only through education and preventive measures. Expansion of the present rudimentary health care facilities and of the availability of drugs would help reduce deaths from the disease.

The existence of mines—especially anti-personnel mines made of plastic—in the western and northern parts of the country present another serious threat to life. According to one NGO estimate, on an average day, 50 persons are injured by mines in Cambodia; that means 18,000 people a year. As the author found during a visit to Cambodia in the spring of 1990, the largest number of patients in the hospitals are young men and women who have lost one or both legs in this way. Clearly one of the priority tasks before repatriating refugees is an extensive de-mining operation—presumably with assistance from foreign military experts. The prosthetic assistance currently provided by the American Friends Services Committee (AFSC) is laudable but woefully inadequate, and much greater aid will be required to rehabilitate the large invalid population and enable it to be productive.

The UNHCR has conducted an exhaustive survey in preparation for the repatriation of Cambodian refugees currently in Thailand. The fact that 64 per cent of the refugees in three major camps polled in 1989 wanted to return to the bordering provinces of Battambang and Oddar Meanchey[6] could make the transfer easier to set into motion, although land mines continue to present a great threat in that area. The government would have to find 52,000–60,000 hectares of land for the returnees to cultivate. While land in the country is still plentiful, refugees may never recover their former land in their native villages. The recently instituted land reform granting titles to those who first cultivate the land is likely to result in the occupation of the best plots. On the other hand, if returnees are provided with financial assistance and tools—as planned by the UNHCR—this could generate jealousy and friction with older residents.

Beyond these immediate steps lies the immense task of ensuring the basic needs of the growing population and restoring the living standard at least to the prewar level—a task that one Cambodian Ministry of Planning document has calculated would take 15 years. Given the destruction of the infrastructure and population growth since 1979, restoring the pre-1970 living standard may require, according to one estimate, a capital investment of $5 billion.[7] Such an investment, however, is likely to be hindered by more than the limited availability of funds, as the absorptive capacity of the country is even more limited.

Thus the first steps toward long-term recovery must address a basic dilemma: While Cambodia requires a significant infusion of foreign aid to rebuild the economy, the country is too weak to *utilize* that aid. Cambodia's physical infrastructure is too poor to absorb such foreign aid, and the country lacks the technical and managerial skills essential to put such assistance to use. In early 1990, the U.N. Secretary General sent a survey team to Cambodia to assess the facilities available for installing a U.N. interim authority and a peacekeeping force. The members returned shocked by the primitive condition of the country. Virtually everything—from housing to transport to potable water—would have to be transported to the country for use by the U.N. officials. The team also found that there were only some 3,000 individuals with education beyond secondary school and not a single person capable of highly sophisticated macroeconomic planning. An earlier United Nations Development Programme (UNDP) study had found that in the whole country there were only 360 individuals with some degree of managerial skill. This dramatic shortage of skilled manpower means that Cambodia can absorb very little economic aid—perhaps not more than $200 million a year.[8]

The managerial shortage also means that the Phnom Penh government is unable to produce any project profiles, not to mention feasibility studies; the only thing it has drawn up is a broad framework of priorities. In this setting, the international community has been loathe to go further in detailing any plan. As the document on reconstruction in Cambodia adopted by the Paris Conference on Cambodia in August 1989 put it: "No attempt should be made to impose a development strategy on Cambodia from outside."

The intent behind such a statement is laudable, but unless one agrees to deal with the Hun Sen regime or with an interim authority such as the Supreme National Council, the task of defining those priorities would have to be left to an elected government when it finally emerges. Moreover, tremendous costs are also involved in waiting for five to ten years until a body of home-grown experts emerges to plan Cambodia's future. A significant return of overseas Cambodians with technical and managerial skills can alleviate the need for human resources to a degree, but international technical assistance to the Cambodian government in helping to define some of the short-term goals will also be essential. Without a broad roadmap indicating the direction Cambodia is to take, piecemeal assistance and construction could turn out to be more of a hindrance than a help in the long run.

Making a start requires an answer to the basic question: Should the emphasis be on construction or on reconstruction? While the limited availability of funds may dictate the latter more modest

course, given the country's outdated and seriously run-down infrastructure, it may be more cost-effective to build new installations
than to keep patching up the old ones. A few examples illustrate the
point: Cambodia will obviously need a huge amount of cement to
build bridges, houses, schools, hospitals, and hotels. But it may be
useless to try to repair the country's only cement plant, built with
Chinese aid in Kampot in the late 1960s. Three Chinese technicians
who made a quiet visit to the plant in 1989 as consultants to a Thai
company told Cambodian officials that the machinery there was so
old that it would be hard even to find spare parts to repair the equipment. They advised Cambodians to buy a new Japanese-made plant
instead.[9] Similarly, power to Phnom Penh is provided by an antiquated French-built power generating station and a very old Soviet
diesel generator. The cost of maintaining the French generator has
been exceedingly high; moreover, as the Soviets themselves now
admit, it was a mistake on their part to install outdated cost-inef-
ficient generators in the late 1980s.[10] Future projects must ease
Cambodia along the path of modernization. In restoring the telecommunications network, it would make economic sense to install
micro-wave stations and digital exchanges rather than wired tele-
phone and telegraph systems. The installation of Soviet as well as
Australian satellite dishes in Phnom Penh for international telecommunication link-up has started Cambodia in the direction of
modernization.

While replacing antiquated equipment with more modern systems in the power generation, telecommunications, and light-indus-
try sectors is a rational course, actual implementation of these systems will, of course, be slowed by the lack of capital and skilled manpower. However, since the training of technical personnel essentially
has to start totally afresh, the most efficient strategy may well be to
focus training on the use of modern machines.

The same approach cannot, however, be applied to agriculture
for the simple reason that modernizing a sector that employs more
than 80 per cent of the population would be an extremely expensive
and unrealistic undertaking. Although Cambodia has made tremendous progress in rice production since 1979, it is barely self-suf-
ficient in food, and some 85 per cent of production is dependent on
rain. Small-scale irrigation schemes providing water during the dry
season could help produce a second annual crop. Utilizing seasonal
labor to dig canals or reservoirs could also generate income for rural
people. While tractors would be appropriate for cultivation in certain
areas of the country, especially for the heavy clay soils of Battambang province and the fertile fields around Tonle Sap, the cost of the

machines and maintenance problems[11] suggest the more modest approach of providing farmers with draft animals. Provision of veterinary care for the existing herd of cattle and buffalo could also help preserve and replenish the stock. Improving the ability of farmers to earn cash from their produce would also prevent distress sales of the cattle, especially in the border areas. Other cost-efficient programs would involve providing farmers with high-yield seeds, fertilizer, and pesticides as well as means of transportation to get their produce to market.

The type of economic system Cambodia should have is a question of fundamental political choice to be determined by the country's future government. But the present reality in Cambodia—the feeble nature of the state apparatus and the acute shortage of skilled manpower—argues for minimal state intervention in the economy. The Khmer Rouge, who announced the abolition of the Communist Party of Kampuchea in 1982, is now publicly calling for a capitalist system; unfortunately, judging from the evidence of internal Khmer Rouge documents, that posture seems designed only to impress the Western world.[12]

In the case of the State of Cambodia, however, the acceptance of free enterprise seems more genuine. In fact, the abandonment of agricultural collectivization and the beginning of the privatization of state-run industrial enterprises, undertaken in 1989 by the Hun Sen government, is an acknowledgment of the weakness of the state. At the same time that it liberalizes economic policies, the government needs to strengthen the administrative apparatus in order to address the poor infrastructure and the total absence of a legal and practical framework for private investment and trade. The Central Bank currently acts as a "treasury department" for the government and has no role either in promoting savings or in providing credit. The creation of a regular banking system and the establishment of a proper tax system, along with the introduction of rules and regulations concerning private investment, could help in developing industry and the trade sector while increasing government revenue. Although three-quarters of the country's economy is now in private hands, and the private trade sector is one of the most prosperous in the economy, only a small percentage of government revenue comes from import tariffs and taxes.

In June 1989, the Hun Sen government enacted a decree concerning foreign investment designed to encourage overseas Cambodians, as well as foreigners and international agencies, to invest capital in the country and provide it with modern technology. However, foreign investors would not flock to Cambodia even if there were peace as long as the implementing regulations are not in place. Foreign technical assistance in that process would be of significant value.

The dramatic shortage of qualified personnel in the country cannot be resolved promptly—not even through accelerated training programs. A temporary and in some cases even a long-term solution might be to encourage Cambodians living abroad to return home. This group includes not only the many professionals who fled the country, but also those who have subsequently acquired skills that Cambodia now sorely needs. The reluctance of prospective returnees to endure the hardships of Cambodia after years of relatively comfortable living in the West could be mitigated by offering them contractual jobs under the auspices of the United Nations or other international organizations. Such a strategy would, of course, pose the risk of creating tensions and antagonisms between the returning expatriates and their "second class" compatriots. Another way to address the shortage—though a less desirable one—would be to send personnel from U.N. and other voluntary agencies to Cambodia on long-term assignment. As motivated foreigners working on a voluntary basis, they would not present the social problems that highly salaried repatriated Khmer would. Mass training of interpreters and teachers inside the country and in camps could begin immediately to meet those needs when peace comes.

While waiting for a peace settlement, training of technical and administrative cadres, too, can begin in the camps and inside the country. In the refugee camps it runs in Thailand, the U.N. Border Relief Operation already has been providing primary schooling and adult literacy programs as well as some vocational training such as knitting, mat making, blacksmithing, and pottery. The UNHCR has also provided workshops for training in auto repair, electrical services, and welding. The people coming out of these programs could in turn train others when they return home.

# A Strategy for the Long Term

In the absence of a political settlement, it is difficult to anticipate the direction Cambodian development planning will take and what type of external assistance will be made available. While it is safe to assume that some kind of political settlement will be reached in the early 1990s, the political stability of the country cannot be taken for granted. Judging by the depth of the Khmer Rouge's continued commitment to radically transform Cambodia and to fight the perceived

Vietnamese threat, one can assume that, whatever the shape of the political settlement, the Khmer Rouge struggle, armed or otherwise, will be a factor of instability for a number of years to come. If the Khmer Rouge emerge as a partner in an eventual coalition, they will attempt to dominate it. And if defeated in an election or left out altogether from an interim political arrangement, the Khmer Rouge will attempt to mobilize the urban poor and dispossessed peasantry to oppose the government.

Given demographic trends and the possibility of large foreign assistance coming into the country, there also will be an increasing danger of a widening economic gap between the cities and the countryside and between the new capitalists and urban workers. The liberalization of the economy in recent years has already led to a significant growth in private trade and the emergence of a moneyed class whose wealth stands in sharp contrast to the vast poverty of the majority of Cambodians. A massive inflow of foreign aid could further widen the gap if it is not judiciously used to create jobs and generate income in the countryside in the pursuit of equity. In 1989, nearly half of Cambodia's 8.4 million population was below 16 years of age, and the economically active population was higher than at any time in the past. The population growth rate—officially 2.8 per cent but estimated to be as high as 4 per cent—will mean a sharply rising demand for employment.[13]

Since the key elements in the Khmer Rouge political campaign will be the "threat" from Vietnam and the exploitation and inequality of Cambodian society, planning should take that into consideration. While fast economic growth certainly requires an open market economy, the development plan should have as its objective a narrowing of the economic disparities between various segments of the population. Special consideration should be given to training Cambodians to branch out from their traditional farming profession. Offering vocational training to Khmer and encouraging their entrepreneurial spirit can help guard against a renewal of the social and ethnic tensions produced in the past by the domination of the fishing, petty trade, and service sectors by ethnic Vietnamese.

Another potentially explosive problem is presented by the unfavorable land/man ratio in Vietnam (64 million people on 6 million hectares of cultivable land), which is likely to encourage emigration across the porous border into relatively underpopulated Cambodia (with one eighth of the population of Vietnam and two-thirds of cultivable land). If unchecked, such migration could over time lead to outbreaks of ethnic conflict. Long-term stability and peace in Cambodia thus require regional development plans that both ensure balanced growth in Vietnam and Cambodia and, through economic development, prevent the search for a Cambodian *lebensraum* by destitute Vietnamese.

## The Pillars of Future Development

Cambodia's long-term development strategy will have to focus on fully utilizing the nation's valuable natural resources, its world-famous temples, and its favorable geographic position as an Indochinese entrepot. The six principal pillars of this strategy must be rice, rubber, fisheries, forestry, tourism, and trade.

Contrary to popular myth, Cambodia is not endowed with very fertile land. Together with the lack of irrigation and of adequate amounts of fertilizer, this makes the Cambodian rice yield one of the lowest in the world. With 85 per cent of the population engaged in agriculture (mainly rice), the expansion of rice production could be of great value, as it not only would provide employment for a growing number of people but also could generate export income. During the 1960s, it was mainly its small population that enabled Cambodia to export its surplus rice (an average of 500,000 tons of rice annually). To develop rice production further, Cambodia could now reclaim some 600,000 hectares of agricultural land, expand the area under dry-season rice through small-scale irrigation projects, and augment the use of fertilizer and pesticides.

Soviet-supplied fertilizer has been one of the factors contributing to Cambodia's impressive recovery in rice production since 1979. However, beginning in 1991, Soviet trade with Cambodia, as with all other socialist countries, will be in hard currency. Unless alternative sources of grants or long-term loans are found, this switch may mean a serious drop in the use of fertilizer in Cambodia. In addition to providing the needed fertilizer and agricultural tools, planning should involve agricultural extension and research, as well as the provision of credit to farmers. The promotion of subsidiary cash crops—maize, soybean, moongbean, pepper, and tobacco—can also enhance peasant income and provide exportable goods. Food processing and cigarette manufacturing industries could also be developed to increase the value of Cambodian exports.

As previously noted, in view of the management and resource constraints, the Cambodian development process will have to begin with promoting small projects and improving traditional methods of farming. Nonetheless, it will be essential to push for modernization in some areas where a beginning has already been made—for example, in instigating the use of tractors in large fields in Battambang. A further and significant boost to agriculture could come from implementing the Mekong Committee's multinational water resource development plan, set up in 1967 under the auspices of the U.N. Economic and Social Commission for Asia. Once a Cambodian government is internationally recognized, it will also be possible to revive the plans of the Mekong Committee to develop projects for irrigation and power generation. Under these plans, water storage projects on the Mekong River and its tributaries would allow for the irrigation of 500,000 hectares. Another reservoir and a hydro-electric station in Stung Treng were also proposed to provide irrigation for one million hectares of land and to generate 2,000 megawatts of electricity. But before such enormously expensive projects are undertaken, Cambodia will have to train engineers and develop a supporting road and communications infrastructure; in 1985, there were only two civil engineers in Phnom Penh's department of hydrology.

The second pillar of development should be rubber production. In prewar Cambodia, rubber was an important item of export; however, negligence and war damage during the Khmer Rouge period led to the loss of more than half of the rubber plantations. Some of the plantations have been put back to use with the assistance of the Soviet bloc. Thus rubber crepe became the second highest export earner in 1989. Rubber wood and furniture, too, could be valuable export items.[14] Domestically, rubber is used in the factories to manufacture tires, sandals, and other products. To fully exploit the potential of this product, the government would have to invest sizable amounts in earth-moving and transport equipment as well as in developing suitable housing for plantation workers. In the past, harsh living conditions and poor wages discouraged Cambodians from working on the plantations, with the result that Vietnamese immigrants provided the principal labor force. Only by improving working conditions in the rubber plantation sector will it be possible to avoid a potentially destabilizing dependence on Vietnamese labor. Cambodia will also need technical assistance in developing rubber plantations and in latex processing. The world's best expertise in rubber research and production is available in neighboring Malaysia. Cooperation with Malaysia in this area would not only benefit both producers but would also help to strengthen regional bonds.

Boasting one of the world's richest fish-breeding grounds— Tonle Sap (Great Lake) and several large river systems—Cambodia has the potential for increasing its own consumption of fish (the principal source of protein for Cambodians) and developing it for export as well. In 1988, freshwater fish production reached barely half the level of the 1960s, while marine fish production was less than half. Deforestation around the Great Lake, the silting of the river channel linking the lake, and ecological changes have brought about a decline in freshwater fish breeding. As the breeding cycle depends on lake water flooding the forest during the monsoon season and on the water-logged wood providing the habitat for spawning, it would be necessary to dredge the confluence of the Mekong and the Tonle Sap rivers and to reforest the edge of the lake to restore those conditions. Since Cambodia lacks fishing trawlers, fuel, and skilled fishermen, it has turned over the marine fishing largely to Thai fishermen. By building a fishing fleet and expanding its refrigeration facilities and fish-processing plants, Cambodia could tap a lucrative export market in seafood. Joint ventures with Vietnamese, Thai, or Taiwanese companies would enable Cambodians to obtain expertise as well as marketing outlets.

Cambodia's rich forestry resources should be the fourth pillar of its long-range development. In 1969, Cambodia had 13 million hectares of forest (of which 30 per cent was rain forest), covering 75 per cent of the country's surface. A decade of war-related damage and uncontrolled exploitation reduced the area by nearly half—to 7.5 million hectares. In the continuing civil war, both sides have taken to savage exploitation of this resource to gain quick cash. To preserve this resource, the government would have to stop this uncontrolled exploitation, undertake a survey of conditions in those regions, and initiate a program of reforestation. Yet in 1979, there were only three university-trained forestry engineers in the country. In addition to training forestry personnel, the country will need other expertise—in developing sawmills and a furniture building industry, for example—to obtain the fullest value of forestry exports. This is another sector where, with proper supervision, joint ventures could help.

While agriculture and fishing could provide employment opportunities to the rural population, a growing number of urban and educated youth will also have to be absorbed by the economy, principally in service sectors such as tourism and trade. (Given material and infrastructural constraints, industrial development in Cambodia would be limited to small-scale agri-processing, consumer production, and handicrafts.) For two decades, Cambodia has dropped off the world tourist map, but once peace comes, the fabled temples of Angkor Wat, Angkor Thom, and other monuments are sure to emerge as some of the most attractive and unexplored frontiers in international tourism. Tourism would not only provide an important source of hard currency, but also a revival of interest in Cambodia's cultural heritage and the rediscovery of its past that could prove to be a valuable healer of the Khmer soul, scarred as it has been by the recent experience of self-destructive radicalism and the humiliation of foreign occupation. The reconstruction of the country and the restoration of its monuments would enable Cambodians to fashion their nationalism around a positive theme rather than define it by invoking the age-old enmity toward Vietnam.

Inevitably, the Thai aviation, road, and railway networks will help to integrate Cambodia into Thailand's highly developed tourist network. With its historic cities and picturesque beaches, Vietnam, too, is likely to emerge as a major tourist attraction. The development of a tourist network linking Indochina to Thailand and Singapore would help promote the critical economic integration of the whole region. In order to exploit this potential, Cambodia will need to develop a road and air transportation system and supporting infrastructure, to build hotels, and to train managers and a corps of interpreters and guides. At the same time, the government will have to resist the temptation of easy money and prevent the environs of the Angkor Wat area from being ruined by greedy developers.

Ironically, one of the very few positive developments to emerge from the destruction and dislocation caused by the Khmer Rouge has been the growing popularity of trade as a profession. Not only did the total absence of consumer products suffered under Pol Pot make citizens hungry for such goods, but the difficulty of earning a decent living through other professions in the People's Republic of Kampuchea led a large number of Cambodians to turn to petty trading—an occupation normally left to the Chinese and Vietnamese.

In recent years, with the opening of the Kompong Som and Koh Kong ports to international shipping, Phnom Penh has reemerged as an entrepot for the whole of Indochina and even for South China. In the 1930s Phnom Penh served as a major trading outpost between Thailand and Vietnam. Now Japanese, Singaporean, and Thai consumer goods find their way to Vietnam and southern China via Cambodia. Properly taxed, this growing trade can both bring revenue to the state coffers and provide employment. While Chinese merchants may still occupy the commanding heights of trade, a growing Cambodian involvement in this domain could help to reduce social gaps and ease ethnic rivalry and jealousy between the two groups.

# Foreign Aid and Coordination

While it is obvious that Cambodia's broken economy and society will require significant developmental aid for a long period, how that assistance is obtained and administered will have to be carefully considered. In 1979, when the incredible suffering of the country was fully revealed by starving refugees pouring into Thailand, the international community was galvanized to provide assistance. The International Committee of the Red Cross (ICRC) and the United Nations Children's Fund (UNICEF) undertook an emergency relief operation (1979–1981), providing $370 million in humanitarian assistance inside the country and at the border. Vietnam and the Soviet bloc countries provided significant assistance as well. But as the threat of famine receded and a guerrilla resistance backed by China and the West took shape, Cambodia faced a harsh economic embargo and near-total isolation. Some thirty non-governmental organizations, the Soviet bloc, and India were the only significant sources of foreign assistance.

Following the collapse of communism in Eastern Europe, aid from those countries has ended. The Soviet Union itself, facing a severe economic crisis, has given notice that it will have to end its grant aid and engage only in hard-currency based trade. As a result, when peace finally comes to Cambodia, Japan, the West, and the multilateral lending institutions will have to be the principal sources of funding.

If peace is achieved through the negotiating efforts of the U.N. Perm Five, and the United Nations plays a role in organizing and supervising the elections, Cambodia will receive immediate attention. As the U.N. survey teams found, just in order to send monitors and supervisors to Cambodia, it would be necessary to undertake significant infrastructural work. Testifying before the Senate Foreign Relations Committee on July 20, 1990, the Assistant Secretary of State for International Organizations, John Bolton, said that the picture that U.N. survey teams have brought back from Cambodia was "sobering." The United Nations, he said, will be faced with a "daunting and unprecedented task." Giving examples, he said that the rail and road systems would have to be substantially rehabilitated; basic radio communications, navigational aid, and air traffic control facilities would be needed to upgrade the civil aviation system to acceptable standards; the country's communication (domestic and international) systems would need urgent improvement; and the ports and inland waterways would require extensive rehabilitation. He estimated that the cost for U.N. involvement in bringing peace in Cambodia would be $3–4 billion.

While infrastructural aid from the United Nations will be extremely valuable, Cambodia will also need a sustained flow of developmental aid for at least ten years.[15] The first task, of course, will be to assess the nation's needs; in 1989, the UNDP undertook a study to obtain indicative planning figures, but the study team did not actually visit Cambodia due to political objections from the

United States and ASEAN. However, following the formation of the all-party Supreme National Council in early September, the UNDP has been allowed to set up a liaison mission in Phnom Penh. One of the first projects of the UNDP would be a human resources study.

The 1989 UNDP report proposed that $450 million be spent in Cambodia over two to three years, with over $300 million allocated to major roads and dams. Some critics have said that the amount proposed by the UNDP is beyond the absorptive capacity of the country within the timeline proposed. Private economists have suggested that an approximate, indicative aid target would be $1 billion for the 1991–95 period, including as much as $500 million in commodity aid, targeted especially to oil, fertilizers, spare parts, and industrial raw materials. Project aid could consume $400 million, of which no more than $300 million should be allocated to large road, energy, and irrigation projects, and $100 million should be used for technical assistance. The economists suggested that in order to prevent Cambodia's debt service ratio from climbing over 25 per cent of exports, it would be necessary to offer aid mainly in donations, and high grant elements with long grace periods at low interest rates.[16]

Whatever the amount of aid made available to Cambodia, a major task will be to channel it in well-planned directions and to prevent duplicated effort, competition, and waste. Japan, which will probably be the key donor to Cambodia, already has proposed the establishment of an International Committee on the Reconstruction of Cambodia (ICORC) "to provide a framework for cooperation among countries and international organizations concerned." The Japanese Foreign Ministry suggested that during the first phase (that of rehabilitation), while Cambodia is under a provisional administrative authority, a U.N. coordinator should have the main responsibility. Then, during the second phase of reconstruction, the ICORC would promote coordination of economic assistance among donor countries and institutions.

The model developed under the Multilateral Aid Initiative (MAI) for the Philippines could prove useful in developing an organization such as ICORC. Under the MAI plan, nineteen donors adopted a program, coordinated by the World Bank, to provide the Philippines $2 billion in loans and grants annually, over a five-year period.

It is increasingly coming to be realized around the world that the Cambodia conflict is not a "proxy war" among superpowers. However welcome the fact that Moscow and Washington can now agree on Cambodia may be, their concord will not necessarily bring peace to the region. But when the Cambodian parties finally come to agree on a peace formula, *international* consensus on the need to rebuild and stabilize Cambodia *will* be vital. Peace and reconstruc-

# 100 INDOCHINA
tion in Cambodia is not only a crying need for the country's hapless citizens. It could be an important factor in the maintenance of peace and stability in Southeast Asia. A weak Cambodia is all too likely to remain what it has so often been in the past—the ground for competing Chinese, Vietnamese, and Thai ambitions—especially if Vietnam itself fails to recover and develop in healthy directions. For Cambodia and the region, the present is therefore not only a time of immediate need but also one of historic opportunity.

## Notes

[1] Naranhkiri Tith, "An Agenda for the Economic and Social Reconstruction of Cambodia," paper submitted at the International Symposium on Cambodia, California State University, Long Beach, CA, February 17–19, 1989, p. 18.

[2] For a fuller treatment of Lao economic development, see Nayan Chanda, "Economic Changes in Laos, 1975–1980," in Martin Stuart-Fox ed., *Contemporary Laos* (St. Lucia: University of Queensland Press, 1982), pp. 116–128; and MacAlister Brown and Joseph J. Zasloff, *Apprentice Revolutionaries: The Communist Movement in Laos 1930-1985* (Stanford, CA: Hoover Institution Press, 1986), pp. 194–218.

[3] Christian Taillard, *Le Laos: Stratégies d'un Etat-tampon* (Reclucs, Montpellier: 1989), pp. 143–49.

[4] For a detailed analysis of the evolution of Vietnam's planning, see David G. Marr and Christine P. White, eds., *Postwar Vietnam: Dilemmas in Socialist Development* (Southeast Asia Program, Cornell University, 1988), pp. 77–133; Stefan de Vylder and Adam Fforde, *Vietnam: An Economy in Transition*, (Swedish International Development Agency, Stockholm, 1988), pp. 123–51; Tetsusaburo Kimura, *The Vietnamese Economy 1975–1986: Reforms and International Relations* (Tokyo: Institute of Developing Economies, 1989), pp. 29–65.

[5] *Cambodia: The Situation of Children and Women* (Phnom Penh: UNICEF, 1990), p. 50.

[6] *UNHCR Absorption Capacity Survey*, January 1990 (Phnom Penh, UNHCR, 1990), p. 4. (Mimeographed.)

[7] K.C. Cherriyan and E.V.K FitzGerald, "Development Planning in the State of Cambodia," NGO Forum, *Phnom Penh and The Hague*, November 1989, p. 17. (Roneo copy.)

[8] Estimate by Phnom Penh-based NGOs, according to David Elder, American Friends Services Committee, March 11, 1990, Washington. Soviet experts reportedly estimate Rubles 200 million a year represents the upper limit of the absorptive capacity of Cambodia. Cherriyan and FitzGerald, op cit, p. 38.

[9] Interview with Vice Premier Kong Samol, Phnom Penh, July 26, 1989.

[10] Interview with the Soviet ambassador, Rachid Khamidoulin, Phnom Penh, April 26, 1990.

[11] In 1988, half of Cambodia's 1,225 tractors were idle because of breakdown and lack of repair. Grant Curtis, *Cambodia: A Country Profile* (report prepared for the Swedish International Development Agency, Stockholm, August 1989), p. 34.

[12] Nayan Chanda, *Cambodia 1989: The Search for an Exit*, Asian Update Series (New York: The Asia Society), p. 20.

[13] A study by the Population Crisis Committee based on mathematical models to study the effect of population pressure and performance of national political institutions found Cambodia to be among the countries facing "extremely high" risk of destablization. *Population Pressures: Threat to Democracy* (Washington, D.C.: Population Crisis Committee, 1989).

[14] Robert J. Muscat, *Cambodia: Post Settlement Reconstruction and Development* (New York: East Asian Institute, 1989), p. 50.

[15] Cherriyan and FitzGerald, op cit., p. 37.

[16] Ibid., p. 38.

# AFTER THE WARS

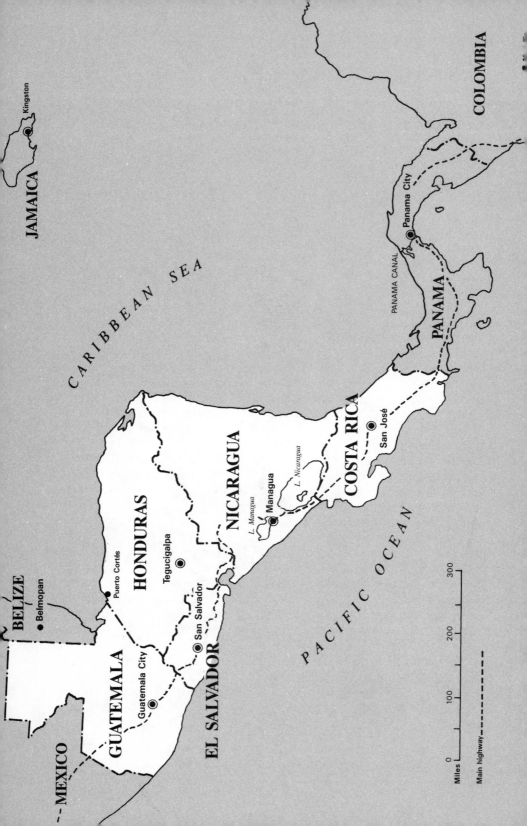

# Chapter 3

# Central America

Benjamin L. Crosby

In the 1970s, Central America was a prospering region. Economic growth averaged around 5.5 per cent a year, by 1978 intra-regional trade had reached nearly a billion dollars, and external debt was virtually nonexistent. With the exception of Costa Rica, all of the region's countries were ruled by the military. In Nicaragua, the 45-year-old Somoza dynasty fell to the youthful Frente Sandinista de Liberación Nacional (FSLN) in 1979; that same year in El Salvador, a group of youngish, reform-minded army officers overthrew the military government of General Humberto Romero. "Civil-military" juntas were established in both Nicaragua and El Salvador. But the euphoria died down, and hopeful beginnings were shattered by civil war. Economic growth in the region plummeted. Per capita income is now well below 1978–79 levels; trade has declined to one-third that of 1979; and debt has skyrocketed alarmingly. Fragile democracies have replaced the military governments, but the region no longer prospers. The isthmus is dependent, disjointed, and fragmented.

The primary factors that produced such unfortunate consequences were of course war and economic crisis. As the models of import substitution and traditional agriculture upon which the Central American economies were based could not respond to eroding prices and deteriorating markets for the countries' goods, they lost credibility. War polarized the populations of El Salvador and Nicaragua, caused governmental expenditures to soar, and drove away investment. Although some degree of economic recovery did occur in

Costa Rica, Honduras, and Guatemala by the mid-1980s, the prolonged civil wars of Nicaragua and El Salvador stifled hope for significant economic progress throughout the region. The conflicts and economic crisis were exacerbated by the ideological demands and expectations of the United States and the Soviet Union. Ironically, although the Cold War protagonists spent about $12 billion in the region between 1981 and 1990, there is little to show for their efforts.[1] The grand strategies relating large-scale economic programs to geopolitical goals proposed by the Kissinger Commission[2] in 1983 were never fully implemented; as the conflicts ground on, even these partial attempts at economic recovery turned into holding actions. Other ideas for recovery, such as those proposed by the Sanford Commission and the United Nations, never found an audience.[3]

On August 6–7, 1987, in Guatemala City, the Central American Presidents took matters into their own hands. Serious progress toward peace in the region began with their signing of the Esquipulas II Agreement, or the "Arias Peace Plan."

The plan has already begun to bear fruit. In 1990, the FSLN was defeated in a fair election. Since mid-1989, each of the region's countries successfully completed a democratic, electoral transition from one government to another for the first time since independence in the nineteenth century. The conflict in Nicaragua has ended, the civil war in El Salvador may have begun to wind down, and the government and the rebels in Guatemala have initiated negotiations. The end of the Cold War, *perestroika* in the Soviet Union, and democratization in Eastern Europe have drastically reduced the strategic component of the conflicts, as well as a significant part of the support for the Salvadoran and Guatemalan rebel groups. Publicly, the Soviet Union has distanced itself from the rebels and has "strongly encouraged" Cuba to do the same.[4]

The election of Violeta Chamorro's UNO coalition brought a shift in U.S. policy toward Nicaragua from complete opposition to cooperation. While there are still significant and daunting economic problems and the political sphere remains highly polarized, the armed conflict has been largely eliminated. Furthermore, Nicaragua's elections have had a spinoff effect in El Salvador, moving negotiations between the government and the Frente Farabundo Marti para la Liberación Nacional (FMLN) rebels forward. Although the war there proceeds, it is considerably diminished; this has restored a sense of hope and opportunity that had evaporated in the wake of the rebels' November 1989 offensive. Still the importance of both the Sandinistas and the FMLN as political actors remains significant.

Both are powerful forces capable of altering the political climate in sudden and dramatic fashion.

The region—and particularly Nicaragua and El Salvador—now faces the task of rebuilding (or constructing anew) political systems rent by a decade or more of polarization and conflict. Furthermore, these countries must rebuild economies destroyed by a near-zero level of investment, bankrupt production models, and exaggerated government expenditures. Finally, the region needs to look toward recovery in the social sphere and the repair of hundreds of thousands of shattered human lives.

Just one of these agendas would be sufficiently challenging, but all three must be faced simultaneously. The task is all the more daunting due to the tenuous nature of the political coalitions and the frailty of the nascent democratic processes in each country. In both Nicaragua and El Salvador, the governments are under the watchful and critical eye of domestic actors with extensive veto capacity in important policy areas, some of whom are merely waiting for the chance to return to power. Complicating the task are the often conflicting or even contradictory demands of international donor agencies that must be heeded because their resources are indispensable for reconstruction.

The problems faced by the region, and especially by El Salvador and Nicaragua, cannot be solved quickly. The recovery process will be slow, quirky, and plagued with setbacks. The path to recovery is not clear; the officials responsible are new to the job and not equipped with all the necessary resources. Their relationship with the private sector, which will play an important role in economic recovery, is still uncertain. And as they wrestle with the economic challenges, the new political leaders also bear responsibility for engendering and consolidating the democratic processes.

The heart of the problem lies in the relationship between the political and economic challenges in each country. The fragility of the governing coalitions in El Salvador and Nicaragua requires that their leaders carefully avoid policies and programs that might alienate key political support. A government in perpetual political crisis is little better than a government overthrown—except that it does preserve the processes and forms of democracy. A government's capacity to obtain and manage its political resources will be critical to its ability to marshall and manage scarce economic resources while deepening the hold of democracy itself. Thus economic reconstruction in the years just ahead must be based on policies that build political support and create confidence—and that requires great caution and flexibility in the application of certain economic reforms. Difficult policies are not easily accomplished in bold strokes; the risks of political failure and the waste of critical economic resources are too great.[5] To be sure, war and conflict have provoked or aggravated economic distortions; however, the standard prescriptions for eradicating such distortions—stabilization and adjustment—will, given the circumstances, prove counterproductive. Such measures will not only sharpen the economic crisis in the short run, but worse, will contribute to a renewed polarization of delicately balanced political forces.

The approach to economic reconstruction and reform in both El Salvador and Nicaragua should be gradualistic, with lower targets for the alignment of macro-economic indicators and for growth than local and foreign economic advisers might prefer. The use of more gradual strategies will also permit each government to manage the costs of reform better and to build on the scarce political resources at its disposal. It will also allow leaders to tackle the equally difficult agenda of rebuilding political systems and nurturing infant democracies.

This essay will address the problems confronting reconstruction efforts across Central America, but its focus will be on Nicaragua and El Salvador. Although it may be argued that Central America would have had grave problems in any case, the conflicts in these two nations have produced the particular nature of the "Central American crisis." Without solutions to the specific problems of Nicaragua and El Salvador, the likelihood of prosperity in the remainder of the region will be severely limited.

The Central American isthmus has undergone wrenching change over the last ten years. As a consequence of that change, it is difficult to predict the state of the region in the year 2000. Both El Salvador and Nicaragua have gone from conservative authoritarian governments to reformist or populist governments and back to more conservative governments over the last years. If the current governments are not successful, chances are there will be another shift. There is much at stake politically as well as economically in the ability of planners to approach the future with flexibility rather than rigid preconceptions and illusions of clear foresight.[6]

# Costs of the Conflict: The Human Dimension[7]

Conservative estimates put the number of dead at about 70,000[8] in El Salvador and at 45,000 in Nicaragua.[9] (The scale of these losses is perhaps clearer if one realizes that for the United States, a death count on the order of Nicaragua's would be three and a quarter million people.) There are no figures for the disabled, but people's losses of limbs from land mines are an immense and growing problem, particularly in El Salvador.[10] Hundreds of thousands of Salvadorans and Nicaraguans have left their countries or have been internally displaced by the war. In sum, about one-quarter of all Salvadorans and about 15 per cent of all Nicaraguans may have been displaced ✓ by the conflicts.[11]

While a portion of the massive displacement and migration is due to fear or repression in both countries, much is also due to the economic crisis. This crisis has had a particularly acute impact on the availability of skilled and white collar workers. Complaints of not being able to find the skilled mechanics, accountants, or mid-upper level managers critical to economic reconstruction and growth are common in the private sector. For example, it has been estimated that 70 per cent of the Nicaraguan graduates (MBAs) of one Central American management institution now reside outside Nicaragua.[12] As companies have closed or reduced operations, better qualified workers have found a market for their skills in other countries, primarily the United States.

Natural disasters, including a hurricane and flooding in Nicaragua and earthquakes in El Salvador, have exacerbated the rate of internal migration. Urban areas have become highly congested with refugees from areas of conflict in the interior of each country. This human tide increases demand and strains the capacity for supplying services in health, education, water, and housing.[13] Because of the extensive destruction of housing both from natural causes as well as aerial bombardment, the growth of slums and "marginal areas" in the capitals of each country has been tremendous.

This rapid urban migration will have serious implications for the future. It is generally accepted that the majority of the recent urban migrants will remain in the cities, creating teeming centers of economic suffering and political tension and pulling badly needed labor out of the countryside and the agricultural sector.[14] For the last several years, the Sandinista government in Nicaragua has had to rely on massive propaganda campaigns, the military, and international volunteer brigades to recruit enough labor to harvest its rapidly diminishing coffee and cotton crops. Salvadoran coffee farmers also complain about the scarcity of labor.

These economic and physical events have had particularly negative effects on the standard of living—and aspirations—of the middle and working classes. Open unemployment in El Salvador was estimated at over 38 per cent in 1985[15] and over 25 per cent in 1988 in Nicaragua.[16] Real wages have fallen precipitously (Table 1); in Managua, as late as President Chamorro's inauguration, it was not

## Table 1.  Evolution of the Real Minimum Wage
### (1980 = 100)

|             | 1983 | 1984 | 1985 | 1986 | 1987 | 1988 |
|-------------|------|------|------|------|------|------|
| Costa Rica  | 95   | 100  | 104  | 106  | 104  | 98   |
| **El Salvador** | **97** | **96** | **84** | **72** | **64** | **65** |
| Guatemala   | 118  | 108  | 93   | 76   | 81   | 83   |
| Honduras    | 91   | 89   | 86   | 82   | 80   | 76   |
| **Nicaragua** | **49** | **70** | **58** | **18** | **20** | **9** |

Source: Consejo Monetario Centroamericano, *Boletín Estadístico 1988* (San José, Costa Rica, 1990).

uncommon to find a secretary making the equivalent of $10 per month. With wages fixed by law and inflation accelerating, the more prosperous companies adopted the practice of paying bonuses in dollars, often several times the nominal wage.

In this setting, a street vendor in Managua selling lemonade in front of a government building was likely to earn several times as much as the professionals working in the building.[17] Over the past 10 years, the growth of the informal sector has been spectacular; it was estimated to include 55 per cent[18] of the economically active population in Nicargua and approximately 38 per cent in El Salvador (despite high levels of out-migration).[19] According to recent studies, the absolute level of poverty in El Salvador (those unable to purchase a minimum basket of necessary goods) has risen from about 31 per cent of the population in 1977 to 64 per cent in 1985.[20] In Nicaragua, 1988 real wages were less than one-tenth of those of 1980. Clearly the populations of both countries, especially the salaried middle and lower classes, are being impoverished.

There has also been a serious deterioration in services and institutions vital to social and economic mobility. The war has caused destruction of the health and education infrastructure; perhaps even more damaging has been the precipitous decline in spending in those areas due to the expenses of the wars.[21] In El Salvador, over six hundred schools were closed in the rural conflict areas, while the migration of nearly half a million people from the conflict zones has strained urban educational facilities at a time when government spending on education has been cut from 1.5 per cent of GDP to 0.5 per cent.[22] As salaries have remained flat, teacher desertion has become a growing problem, and student absenteeism is rampant. On average, it now takes a student who actually finishes sixth grade about ten and a half years to do so.[23] As the head of planning in the Ministry of Education put it, "we have lost a whole generation."[24]

Although no serious deterioration in overall health standards is perceptible from the available data, the implications of virtually no investment in either education or health are obvious. Medical equipment is old and obsolete; what breaks down does not get replaced.[25] Ministry of Health officials in El Salvador worry about the flight of physicians to other countries and a massive deterioration in the standards for training in the health sector—both of which will have repercussions well into the future.[26]

Economic and political reconstruction must rely on capable and trained individuals to put economic and political policies and strategies into practice. Without talented managers, the options for reform will be extremely limited and plagued with errors. Just to replace the talent that has left these countries will require a vast, costly, and coherent effort. The effects of massive human dislocation are clear; not only is the human plight intense, but governments have been left with less capacity to cope with the tragedy as well.

## Economic Dimensions of the Conflict

Precise figures on the economic costs of the conflicts in Nicaragua and El Salvador are not available, but clearly the impact has been staggering. It is now almost a cliché to describe the economies of both countries as bankrupt or basketcases. Losses have been generated not only through war-inflicted destruction, but also through abandonment, deterioration, obsolescence, and the effects of little or no investment in the past ten years. Furthermore, under current conditions, there is virtually no likelihood of the new investment that will be so critical to leading these economies toward a sound footing in the 1990s.

The costs of the wars can be divided into two main areas: first, property damage and production losses (through crop damage and abandonment of crop lands in conflict areas), and second, the decline in economic capacity brought about by investors' loss of confidence, capital flight, emphasis on military spending rather than social programs and capital investment, and massive financial imbalances. Estimates of 1980–89 losses directly or indirectly attributable to the war total some $1.076 billion in El Salvador (Table 2), and approximately $1.420 billion in Nicaragua (Table 3). In addition, indirect costs of the U.S. embargo imposed during the Reagan administration are estimated at nearly $1.1 billion.[27]

## Table 2.  El Salvador: Damage Estimates, 1980–89 ($ millions)

| | |
|---|---:|
| **Conflict, 1980–88** | |
| Agricultural Production Infrastructure | 597 |
| Agro-Industry | 65 |
| Commerce and Industry | 179 |
| Public Transport | 23 |
| Public Infrastructure | 212 |
| Subtotal | 1,076 |
| **Earthquake, 1986** | |
| Production Losses | 350 |
| Property Damage | 1,050 |
| | 1,400 |
| **Total** | **3,150** |

Source: Ministerio de Planificación y Coordinación del Desarrollo Economico y Social, "Cuantificación de Daños Materiales y Humanos Derivados de la Violencia en El Salvador, 1979–1987, 1988"; (San Salvador, El Salvador, 1988, 1989); FUSADES, "Evaluación de Perdidas Humanas y Daños Físicos Provocados por la Agresión Insurgente," Boletín No. 49 (December 1989).

In El Salvador, the Ministry of Planning estimates that increases in security and defense costs between 1981–89 were about $674 million dollars.[28] In Nicaragua, though there is no precise data, increases in defense and security, which are the two most important factors responsible for the massive distortions in its economy,[29] have been even higher. Natural disasters—a hurricane in Nicaragua in 1988 and an earthquake in El Salvador in 1986—have added to the devastation. In fact, both disasters caused more physical damage in just a few minutes than was wrought in ten years of war—roughly $1 billion in El Salvador and $700 million in Nicaragua.[30]

Worse still, the estimates cited above do not include the costs for rehabilitation of abandoned or shuttered assets. In El Salvador, 85 per cent of lands under cotton production have not been cultivated since 1982–83.[31] In Nicaragua, where cotton was the leading foreign exchange earner in 1978, only one-quarter of the total prewar acreage was still under cultivation in 1990.[32] Meat production, important for both local consumption as well as export, was gravely

# Table 3. Nicaragua: Damage Estimates, 1980–89 ($ millions)

| | |
|---|---:|
| **Conflict, 1980–88** | |
| Production losses | 1,194 |
| Property damage | 226 |
| **Losses from U.S. Embargo** | |
| Includes loss of markets, higher import costs, exchange loss, higher intermediary costs | 1,092 |
| **Hurricane Joan, 1988** | |
| Production losses | 99 |
| Property damage | 718 |
| **Total** | **3,329** |

Source: Economic Commission for Latin America and the Caribbean (ECLAC), *Economic Survey of Latin America and the Caribbean, 1988* (Santiago, Chile: United Nations, 1989), p. 170; Oscar Neira, et al., "Nicaragua: La Guerra y la Tentativa de Crecimiento con Equidad Social," in *Economía de America Latina 18–19 (1989)*, Mexico, p. 234.

affected by a dramatic reduction of herds through slaughter and smuggling to nearby countries and will require major investments in breeding stock to regain pre-conflict levels.[33] In El Salvador, the conflict forced as many as 254 firms of which 35 per cent were industrial manufacturing enterprises to close their doors.[34] In Nicaragua, the Consejo Superior de la Empresa Privada reported the closure of large numbers of commercial and manufacturing firms. Many of the Somoza holdings, which had accounted for a significant portion of Nicaragua's output, were taken over by the Sandinista government and run as state enterprises but later fell into serious decline or were closed.[35]

In some cases, rehabilitation may only mean reactivation of idle capacity, but in others, assets that have been lost through abandonment, sale, and export—or assets that have deteriorated beyond repair (tractors, farm machinery, trucks, industrial machinery)— will have to be replaced. During the past ten years, the Nicaraguans have imported massive stocks of agricultural equipment, machinery, trucks, and buses from the socialist bloc. Much of this equipment has deteriorated, and replacement parts will likely be hard to find.

Finally, the emphasis of much of the pre-conflict manufacturing in El Salvador and Nicaragua was on import substitution. With vastly reduced levels of demand and consumption and a new emphasis on export of non-traditional goods, many of these industries have become obsolete. In sum, these economies will require a massive reorientation.

The conflict has also prompted significant numbers of the entrepreneurial class to leave their native countries and take up residence elsewhere—both within the Central American region and in the United States. A number have tried to maintain activities in both their new and old homes: Nicaraguans have established organizations of businessmen in exile in San José, Costa Rica, and in Miami. Many prominent Salvadoran businessmen maintain homes in Miami or Guatemala, commuting to San Salvador. But while these entrepreneurs may maintain businesses in their home countries, they appear to have little inclination to invest or re-invest there. Proceeds and profits are converted into hard currency and removed. Moreover, many businessmen now have established profitable activities in other countries where they are investing those funds. Such commitments will make it difficult to unlock capital for investment in either El Salvador or Nicaragua.

The fundamental productive capacity of both El Salvador and Nicaragua has been seriously eroded by ten years of conflict. In both countries, performance in a number of areas has been starkly worse than that of their neighbors, despite the fact that these neighbors too, have been afflicted by severe economic crisis throughout the 1980s. Agricultural growth (the mainstay of the Central American economies) in Nicaragua and El Salvador has been consistently negative, while it has been low but consistently positive in neighboring countries. El Salvador's and Nicaragua's capacity to feed themselves has also declined more significantly than in the neighboring countries (Table 4). Food imports to Nicaragua and El Salvador have grown from 5 metric tons in 1974–75 to 262 tons in 1986–87. At the same time, Nicaraguan and Salvadoran exports have declined vertiginously from the levels achieved in the late 1970s. In the neighboring countries, while exports first declined, they have since recovered or surpassed the export levels of 1979. And while dependency on food imports has grown, so has dependency on foreign aid and assistance of all types; by 1987, disbursements had approached 16 per cent of El Salvador's GDP, and by 1988 they reached a staggering 27 per cent of GDP in Nicaragua.

Interestingly, El Salvador and Nicaragua have diverged rather dramatically in their attempts to manage economic devastation. El

## Table 4. Per Capita Food Production Index
### (1979–81 = 100)

|  | 1983 | 1984 | 1985 | 1986 |
|---|---|---|---|---|
| Costa Rica | 88.7 | 91.5 | 92.0 | 92.8 |
| **El Salvador** | **83.9** | **91.5** | **90.1** | **83.6** |
| Guatemala | 101.7 | 99.5 | 97.5 | 94.9 |
| Honduras | 86.7 | 83.3 | 84.8 | 90.1 |
| **Nicaragua** | **83.1** | **77.4** | **76.3** | **74.3** |

Source: Economic Commission for Latin America and the Caribbean, *Statistical Abstract for Latin America*, Vol. 27 (Santiago, Chile: ECLAC, 1988).

Salvador has pursued conservative fiscal and demand management policies, producing a deep recession. Nicaragua, on the other hand, produced both hyperinflation and a profound depression through a combination of indulgent economic policies and mismanagement. El Salvador has maintained relatively modest fiscal deficits (averaging 2.1 per cent between 1983 and 1988), but the approach has been to make deep cuts in expenditures (except the military) instead of trying seriously to increase revenues (the latter actually shrank from 12.4 per cent of GDP in 1983 to 10.7 per cent in 1988). The strategy has been different in Nicaragua; revenues have been consistently higher than in neighboring countries (averaging 30 per cent of GDP between 1983 and 1988), but public expenditures have averaged over 50 per cent of GDP since 1983, and fiscal deficits have averaged over 20 per cent of GDP for the same period.[36]

The crux of the challenge in both El Salvador and Nicaragua is a dramatic need for a rapid increase in investment levels just to generate the capacity to satisfy even minimal economic and social demands. In El Salvador, investment levels have been extremely low; in Nicaragua, they have been considerably higher due to public sector spending. The sad similarity between the two countries has been the low or negative return on those investments (Tables 5 and 6). Any strategy or plan for economic reconstruction should focus sharply on the need to increase and stimulate investment. But more than an increase is necessary. A strategy for recovery must also pay close attention to how those funds are used—to ensure not only that a maximum return is generated, but also that the allocation of those investments assures positive social and political consequences.

## Table 5.  Gross Domestic Investment as a Percentage of GDP

|             | 1983 | 1984 | 1985 | 1986 | 1987 | 1988 |
|-------------|------|------|------|------|------|------|
| Costa Rica  | 24.2 | 22.7 | 25.9 | 25.2 | 28.2 | 27.8 |
| El Salvador | 12.1 | 12.0 | 10.8 | 13.3 | 12.6 | 12.2 |
| Guatemala   | 11.1 | 11.6 | 11.5 | 10.3 | 13.8 | 14.0 |
| Honduras    | 14.9 | 19.0 | 18.1 | 14.1 | 14.7 | 13.3 |
| Nicaragua   | 22.5 | 22.2 | 23.1 | 16.9 | 15.8 | 31.1 |

Source: Consejo Monetarío Centroamericano, *Boletín Estadístico 1988* (San José, Costa Rica, 1989).

## The Political Dimension: Winners and Losers

Since 1979, Nicaragua and El Salvador have undergone wrenching processes of political change. Despite the fact that the current crisis in both countries began with the overthrow of conservative, authoritarian, military dictatorships, they have had strikingly different evolutions. Political change has not followed a straight line; in Nicaragua, for example, the path followed for nearly ten years now appears to have been totally reversed. El Salvador, on the other hand, has been characterized by a zig-zagging to the left and right in both political style and content. The crucial point is that in neither country has there been sufficient stability for the government to accumulate the necessary political resources to carry out substantial reform policies.

Nicaragua's Sandinista-led insurrection and revolt, which culminated in the downfall of the Somoza dictatorship in July, 1979, was sudden, profound, and dramatic. The thwarted attempts to install a one-party state and socialist economy under the guidance of the FSLN leadership produced far-reaching changes in the economic and political landscape. At first, anti-Somoza, non-Sandinista elements of the elite, including current President Violeta Chamorro, gained high visibility and participation as members of the junta or the cabinet and through their economic status. However, by the end of 1981, their power and position had evaporated as they were replaced by Sandinista loyalists and excluded from virtually all decisionmaking regarding the economy.[37] As a result, the economic elite became an embittered and polarized opposition. Meanwhile, the FSLN created a series of new organizations to fill their shoes.

## Table 6.  Return on Investment
## (growth of GDP/gross investment)

|  | 1984 | 1985 | 1986 | 1987 | 1988 |
|---|---|---|---|---|---|
| Costa Rica | .38 | .03 | .23 | .18 | .15 |
| **El Salvador** | **.19** | **.18** | **.04** | **.21** | **.03** |
| Guatemala | .04 | − .07 | .02 | .29 | .34 |
| Honduras | .13 | .15 | .18 | .27 | .24 |
| **Nicaragua** | **− .07** | **− .19** | **− .02** | **− .05** | **− .38** |

Source: Author's calculations based on data from Consejo Monetario Centroamericano, *Boletín Estadístico 1988* (San José, Costa Rica, 1989).

Organizations for farmers, professionals, and labor became the privileged sectors. Much of this will certainly·change with the election of Chamorro; already, promises have been made to restore a large part, though not all, of the elite's property, dismantle state control of the economy, and vastly reduce the size and scope of the state. In sum, the winners under the FSLN will become the losers under Chamorro, creating a new, highly mobilized, and potent opposition.

In El Salvador, the military coup of October 1979 that overthrew General Humberto Romero produced a much more tentative and less predictable change than in Nicaragua. While certainly not devastated, the power of El Salvador's traditional economic elite was at least temporarily curbed. The civil-military junta instituted a series of redistributive measures, including land reform and nationalization of both banks and the coffee marketing system. Meanwhile, El Salvador's disparate rebel groups put together the FMLN coalition in 1980 and in January 1981 launched a guerrilla war aimed at a more fundamental realignment of the political and economic balance.

The outbreak of the guerrilla war contributed to a new mobilization of the right, particularly of the private sector, which launched a highly effective campaign to halt further reforms and to end the leadership of junta President Jose Napoleon Duarte. Duarte's inability to either consolidate support behind his policies or to end the guerrilla war led to the victory of a right wing opposition coalition composed of the Alianza Republicana Nacionalista (ARENA) and the Partido de Conciliación Nacional (PCN) in the Constitutional Assembly election of 1982. Once in power, however, the right was likewise incapable of consolidating support and, in the country's first freely contested elections in 1984, Duarte returned to power. Though Duarte's party also won the Congressional elections in 1985, worsening economic problems, a confrontation over economic policy with the private sector, and futile attempts to negotiate a solution to the war exhausted Duarte's credibility, reducing him to the role of caretaker president for the last two years of his term.[38] Meanwhile, the right, under ARENA leadership, reasserted itself with a sweeping victory in the Legislative Assembly elections in 1988, and with Alfredo Cristiani's triumph in the 1989 presidential elections.

In both countries, the events of 1979 eventually led to a polarization of society and, by 1981, produced civil wars. These conflicts sapped the energies of the ruling governments and did not allow for either the institutionalization of a policy process, or for putting into place mechanisms to carry out those policies. In El Salvador, that failure was reflected in pendulum shifts of governments and policies, whereas in Nicaragua, it led to a rapid and devastating deterioration of the economy that produced a high turnover of government officials and unpredictable shifts in policy.[39] In both countries, these changes have produced governments only marginally stronger than the opposition. As a consequence, any attempt at significant reform has produced often violent opposition that narrowly restricted the government's options.

The East–West Cold War competition also contributed to the exacerbation of civil conflicts in both El Salvador and Nicaragua. Between 1979 and 1986, what were small insurgencies grew into full-scale civil wars. Central America, a region of only 22 million people, became a major focus of American foreign policy. The Reagan administration spent over $500 million in arming the contras and considerable political capital in promoting the contra campaign to rid the region of the Sandinistas. The Soviet Union, on the other hand, spent over $3.5 billion trying to keep them in power.

The policies of both countries began to change course in the latter part of the 1980s. *Perestroika* and the ending of the Cold War, brought an emphasis on peaceful solutions in both Moscow and Washington and presented both Nicaragua and El Salvador with the likelihood of declining levels of assistance from their respective allies. After President Chamorro's election, Nicaragua lost the vast majority of assistance from the Soviet Union. The United States, however, approved a $300-million assistance package. In the case of El Salvador, the United States cut ESF assistance from $191 million in FY1989 to $144 million in FY1990. For FY1991, Congress cut military aid to El Salvador by over one-half in the hope of maintaining pressure for a peaceful solution.

Soviet pressure certainly helped push Nicaragua down the road to free elections and has helped isolate the FMLN rebels in El Salvador. Moreover, the democratization of Nicaragua provided the opportunity for the Soviets to escape a heavy financial obligation. Peace in El Salvador could provide the United States with similar (if not as large) benefits. For the governments of El Salvador and Nicaragua, however, less foreign aid has meant an erosion in their ability to maintain programs that keep their political constituencies on board—again narrowing their options.

# The Political Tasks of Reconstruction

Over the next several months and years, the governments of El Salvador and Nicaragua face three daunting political tasks. They must bring to an end the armed conflicts that have plagued them over the last decade; they must find a way to consolidate their power in order to execute the difficult political and economic tasks that lie ahead; and they must strengthen their infant democratic institutions. These are not simple tasks, and the mechanisms to accomplish each are not necessarily obvious. Moreover, the environment in which these tasks must be carried out is not particularly hospitable. There will be considerable unevenness in the implementation of each, and timing will be difficult.

### Ending the Wars

In Nicaragua, despite the election and vastly reduced conflict, the society remains highly polarized, with one group coalescing around the new government and the other around the FSLN opposition. In El Salvador, the situation is more complicated, with major opposition groups on both the left and right and the FMLN challenging the political order altogether. Furthermore, in neither country is there a tradition or long-standing precedent for democratic behavior—changes of government have come through authoritarian imposition, not through the give and take of democratic procedures. Extreme, even violent tactics have long been considered standard behavior for groups in opposition.

The conclusion of the wars and their aftershocks is important both for ending violence and further loss of human life and for the savings in economic resources that will follow. The *potential* peace dividend is significant: In both countries, defense consumes 40–50 per cent of the annual budget and is responsible for much of the financial disequilibrium.[40] But a peace dividend will be difficult to produce in the short run.

In Nicaragua, the contras have disbanded, and most have turned in their arms; nevertheless the threat of terrorist and bandit activities from isolated dissident "contra" and Sandinista groups does argue to some extent for maintaining a security apparatus.[41] More important, President Chamorro's decision to leave control over the security apparatus with the FSLN gives it an extremely valuable political resource, providing it with an independent political base and the capability of vetoing crucial decisions by the president. Ironically, this same security apparatus is also needed by the government to control the actions of FSLN-led public sector unions, whose general strikes provoked major disorders shortly after President Chamorro took office. While the economic future of the country depends in large measure on a serious reduction in the military, political calculation is unlikely to lead the FSLN's Humberto Ortega, chief of the armed forces, to allow erosion of an instrument that offers so much leverage. Thus while the FSLN has agreed to a 30 per cent reduction of force in the military, closer analysis of the proposal reveals that the reduction would be achieved simply through releasing conscripts.

In El Salvador the situation is similar, though without the ideological overtones encountered in Nicaragua. The armed forces have been the pre-eminent political factor for the past ten years, rising from a strength of 12,000 to over 55,000 and creating powerful vested interests. Even if the conflict should end in reasonably short order, little thought has been given to de-mobilization. Moreover, military leaders argue that the armed forces are vital to that stage of transition process during which the reincorporation of the FMLN rebels into civilian life takes place.[42]

In Nicaragua and especially in El Salvador, the governments must exercise caution in reducing the military and its budget in order to avoid the very real threat of military coups. Therefore it is unlikely that major gains in resources from the peace dividend will be forthcoming very rapidly.

### Consolidating the Governments

Although both Cristiani and Chamorro won impressive electoral victories, the degree of their control over their own governments is unclear. In both countries, the President's party also controls the Congress and the Judiciary. However, Mr. Cristiani's ruling party in El Salvador, ARENA, is a murky alliance over which Mr. Cristiani

has only partial control. While Mr. Cristiani is concerned about solv-
ing the mammoth economic problems facing El Salvador, Major
Roberto D'Aubuisson, who controls the most powerful faction of
ARENA, is more concerned with winning the March 1991 Congressional election. Mrs. Chamorro's situation is even more precarious.
Her ruling UNO "party" is a loose coalition of eleven political parties and three associated groups including communists and conservatives, labor, and business. Chamorro lost her first two challenges
within the party before she had even taken office. First, she backed
one candidate for the presidency of the Congress while her Vice President, Virgilio Godoy, openly opposed her by backing another. Chamorro's candidate lost. Subsequently, two prominent supporters
refused to join her cabinet after having been named publicly,
because Chamorro had decided to keep Humberto Ortega on as chief
of the armed forces. This lack of unity within UNO contrasts sharply
with the internal cohesion of the FSLN opposition, which controls 40
per cent of the Congress.

Even more difficult if less obvious is each president's lack of
power over either the armed forces or the bureaucracy. In the case of
El Salvador, the President has only nominal control over the military budget and is not in a position to control the internal command
structure of the armed forces. To demonstrate its autonomy as well
as the importance of its continued support, the General Staff of the
Salvadoran Armed Forces held a press conference in November 1987
to announce that the members had "decided to confirm President
Duarte for the remainder of his constitutional term of office." In Nicaragua, Mrs. Chamorro will have to rely on good faith and international public opinion and support to have some, albeit minimal,
degree of control over the military. While she is nominally Com-
mander-in-Chief of the Armed Forces, the Sandinistas in fact control
the military. If stripped of conscripts, the army would be almost
exclusively made up of Sandinista loyalists, who owe their
priveleged position to the former Sandinista government.

Nor can either president count on a loyal bureaucracy. In Nicaragua, the bureaucracy is largely a product of ten years of Sandinista rule, during which time it nearly quadrupled in size to over
300,000 employees. It has come to be the principal source of employment in an economy with more than 30 per cent unemployment.
This—and the fact that the Sandinistas organized the bureaucracy
under a single, powerful labor confederation shortly before the
Ortega government left office—will make paring the size of the
bureaucracy and gaining its support a difficult and long-term task.
Early faceoffs with the Sandinista-controlled bureaucracy resulted

in President Chamorro's having to make major and potentially very damaging concessions.

A similar problem is faced by the Cristiani government in El Salvador. Here much of the large increase in the public sector came during the Duarte years. Salvadoran public sector employees are also organized in labor unions affiliated with the major union confederations. As in Nicaragua, the capacity of top government officials to change personnel or to fire employees is extremely limited. The president of the Central Bank has said that one of the difficulties he has faced in the implementation of his economic reform package is his inability to reduce the size of the public sector work force—even within his own organization.[43]

Not having sufficient control over the instruments of government is somewhat like having a car that functions on only four of its six cylinders. It runs but only sputters along.

### Institutionalizing Democracy

El Salvador's and Nicaragua's new governments also face an interesting dilemma. They need to consolidate their governments, but at the same time they must attend to the task of encouraging and strengthening democratic institutions. This includes giving a real role to the congress, respecting the independence of the judiciary, and allowing interests (no matter how much of an anathema) to flourish. But by encouraging and strengthening such institutions, the president also inevitably cedes some degree of control over the instruments of government.

A credible and vigorous legal system is vital to democracy—not only to bring murderers to trial but also to process those accused of corruption or tax evasion. Without firm and meaningful sanctions against such violations, economic reform policy cannot be implemented. However, while an independent judiciary is the guarantor of democracy, it can also defeat the laws needed for economic reform—as happened in El Salvador in early 1987, when the judiciary annulled a tax on capital assets of firms, a measure deemed vital to implementation of fiscal and economic reform. The incident reinforced the role of the court but undermined the government's reform policies.

Strengthening the role of Congress, especially if it is highly factionalized, as in Nicaragua, means that the legislative process will often be characterized by long and arduous negotiations. Economic measures that are intended to be tough will become diluted in the bargaining process. When Congress is controlled by the ruling party, cooperation generally increases but can be torpedoed by ambitious and influential congressmen looking to enhance their stature for a future presidential bid.

Encouragement of participation and pluralism requires not only a highly conciliatory attitude on the part of the government but also their actual facilitation. This means that the government must encourage the involvement of former opponents and, particularly in the case of Nicaragua and El Salvador, mortal enemies. It is one thing to declare peace in a civil war but quite another to instill enough trust in the former enemy to get him first to lay down his arms and then accept the policy dictates of his former enemy. Repressing—or, perhaps worse, ignoring—such groups will only prompt their continued hostility. It is important that they receive periodic satisfaction of demands . . . if not, the government will only vindicate the suspicion that the system is incapable of satisfying their demands, leading them to revert to anti-system behavior. In that sense, the Chamorro government should not pursue vindictive policies against the FSLN; instead, it should seek to give them at least some minimal degree of satisfaction. Likewise, the Salvadoran government must seek ways to incorporate rather than to exclude, or worse repress, the FMLN. In that regard, the efforts of the Colombian government in incorporating former rebels is noteworthy.

The test of the systems in both El Salvador and Nicaragua will be their capacity to solve disputes in an orderly and equitable manner and to satisfy at least some of the demands of those elements in society that are likely to be most disruptive. To accomplish this task, the political leadership needs sufficient resources at its disposal— and these are most scarce during periods of economic crisis.

# The Economic Tasks of Reconstruction

The economic tasks that lie before Nicaragua and El Salvador are straightforward and not terribly dissimilar from those facing the other crisis-ridden countries of the region. It is the relatively greater depth of crisis confronting the two countries and their relatively weaker capacity to address it that distinguish them from their neighbors. It must also be emphasized that none of these tasks can be accomplished unless the conflicts are ended and financial imbalances redressed.

## Economic Stabilization and Investment

Among the economic tasks, the highest priority should be given to the stabilization of national finances and to the restoration of local investor confidence. The two tasks are complementary. Stabilization can be achieved through budget cut-backs (especially by reducing the size of government and defense expenditures), rationalization of government expenditures, alignment of the currency, reduction or elimination of subsidies, reduction of fiscal incentives, tax reform, and increased external financing.

Gains in any of these areas will only be temporary, however, unless investor confidence is restored. What the potential investor in a product or service looks for above all else is a *market*—and that requires a minimum domestic capacity to consume (especially in the absence of a strong outlook for exports). The investor also wants access to credit at low rates, low or predictable levels of inflation, a convertible currency, low taxes and/or fiscal incentives, access to cheap services, and minimal government intervention. Unfortunately, some of the measures customarily used to stabilize national finances are not always compatible with the short-term interests of the traditional investor.

The serious disequilibria present in the economies of both El Salvador and Nicaragua make the restoration of balance difficult. In Nicaragua inflation, which had dropped to an annual rate of 3,500 per cent in 1989 from a high of 33,600 per cent in 1988,[44] had again increased sharply by May 1990. While much less impressive, inflation in El Salvador began to creep upward in the first quarter of 1990 to an annual rate of around 50 per cent.[45] Early 1990 figures indicated that El Salvador had a balance-of-payments deficit of $395 million; Nicaragua, $525 million.[46]

### Job Creation

Another task will be that of job creation. At present, both countries have open unemployment rates of over 25 per cent. Should peace be restored and, by some happy circumstance, the military rapidly demobilized, each country would be faced with accommodating 35,000–50,000 new entrants into the private job market. These numbers are additional to the 40,000 that normally enter the Nicaraguan work force annually and the 60,000 in El Salvador.[47] Neither appears to have had the capacity to absorb even the normal levels of entrants. The rebuilding of local markets is vital to the restoration of investor confidence. A substantial portion of the local economic infrastructure is geared to the local market, and both have been hard-hit in the economic crisis. But for local markets to expand, per capita income must expand.

## Rebuilding Infrastructure

Much of the productive infrastructure of the region has either deteriorated through underuse or abandonment or been destroyed in the fighting. Since replacement investment has been low over the past decade, much of the existing equipment is now obsolete. Just bringing existing infrastructure back into use would require a major investment of funds; replacing it with current technology would require a much greater commitment. To make investment in productive areas effective, there will also be a need for parallel spending in public works to counter the estimated $212 million in damage to bridges, to electrical generation and distribution networks, and to communications.

## Agriculture

In the more productive areas of agriculture, such as cotton, coffee, and sugar, there are serious impediments to quick fixes. In both El Salvador and Nicaragua, numerous coffee and sugar processing plants have been destroyed and will require extensive investment in replacement machinery to make them operative. Major investments will also be needed to restore cotton lands and sugar plantations to previous levels of productivity. Getting meat and milk production back to prewar levels will require the purchase of new breeding stock. Much of the agricultural equipment that has been sold and exported or has deteriorated through lack of use will have to be replaced. Moreover, in this sector, Nicaragua has large stocks of socialist bloc machinery and equipment; obtaining compatible spare parts is likely to be an increasing problem in the changed political and economic setting.

Another major task is that of generating external confidence, especially among major donors and potential investors. Consistency and effectiveness in economic policy along with political stability should help, but it cannot be achieved quickly and is by no means a sure thing. In other Latin American countries that are much more politically stable (Bolivia, Colombia, Dominican Republic), investment has been consistently low and the economies stagnant.[48]

Some economic tasks will require policies that conflict with political goals. Economic reform implies reduction of resources available to the government in the short to medium term, lessening the ability of the government to satisfy demands and thus to maintain political support and legitimacy. Economic measures should be carefully crafted in order to avoid the wrath of a powerful political, and potentially anti-systemic, opposition. For example, the Chamorro government's proposed reductions of staff in the bureaucracy, enacted to tackle Nicaragua's crushing public deficit, collided with the interests of the powerful FSLN public sector unions and ultimately led to violent confrontations.

## Macroeconomic Policy Options

The choices available to the governments of El Salvador and Nicaragua for fulfilling the economic tasks they face are limited. The approach most often prescribed and followed in Latin America is that of stabilization and adjustment.[49] The principal thrust of stabilization is to make price corrections in order to align current-account, balance-of-payments, and exchange disequilibria, and to cut the public deficit. Such measures generally have the effect of severely reducing demand and, at least at the outset, spurring inflation and inducing recession. The consequences are often increased unemployment, reductions in real wages, impoverishment, cuts in social services, price increases in services and necessities, and reductions in investment. The second part of the prescription calls for the adjustment of the productive mechanisms of society—generally toward the promotion of an export-driven model concentrating on non-traditional exports. This involves the reduction or elimination of incentives, tax exemptions, and modifications in the tariff structure to reduce the protection of import-substitution manufacturing while creating incentives and structures to promote exports. The timing with which these policies may be adopted varies from "shock" therapy—imposing them all at once—to a more gradualistic format. Each has its risks and its advantages.

The second possibility is to stimulate demand with the expectation that there will a quick and appropriate supply response.[50] The implementation of this policy generally involves pump-priming mechanisms and often includes such policies as job creation (largely in the public sector), wage increases, tax reduction, creation of incentives, greater access to and availability of cheap credit, maintenance of subsidies, and protection of the productive sectors through tariff barriers. The risk inherent in this choice is that liquidity could rise too rapidly, increasing the likelihood of inflation. This approach also relies on a strong supply and investment response that requires an environment of investor confidence. If not balanced and controlled, the process runs the risk of turning in on itself and creating a hyperinflationary spiral. This alternative also requires considerable capacity for timing and astute political management.

# Economic Choices and Political Realities

In deciding which economic strategy to adopt, particular attention must be paid to the political environment. The governments of both El Salvador and Nicaragua are based on relatively fragile political coalitions; relations with major political figures are not always well defined and in some cases are hostile. If the strategy is not feasible in political terms—if it is likely to weaken the government's capacity and make it unable to induce compliance—then it simply is not a viable strategy; in the end, the government will fail to accomplish its desired objectives.

There appear to be three major requirements for a feasible economic strategy:

*1. The government must have the will to proceed and the capacity to manage.* Is the government sufficiently committed to the policy choices it made to "stay the course," even in the face of hostile reaction? Does the government command the technical and managerial talent required to design, manage, and sequence policy implementation, and will it carry the policy through even when things get tough? Will the bureaucracy cooperate? Such elements are not automatic.

The window for tough economic policy is narrow and highly dependent on showing quick progress. Once a cabinet (or economic team) has exhausted its political vitality, a new team can be called—but once the first has fallen, the second will fall even more readily. And the replacement cabinet's window for tough decision-making will be even narrower than the first.

*2. The government must possess or have ready access to the economic or financial resources needed to make the strategy work.* At times, a government will undertake the first steps of major economic reform without actually having the resources necessary—in the hope that such resources will be forthcoming once it is demonstrated to the international financial institutions that the government is serious.[51] Reforms might begin on the basis of projections of increasing tax collections or maintaining a tendency toward increasing prices for major exports. But increasing tax collections is a major challenge in countries accustomed to major tax evasion, and prices of exports can weaken.

The problem of taking such steps without firm assurance of financing is twofold: Even if financing is virtually certain to be obtained, it may be difficult to predict the timing of the disbursements, which can greatly jeopardize the prospects of an otherwise workable strategy.

3. *Powerful non-governmental actors must agree with the strategy enough to cooperate—or at least to not block it.* Any real "agreement" means commitment and sacrifice, especially when protected interests are concerned. Will the military be supportive if its budget is to be cut by 15 per cent? Does the bureaucracy have an independent political base to which it can appeal? Will the private sector continue to support the program even if taxes rise, protective tariffs are reduced, and exemptions are eliminated; or will it take its capital elsewhere? To what degree will it be possible to get around policy through corrupt mechanisms, or to seek favored or exceptional status through political connections? Any of these relations can clearly dilute compliance and make the achievement of reform objectives just that much more difficult.

The three requirements outlined above are not easy to fulfill, and they are much more difficult in a polarized society emerging from conflict. This is certainly the case in El Salvador and Nicaragua, where the leaders have only marginal control of the government, resource bases are in tatters, and powerful interests are waiting for the government to stumble.

### El Salvador

In July 1989 the Cristiani government in El Salvador undertook the first steps of a rather orthodox stabilization and adjustment economic reform package. The first steps included devaluation of the currency, a raising of interest rates, and hikes in the public service rates. In August, adjustment measures were initiated, including the reduction of tariffs, the liberalization of prices in over one hundred product categories, and the reduction of some incentives, including a reduction of export tax credits from 15 per cent to 8 per cent.

An economic team with excellent technical qualifications and a high degree of commitment to reform was recruited from a private sector thinktank.[52] Its members were non-political technocrats with only weak links to the ruling ARENA party. Beginning in March 1990, they came under increasing criticism from various sectors of the party, especially from those concerned with the impact that the economic reform measures might have on ARENA's electoral possibilities in March 1991. A leader of one of ARENA's major factions said in a confidential interview that if the government failed to produce positive results by the end of the year, it would have to come up with new policies.[53] Resistance had also begun to grow within the D'Aubuisson faction of ARENA in Congress. Questions were being raised by the armed forces. Although these rumblings did not reflect a withdrawal of support for economic reform, limits to the commitment of critical support groups were being expressed.

With respect to the control over resources needed to finance the reforms, the situation is a bit more difficult. Three unforeseen variables produced a balance-of-payments financing shortfall of $350 million in 1989.[54] First, coffee prices plummeted, costing the government an estimated $150 million in revenues. USAID cut Economic Support Fund (ESF) financing by $50 million. And the November 1989, FMLN offensive cost $150 million in additional expenditures for imports. Moreover, an expected agreement with the IMF for funds to be disbursed by December 1989 had not materialized by the following May. In January, with substantially diminished foreign-exchange inflows, the devaluation of the Salvadoran *colon* against the dollar increased, and inflation accelerated. Import permits were delayed, and complaints of a lack of liquidity began to grow. Finally, according to both a private sector leader and the head of the Central Bank, by November there was a sharp decline in investment which still had not begun to rebound by July 1990.[55]

Less than a year after President Cristiani's inauguration, several of his important early support groups began to back away from their commitment to his reforms and expressed concern about, if not downright criticism of, the government's economic strategy. The National Association for Private Enterprise (ANEP) published a critique of the program concentrating on the severity, timing, and perceived inconsistencies of the reforms.[56] Coffee growers criticized the government for discriminatory treatment in foreign-exchange transactions. Labor organizations began a series of strikes and protest demonstrations calling for drastic modifications in the reform package. Finally, and most importantly, rumblings of discontent within the armed forces began. None of these groups were seeking the overthrow of the government, but their opposition did signify limits on what the government could achieve.

Over the short run, it should not be expected that the situation that the Cristiani government faces will improve much. President Cristiani is already suffering a deterioriation in political support on account of his economic program. Increasing pressure for change in the economic team will further diminish his political maneuverability. If he is forced to fire his economic team, the successor group is not likely to be as strong or capable of withstanding pressure. But forcing greater compliance through repressive tactics would be a blow to the democratization process. The situation is further complicated by the ongoing negotiations with the FMLN, for which Cristiani will need as much internal support as he can garner.

Should his support from the private sector, Congress, or the armed forces erode rapidly, then negotiations could be crippled—along with the likelihood of producing the economic reform.

### Nicaragua

The balance in Nicaragua is still more delicate and the prospects even more daunting. The original strategy proposed by the incoming government to cope with the economy was unorthodox. It rested on the twin pillars of a strong supply response from the agricultural sector and liberal (as well as quick) financing to cover an estimated $600 million gap in its balance of payments.[57] The former was to come from the release of resources to a newly energized private sector, while the latter was to be covered by grants from the United States and other donors. Nicaragua's hyperinflation and the reduction of its liquidity would be treated through the introduction of a new currency at a rate consistent with the availability of foreign exchange. Redistribution of land, sale and liquidation of state enterprises, and major reductions in the size of the state were also proposed. Finally, the massive public deficit was to be attacked through the reduction of the armed forces and the bureaucracy.

From the outset of the Chamorro administration, political realities presented major impediments to the implementation of the government's proposed strategy. The new administration began with little real control over the bureaucracy or other branches of government and with a relatively high degree of criticism, even opposition, within Mrs. Chamorro's UNO coalition. The complaints centered on a lack of real participation. UNO was offended because it was given little say in the selection of the President's cabinet—a largely technocratic group with little or no connection to any of the political forces within the coalition. Resentment was exacerbated by the near-monopoly on power of Chamorro's son-in-law, Antonio Lacayo. Furthermore, former leader Daniel Ortega's assertion that the FSLN was still the largest and best organized political group in Nicaragua, and that it would continue to rule from below, was reinforced by the retention of FSLN control over the armed forces and the unionization of the public sector shortly before the Sandinistas left office.

President Chamorro's lack of control over critical political actors was clearly demonstrated when the FSLN-controlled state employees' union called two general strikes within two months of her taking office. The first strike resulted in a wage concession of 50 per cent. The second was even more disastrous for the government and its economic plans. The political symbolism was bad enough: It was necessary to convince the FSLN-led army to put down a strike arguably started by an FSLN-directed organization. Worse yet, the government was forced to grant another major wage hike and to back away from several of its economic proposals. And worst of all, the disorders of the second strike caused the suspension of much planting activity, drastically reducing expectations for major gains in agricultural productivity. Ironically, in carrying out these strikes, the FSLN was opposing the same sorts of measures that it had taken while still in power in 1988; the real point of the FSLN opposition, however, was to establish its political clout and to weaken Mrs. Chamorro's control. Finally, to settle the mounting disputes over land ownership, cooperation will be required from the courts, staffed largely by Sandinista judges and magistrates.

Nicaragua obtained an initial $300 million from the United States just in time for the 1990 planting season. Through funding from a combination of sources in Europe and Japan, it managed to cover the rest of its financing needs through 1991. However, for all the financing to be disbursed and for it to have the desired impact, other elements of the government's economic strategy must also work, particularly measures in the area of budget-deficit reduction. Although major budget reductions are theoretically possible, they seem less realistic politically. The major sources of expenditures—the gigantic bureacracy and the military—are controlled by the FSLN, which has already demonstrated an ample willingness to veto major cuts. To the extent that President Chamorro is politically unable to put her economic strategy to work fully, international sources of financing (not to speak of investment) will be reluctant to risk significant funding, and the promises of several hundred million dollars could remain unfulfilled.

Neither the government of El Salvador nor the government of Nicaragua possesses the resources or capacity to implement fully the reforms proposed. Although the government of El Salvador is somewhat better equipped than Nicaragua, neither fulfills the three requirements for implementation: control over the major instruments of policymaking is only partial; resources for financing the programs cannot be assured; and essential political support for the reforms is at best weak.

A stable political coalition in either El Salvador or Nicaragua cannot be assumed. Given the constraints under which these countries' current governments must operate, economic resources will be scarce and competitive claims for those resources fierce. The regimes will likely become weaker rather than stronger as they progress through their constitutionally mandated terms, and their capacity for tough decisionmaking over time will diminish.

# Policies and Priorities

Successful policies must pass two tests: They must make economic sense; and they must generate political capital. Unfortunately, in the cases of El Salvador and Nicaragua, policy that makes economic sense may have disastrous political consequences.

The conventional wisdom is that a new government should strike quickly on economic reforms—during the first blush of the political honeymoon. But that can only be done if the new administration knows that resources will be available and that all the necessary institutions will indeed cooperate.[58] When Mrs. Chamorro entered office, she was faced with a depleted treasury and a huge deficit. Though there were promises of $300 million from the United States, the measure was bogged down in the U.S. Congress. The still powerful FSLN called for a public sector strike one week after Mrs. Chamorro took office; clearly there was no honeymoon.

Mr. Cristiani came into office under rather more fortuitous circumstances; the outgoing regime was thoroughly discredited, and the new government had been given an apparently broad mandate. Nonetheless, his economic policies soon got bogged down by a hostile bureaucracy, inadequate control over the military, and resources that failed to materialize.

In both nations, the attitude of the private sector has been and will continue to be one of "wait and see." Having shown no serious commitment to risk at the out-set, business will demand access to credit and guarantees, as well as macroeconomic and political stability. On the other side, the displaced and the unemployed will want jobs, land, and a roof over their heads. Although there will be considerable pressure to solve all these problems at once, it is important that the governments be modest in setting targets for reconstruction. They must also avoid the temptation for simplistic panaceas and not be overly optimistic about what they can achieve. Since donors prefer plans that show decisiveness and determination, the governments will be tempted to look for grand solutions and to outline ambitious and often unflexible objectives. Unfortunately, such objectives often ignore political realities, and credibility will suffer as goals are unmet. What, then, might be done that *will* be feasible, *will* generate political capital, and *will* stimulate investor confidence?

Given the serious decline in agricultural productivity in Nicaragua and El Salvador over the past ten years, one can assume that there is considerable slack, and that relatively modest incentives could show quick and substantial returns in production gains.

Therefore, reconstruction policy should emphasize agricultural infrastructure, including the rebuilding of roads, drainage systems, and water resources—especially in those rural areas where there is the greatest likelihood of a satisfactory supply response. The governments must bear the major responsibility for funding these projects and for creating related jobs.[59] Priority should be given to providing employment for resource-poor small farmers who invest their earnings in their own farm production. Credit availability for the agricultural sector, both for basic grain production and for export crops, should be flexible enough to promote demand for credit, with the proper measures to ensure accountability. In the short run, such policies might boost inflation, but that danger could be reduced either through the use of external financing and/or the reduction of government expenditures in non-agricultural related areas. While the latter would alienate the losers, the benefits to the agricultural sector would produce support that could compensate the other losses.

The emphasis on infrastructure and demand stimulus is not aimed at avoiding the more difficult tasks of establishing firmer financial grounds for the economy through exchange-rate ordering, cutbacks in government spending, and liberalization of prices. It is aimed at promoting a sounder base for such measures. Steps can be taken in that direction only when it is reasonably certain that the measures will work and that the likely subsequent erosion of political support is manageable.

Joan Nelson has pointed out that one reason for the success of the Costa Rican stabilization program was that the measures produced benefits quickly.[60] Instead of undergoing a long period of stabilization or adjustment with little or no progress, as is typically the case, real gains were made quickly, allowing the government to ease off somewhat. But Costa Rica had few of the problems of its conflict ridden Central American neighbors. It has had no serious political turmoil since 1948. Its governments alternate in a regular and orderly fashion, and the underlying "rules of the game" vary only slowly and rather predictably. During the economic crisis of 1980–83, little capital flight occurred, and factory closings were rare. While unemployment surged to 12 per cent, it never reached the astronomical proportions of El Salvador's 40 per cent rate. Roads were not destroyed, and there was still a comparatively efficient system of electrical distribution, a good health system (reflected in infant mortality rates comparable to those of the more industrial nations), and a competent if not always efficient educational system. Finally, there was a fundamentally solid infrastructural base upon which the stabilization process could work.

The same cannot be said for Nicaragua and El Salvador, where the process of economic recovery will be far more difficult. However, certain policy choices will facilitate the process and mitigate the political impact of economic reform. For example, emphasis on infrastructure rehabilitation will provide tangible examples of the progress being achieved by the new government, thus allowing it to build political capital among constituents. Once there is solid progress to point to, it will be simpler to begin the institution of economic reforms.

Civil wars understandably tend to breed disconfidence, low to nil investment, capital flight, speculation, nil savings, human resource flight, and propensities toward "rent-seeking" behavior. Under these circumstances, demand dampening policies do little to restore the confidence needed to spur investment and risk-taking[61]; instead, such policies may promote hostile reactions even among the government's own constituents.

The rehabilitation of economic infrastructure can send a signal to the private sector that the government is serious about the restoration of the economy and its productive capacity. Temporary tax incentives and expeditious bureaucratic treatment of licenses and permits would be further positive signs. Unless flight capital is given special treatment—through tax amnesty or attractive interest rates for instance—there will be little incentive to expedite its speedy return.

Employment generation programs, even if temporary, will put liquidity back into the economy and restore some degree of demand, encouraging the private sector to reinitiate serious investment. This investment will be needed to increase the country's productive capacity, thereby avoiding the dangers of an inflationary push. Eva Paus has pointed out that political stability and favorable growth prospects are important prerequisites for increased direct foreign investment.[62]

It does not seem unreasonable to assume that the local investment will require similar conditions. Several Nicaraguan businessmen interviewed in March and April 1990 expressed interest in investing in Nicaragua, yet indicated that they would pursue a go-slow, "wait and see" approach before they actually put in significant sums. After all, what incentive is there for the private sector to invest in a shrinking market or a "repressive" economic environment? Although private investment in developing countries has risen from the very low levels recorded in the mid-1980s, overall investment remains 20 per cent lower than the levels recorded in the late 1970s and early 1980s.[63]

Markets in Central America are not attractive—and further recession will make them even less so. The problem of attracting flight capital and stimulating investment could be addressed through certain groups, such as businessmen's associations in exile (associations of Nicaraguan businessmen exist in both Miami and in Costa Rica). These groups could mobilize entrepreneurial spirit and capital to El Salvador and Nicaragua both in pursuit of their own investment interests and by acting as intermediaries for other possible investors. Such groups could also be enormously valuable for establishing contacts with marketing outlets, suppliers, and financial institutions.

Another positive sign is that the success of the Arias Peace plan has encouraged Central American presidents to work together on regional economic development and trade.[64] These initiatives have been reinforced through ongoing meetings of the region's economic ministers and offer hope that reconstruction in El Salvador and Nicaragua can be assisted through regional efforts. In part as a result of the conflicts, most Central American regional institutions have deteriorated badly. The Central American Common Market (CACM) lost the vigor it displayed in the 1960s and 1970s; its monetary clearinghouse did not function for nearly ten years; and, since much of its activity was based on import substitution, even its *raison d'etre* has been thrown open to question. But the efforts of the Central American presidents should be encouraged. The group can certainly be effective in promoting common interests in the area of debt reduction, promotion of investment, development of trade links, and the establishment of regional infrastructure (especially in communications, energy, and transportation). Mutual agreements could also solidify the current tendencies toward liberalization of the region's economies and the institutionalization of democratic processes. And their cooperation offers foreign governments and international institutions a new opportunity to approach the region as a whole rather than only through its separate pieces.

A cautionary note is nevertheless in order. There have been regional schemes before in Central America, and they have done little to solve the region's fundamental problems. Indeed, the economic model of import substitution was the linchpin of the Central American Common Market; that model is now in disrepute and given much of the blame for the crisis state of the Central American economies.

International development assistance moves slowly. While it can produce major projects with potentially large benefits over the medium to long term, the new presidents in El Salvador and Nicaragua need virtually immediate results. Experience seems to argue that, given the frequency of short-term failures, adjustment success occurs over the long haul.[65] Reactivation of existing productive infrastructure including factories, shops, farms, and the like, as well as food production, are highly visible outcomes that can be accomplished rapidly—given the proper incentives to the entrepreneur. The repair of roads, bridges, and agricultural infrastructure can also be done quickly and promote political stability.

At the outset, subsidies will be necessary for transport, food, and basic services. Some of the inefficiencies of these subsidies can be avoided by careful targeting. For example, lower fares can be limited to bus routes servicing poor areas; food subsidies can be limited to a narrow but essential range of goods sold only through small stores in the poorer areas; and consumption criteria can be applied to usage rates for water, sewage, and electricity.[66]

There is certainly much in these suggestions that will make the international financial institutions uncomfortable. But the objective is not to avoid the hard decisions implied by the need for financial stabilization and economic adjustment. Rather, it is to equip the governments with the political tools necessary to give the implementation of such policies a reasonable chance of success without causing an erosion of support to the point where the governments become paralyzed or are overthrown. Thus the international financial institutions need to be flexible regarding compliance with certain programs, recognizing that it may not be politically viable for a government to implement a particular measure. For example, powerful political interests may at times require that certain subsidies remain in place; in Costa Rica, for instance, rice farmers have been very successful in retaining subsidized prices for their crops because of the importance of rice in the national diet.

Moreover, targets for achieving certain objectives or goals may have to be phased in over longer periods. The possibility of political violence may compel the government to reduce service subsidies incrementally over a long period of time. In normally peaceful Costa Rica, President Luis Alberto Monge tried to raise electricity rates by 60 per cent in one blow in 1983, but the reaction of consumer groups and ensuing violence caused him to retract the measures and raise rates much more slowly.

The role of bilateral donors and of the international financial institutions should be one of support for the reconstruction process in both the political and economic spheres:

- El Salvador and Nicaragua will for some time have major balance-of-payments deficits (projected at some $400 million and $600 million, respectively, for 1990–91); these gaps are on a scale that only the international financial institutions (IFIs) and the major bilateral donors are in a position to help alleviate.

- Given their role in the conflicts, the bilateral donors also have an obligation to help repair some of the damage done. They also can and should assist in formulating and monitoring economic strategies.

- The IFIs and the major donors should also help Nicaragua and El Salvador to achieve favorable trade status and broker agreements with other sources of financing.

- Bilateral donors and the IFIs must also be patient; they should not be too quick to pull the financing plug when deviance from objectives occurs—especially when such deviance helps maintain or build political support. It is, after all, difficult to predict the impact of certain variables; and donors *should* help cushion the impact of external shocks. No one predicted the collapse in coffee prices that occurred in the fall of 1989, yet it cost the government of El Salvador $150 million in lost revenues. Worse still, President Cristiani had to suspend taxes on the coffee exports that his administration had counted on to reduce the fiscal deficit.

- Finally, the IFIs need to be politically sensitive. They cannot demand the same performance from a fragile coalition trying to govern in the wake of a civil war as they expect from a stronger and more stable government.

The task of reconstruction will be long and arduous. In an age of declining resources and increasing demand for aid, it may be difficult to justify continued large assistance, especially when results appear small. But the price of failure and a return to conflict or military rule and continued human suffering is much higher.

## Notes

[1] This figure includes military as well as economic assistance by the United States to Central America. It might be noted that the figures for assistance from the Soviet Union are calculations based largely on reported financing gaps. Since only modest figures can be accounted for from non-Soviet sources, it is assumed that the Soviets made up the rest of Nicaragua's huge balance-of-payments financing needs suffered over the last 8–10 years.

[2] The Commission recommended spending 8 billion over a period of five years, beginning in 1985. *Report of the President's National Bipartisan Commission on Central America* (New York: Macmillan, 1984). In 1988, the U.S. Agency for International Development predicted that there would be a $3-billion shortfall, assuming no change in levels

of obligation and disbursement. Since then, there has been (except for Nicaragua) a downward trend in assistance flows.

[3] For the Commission's recommendations, see *The Report of the International Commission for Central American Recovery and Development* (Durham, NC: Duke University Press, 1989).

[4] The Soviet Union's growing disenchantment with wars of national liberation in general, and Marxist guerillas in Central America in particular, is described in Susan Kaufman Purcell, "Cuba's Cloudy Future," *Foreign Affairs,* Vol. 69, No. 3 (Summer 1990), pp. 114–18.

[5] Though not generally referred to as a "waste of resources," there is a clear sense of disappointment over the lack of results of economic reform programs. See John Williamson, *Progress of Policy Reform in Latin America* (Washington, D.C.: Institute for International Economics, 1990; and Manuel Pastor, "The Effects of IMF Programs in the Third World: Debate and Evidence from Latin America," *World Development,* Vol. 15, No. 2, 1987, pp. 249–62; and World Bank, *World Development Report: 1990* (Washington D.C.: World Bank, 1990).

[6] Economists and politicians of course employ different models or paradigms of analysis—which may account for why economists seem so confident of their ideas and why politicians often view them with skepticism. The economist generally employs a "rational" model that emphasizes the maximization and efficient use of resources. The politician on the other hand, is a negotiator equipped with a bargaining mode. His view of the world is not dependent on a series of hierarchical premises, and thus he is often willing to compromise in order to move the process along. See Graham Allison, *The Essence of Decision* (Glenview, IL: Scott, Foresman, and Company, 1972), for a more comprehensive analysis of this view.

[7] Accuracy and agreement on aggregate data in Central America is scarce, especially in the case of Nicaragua and El Salvador. The problem is owed to poor data gathering, politicization of the data, and subsequent unfiltered citation of such data by myriad sources. Thus, some of the data cited come from sources that cannot be viewed necessarily as unimpeachable but nevertheless are cited to give an idea of magnitude.

[8] Cited by Rafael Menjivar in "El Salvador: Opciones y Desafíos Hacia el Ano 2000" in *America Central Hacia el Ano 2000* (Caracas, Venezuela: Editorial Nueva Sociedad, 1989), p. 5. According to UNICEF, El Salvador's dead numbered 60,371 (through 1986). In stark contrast is an estimate of 26,700 through 1989, cited by the Ministerio de Planificacion (MIPLAN) de El Salvador, "Cuantificación de Daños Materiales y Humanos Derivados de la Violencia en el Salvador," San Salvador, El Salvador, June 1988. (Mimeographed.)

[9] Cited by Juan Valverde in "La Crisis y las Distorsiones de la Economía Nicaraguense" in *Boletín Socioeconómico* (Managua, Nicaragua: 1988), p. 7. Oscar Neira puts the estimate at 40,000 in "Nicaragua: La Guerra y la Tentativa de Crecimiento con Equidad Social," *Economía de America Latina 18–19* (1989), p. 223. Also, David Ronfeldt and Brian Jenkins, eds., *The Nicaraguan Resistance and U.S. Policy* (Santa Monica, CA: The Rand Corporation, 1989), p. 50.

[10] Posters displayed throughout El Salvador with photos of maimed children are eloquent reminders of the problem.

[11] Richard Feinberg and Cynthia Carlisle, "Immigration from Central America," Commission for the Study of International Migration and Cooperative Economic Development, Working Papers, No. 6 (July 1989), p. 16.

[12] Interview with Director for External Affairs, Instituto Centroamericano de Administración de Empresas, Alajuela, Costa Rica, April, 1990.

[13] Feinberg and Carlisle, op. cit., p. 6.

[14] International Science and Technology Institute, Inc. (ISTI), "El Salvador: Income, Employment, and Social Indicators Changes over the Decade 1975–85" (Washington D.C.: ISTI, January 1988), pp. 18–21.

[15] MIPLAN's estimate for 1985 cited in ibid., p. 13.

[16] *Boletín Estadístico,* Consejo Monetario Centroamericano, San José, Costa Rica, 1989, p. 13.

[17] Valverde, op. cit.

[18] Ibid.

[19] ISIT, op. cit.

[20] CENITEC, "Las Dimensiones de la Pobreza Extrema en El Salvador," *Cuadernos de Investigación,* Vol. 1, No.1 (February 1989) p. 12.

[21] Ministerio de Hacienda de El Salvador as cited in FUSADES, "Informe Trimestral de Coyuntura," No. 4, 1989, pp. 79, 81. In Nicaragua the decline in spending in education over the last five years has been less steep than in El Salvador. See Juan B. Arrien

and Roger Matus Lazo, *Nicaragua: Diez Años de Educación en la Revolución* (Mexico D.F.: Claves Latinomericanos S.A., 1989), p. 517. In health, spending rose, both as a percentage of GDP as well as of budget expenditures. Inter-American Development Bank, *Report on Economic and Social Progress in Latin America, 1988,* Washington D.C., 1988, p. 37.
    [22] FUSADES, op. cit.
    [23] Interview with Roberto Gavidia, Education Officer, United States Agency for International Development, El Salvador. These data also appear as background for the Education Program's strategy statement, San Salvador, El Salvador, March 1990.
    [24] Interview, Jefe de Planeamiento, Ministerio de Educación, San Salvador, El Salvador, March 1990.
    [25] The average age in 1987 of health equipment in Nicaragua and El Salvador was 11.3 and 10.9 years respectively, as compared to 6.7 for Costa Rica. In Nicaragua, 28 per cent of equipment was paralyzed, 23 per cent in El Salvador, but only 1.5 per cent in Costa Rica. See Los Servicios de Salud en las Americas: Análisis de Indicadores Básicos (Washington, D.C.: Organización Panamericana de la Salud, 1988), p. 194.
    [26] Interview with Minister of Health, San Salvador, El Salvador, March 1990.
    [27] *Barricada* (Managua, Nicaragua, November 6, 1989), p. 4.
    [28] Ministerio de Planificación, San Salvador, El Salvador, "Estimado de los Costos del Conflicto: 1980–89," (Mimeographed.)
    [29] Economic Commission for Latin America and the Caribbean (ECLAC), *Economic Survey of Latin America and the Caribbean, 1988,* (Santiago, Chile, 1989), pp. 470–72.
    [30] Neira, op. cit., p. 234.
    [31] ISTI, op. cit.
    [32] Data prepared by Francisco Mayorga, President of Central Bank of Nicaragua, undated, mimeographed.
    [33] ECLAC, op. cit.
    [34] Menjivar, op. cit.
    [35] For a very thoughtful study of some of the problems encountered by Nicaragua's state enterprises during the Sandinista period, see Forrest D. Colburn, *Managing the Commanding Heights* (Berkeley, CA: University of California Press, 1990).
    [36] These figures are taken from tables in *Boletín Estadístico,* Consejo Monetario Centroamericano, San José, Costa Rica, 1988.
    [37] Stephen M. Gorman, "Power and Consolidation in the Nicaraguan Revolution" in *Journal of Latin American Studies,* Vol. 13, No. 1, pp. 133–49.
    [38] Sam Dillion, "Dateline, El Salvador" in *Foreign Policy,* Vol. 73 (Winter 1988); James Lemoyne, "El Salvador's Forgotten War," *Foreign Affairs,* Vol. 68, No. 3 (Summer 1989), pp. 104–25; and Benjamin L. Crosby and Angel Interiano, "Democratización y la Política de Oposición de los Grupos de Presión en Centroamérica," Technical Note No. 14336, (San José, Costa Rica: INCAE, 1989).
    [39] A discussion of some of the effects of this shifting can be found in Ann Helwege, "Is There any Hope for Nicaragua?" in *Challenge* (November-December 1989) pp. 22–28; David Ruccio, "The Costs of Austerity in Nicaragua" in Howard Handelman and Werner Baer, *Paying the Costs of Austerity in Latin America* (Boulder: Westview Press, 1989); and Neira, op. cit.
    [40] Menjivar, op. cit., p. 1, "Informe Especial: Distensión no Pasa por Centroamérica," in *Inforpress Centroaméricana,* No. 866, (December 7, 1989); and Valverde, op. cit.
    [41] During the general strike of the public sector unions in June 1990, it was widely reported that armed "contras" had come out in defense of the government and had fired on the strikers.
    [42] Interview with Colonel Rene Emilio Ponce, Chief of Staff of the Armed Forces of El Salvador, San Salvador, El Salvador, March 1990.
    [43] Interview with Roberto Orellana, President of the Banco Central de Reserva de El Salvador, San Salvador, El Salvador, March 1990.
    [44] Comisión Económica para America Latina y el Caribe (CEPAL), "Balance Preliminar de la Economía de América Latina y el Caribe: 1989" (Santiago, Chile: CEPAL, 1989), p. 20.
    [45] FUSADES, op. cit.
    [46] CEPAL, op. cit., p. 24.
    [47] These calculations are based on Central American labor force projections made by Stewart F. Tucker in "The Caribbean Basin Initiative and Job Creation in the Basin," paper presented at the XV International Congress of the Latin American Studies Association, Miami, Florida, November, 1989, p. 18.
    [48] See John Williamson, *The Progress of Policy Reform in Latin America* (Washington D.C.: Institute for International Economics, 1990); Manuel Pastor, "The Effects of IMF

Programs in the Third World: Debate and Evidence from Latin America," *World Development*, Vol. 15, No. 2 (1987), pp. 149–62; and World Bank, *World Development Report: 1990*, (Washington D.C.: World Bank, 1990).

[49] A description and definition of stabilization policies can be found in Pastor, ibid.; William R. Cline and Sidney Weintraub, eds., *Economic Stabilization in Developing Countries*, (Washington, D.C.: The Brookings Institution, 1981).

[50] Some of the difficulties of this approach are outlined by Rudiger Dornbusch and Sebastian Edwards in "Macroeconomic Populism in Latin America," NBER Working Paper Series No. 2986 (Cambridge, MA: National Bureau of Economic Research, May 1989).

[51] Recently, countries such as Ecuador, El Salvador, and Honduras have all begun programs of economic reform without prior agreements from the major international financial institutions in the hopes that, after demonstrating their serious intentions, major resources will be forthcoming. The results have been mixed, and have tended to erode political support in each of the countries cited.

[52] The organization, Fundación Salvadoreña para el Desarrollo Económico y Social (FUSADES) is a private, non-profit "think tank" established to analyze and comment on economic policy. It is financed in large measure by the United States Agency for International Development. The former Executive Director and Director of Economic Studies are now the President of the Central Bank and Minister of Planning, respectively.

[53] Confidential interview with member of the executive committee of ARENA, March 1990, San Salvador, El Salvador.

[54] Interviews with Ernesto Altschul, op. cit.; and Roberto Orellana, op. cit.

[55] Interview with Roberto Orellana, op. cit.

[56] "Reflexiones Sobre el Programa Económico," *Unidad Empresarial*, Vol. 1, No. 1 (Enero-Febrero 1990), pp. 17–31. This magazine is a publication of Salvador's National Association for Private Enterprise (ANEP).

[57] From discussions with Francisco Mayorga, President of the Central Bank of Nicaragua (March 1990).

[58] While the President makes the decisions regarding policy reform, it is the bureaucracy that implements the decisions. As Thomas Callaghy points out in "Toward State Capability and Embedded Liberalism in the Third World: Lessons for Adjustment" in Joan M. Nelson, *Fragile Coalitions: The Politics of Economic Adjustment* (Washington, D.C.: Overseas Development Council, 1989) p. 131, that the bureaucracy is often threatened by reform and runs the risk of sabotaging efforts merely by doing nothing. Reform requires active cooperation.

[59] A recent study by CEPAL criticizes the lack of attention to the problem of job creation and questions the capacity of adjustment strategies to cope with the problem. CEPAL, "Recursos Humanos, Pobreza, y las Estrategias de Desarrollo," October 1989, mimeographed, pp. 12–16.

[60] Joan M. Nelson, "The Politics of Adjustment in Small Democracies" in Joan Nelson, ed., *Economic Crisis and Policy Choice* (Princeton, NJ: Princeton University Press, 1990) pp. 183–86.

[61] Manuel Pastor, op. cit.

[62] Eva Paus, "Direct Foreign Investment and Economic Development in Latin America: Perspectives for the Future" in *Journal of Latin American Studies*, Vol. 21, pp. 221–39.

[63] Guy Pfeffermann and Andrea Madarassy, *Trends in Private Investment in Thirty Developing Countries* (Washington D.C.: International Finance Corporation, 1989).

[64] A meeting of the Central American Ministers of Economy was held in Antigua, Guatemala during June, 1990, to discuss possible new regional initiatives.

[65] World Bank, *Adjustment Lending: An Evaluation of Ten Years Experience* (Washington D.C.: World Bank, 1989).

[66] World Bank, "How Adjustment Programs Can Help the Poor," mimeographed, (Washington, D.C.: World Bank, 1989), pp. 12–14.

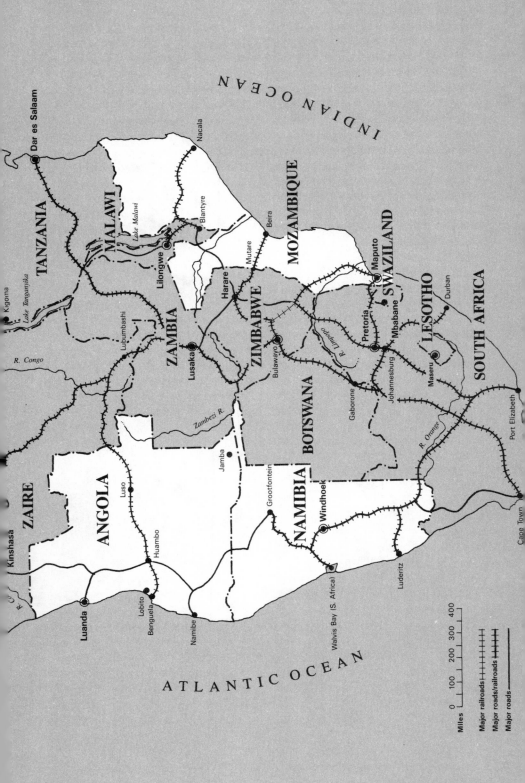

# Chapter 4

# Southern Africa

## Mark C. Chona and Jeffrey I. Herbst

In few areas of the world does the weight of history lie more heavily than in Southern Africa. To understand the full dimensions of the tasks of reconstruction there, one must begin with the multiple penalties that colonialism left in its wake. The colonial powers—Portugal in Angola and Mozambique; South Africa (a colonial power whatever the legal distinctions it made) in Namibia; and the British in Southern Rhodesia, now Zimbabwe—first ruled through violence, and then relinquished that rule in ways that created still more suffering and destruction. In contrast to most African nations, the nationalists in all four countries had to wage prolonged guerrilla wars to gain independence. In Zimbabwe, a white settler regime clung to power for over a decade of brutal civil war. Extended wars of independence in the Portuguese territories ended with a military coup in Lisbon in April 1974. And in Namibia, South Africa disregarded the withdrawal of its trusteeship by the United Nations in 1966 and waged a bitter fight against the armed rebellion.

The tragedy was compounded when the sudden collapse of white rule in Angola and Mozambique was followed by the continued conflicts among local forces—conflicts exacerbated by the policies of the superpowers, of Cuba, and, most notably, of South Africa, which routinely interfered violently in efforts to destabilize the independent governments of its neighbors.

Mozambique, Angola, and Namibia vividly bear the scars of

colonial and post-colonial violence. A 1989 United Nations report on casualties concludes that:

> When put together with other war deaths in the region, the total reaches 1.5 million lives lost over 1980–88 as a direct or indirect consequence of South Africa's regional strategy. In Mozambique, the total was almost 900,000 or 6 per cent of estimated 1988 population and in Angola 500,000 or 5.5 per cent. The total for the rest of the region was about 100,000.[1]

According to the same report, half the populations of Angola and Mozambique are now refugees or are displaced.[2] In addition, the economic cost of South African acts of destabilization and aggression is estimated by the U.N. report to have been about $10 billion a year. Angola alone is estimated to have lost $4.5 billion in 1988 and $27–$30 billion between 1980 and 1988. Mozambique's burden is put at between $2.5 and $3 billion in 1988 and at about $15 billion for the period.[3]

Despite this destruction, we have arrived at a time of new hope. After years of competitive, harmful interventions in the region—most notably in supplying weaponry to their favored factions in Angola—the United States and Soviet Union have reduced (but not yet ended) such involvement and have even worked together in diplomatic efforts to resolve the Angolan conflict. While the South Africans and Cubans both sent their troops into Angola for reasons related more to their own national interests and aspirations than to the Cold War, the change in U.S.–Soviet relations was crucial to their agreed withdrawal. Thus in Angola and elsewhere in the region, the overlay of international rivalries no longer exacerbates the region's conflicts to the degree it did in the early and mid-1980s. In addition, events in Eastern Europe have contributed positively by encouraging flexibility on the left and democratic sentiment generally.

While fighting continues in Angola and Mozambique, signs of hope can be found everywhere: Zimbabwe, independent since 1980, has been able to make substantial progress in reconstructing its economy, with particular success in smallholder agriculture. Namibia gained its independence in 1990. In addition, for the first time since the outbreak of the civil war in 1975, the leaders of the parties in the conflict in Angola met in June 1989 in Gbadolite, Zaire, under the auspices of the African heads of state to talk peace. While no immediate results came of the Gbadolite initiative and other contacts made since then, the fact that the adversaries were able to talk after years of conflict suggests that some progress has been made in building a climate for ending this tragic war. Finally, the government of Mozambique and the rebel Mozambique National

Resistance (MNR) appear to have made definite moves toward resolving the conflict. Two rounds of peace talks, held in July and August of 1990, were characterized by the delegations as fruitful. Moreover, in its August 1990 meeting to propose rules for multi-party elections in 1991, the Front for the Liberation of Mozambique (FRELIMO) included specific provisions to meet the MNR's demands—e.g., lowering the age of presidential candidates from 40 years to 35 so that MNR leader Alfonso Dhalkama might run, and giving a party legality if it registers only 100 people in each of eleven provinces.[4]

In South Africa, measures taken by the government under President F. W. de Klerk in February 1990, including the un-banning of the African National Congress (ANC) and the Pan African Congress and the release of political prisoners including Nelson Mandela, suggest a potential willingness on the part of the National Party to abandon apartheid and create a new climate for a possible negotiated settlement in that troubled country. South Africa seems to have re-evaluated its policies toward the region, offering grounds to believe it will be less aggressive toward its neighbors in the future.[5]

The result of the concurrence of these events is a temporary relaxation of tension that, with wisdom and good will, could lead to a permanent process that might end the era of conflict and bloodshed in the region as a whole. The "peace dividend" could be substantial—in individual freedom and racial harmony, in budgetary terms, and in vast opportunities for economic and social development and trade. Peace, accompanied by an enabling environment for private sector growth, would open opportunities for the flow of new investment. It is therefore appropriate to ask what political and economic steps need to be taken now to help Angola, Mozambique, and Namibia build governments and economies that will put their troubled history behind them and open opportunities with real benefits to the approximately 25 million people who live in them.

But the hope for a healing future is tempered by another legacy of the colonial past. The massive exodus of Portuguese military and civilian personnel from Angola and Mozambique in 1975 left a near void of trained public and private administrators, teachers, medical personnel, and the like, due to colonial policies that left massive illiteracy and poor educational facilities in their wake. Nor were the exclusivist institutions and philosophies of colonial governance—economic and political—suitable to independence. Thus the challenge is not merely one of reconstruction. The region faces the burden, as well as opportunity, of new construction.

Despite their common plight and despite their similar histories of conflict, the reconstruction needs of the three nations are quite different. Mozambique is one of the world's poorest countries, yet it has embarked upon an economic reform program that has already increased small-farm output and attracted donor support. Angola has a much higher per capita GDP than Mozambique and well-developed oil and mineral resources, but it has not yet implemented the kind of economic reform needed to reschedule its massive debt. Namibia has the highest per capita GDP and the best developed infrastructure of the three but must transform its economy to one that benefits its own people.

The needs of all three nations exceed their internal capacities. International sympathy is likely to be greater than the foreign assistance made available to meet them. As generous as the contributions of some donors will be, the largest recipient, Mozambique, is already experiencing some donor fatigue. As needs in each country shift from humanitarian relief to reconstruction, they may fall between the cracks in many assistance agencies that are geared toward providing either disaster relief or long-term development assistance. Finally, if there is political and economic progress in South Africa, it will undoubtedly attract international donor support and may shift attention and assistance from the real needs of neighboring states. Therefore it is especially important in recovery planning to focus clearly on *priorities,* regional and national, and to have a careful strategy. If such a strategy is lacking, efforts to accomplish everything at once could lead to a failure to achieve anything in satisfactory fashion.

## An Overarching Strategy: Setting Priorities

Any attempt at reconstruction will take many years and long-term commitments on the part of the governments involved and the international community to show enduring results. In this paper, we sketch a strategy for reconstruction that encompasses the following points:

- The focus should be on Angola and Mozambique. While the needs of Namibia are great, given its small population (one-ninth the number of people in Angola and one-fifteenth those of Mozambique) and the international attention that the long struggle of the South West Africa People's Organization (SWAPO) received, Africa's newest nation will probably not face a dearth of foreign aid, at least from European donors, in the foreseeable future.

- Although in the end peace will be largely dependent on the decisions made by the Angolans and Mozambicans involved, the international community must take all possible steps to help end the war and promote peace and political reconciliation in all three countries. There should be an immediate end to external military support (overt and covert) for the warring factions in Angola, with simultaneous increases in certain forms of humanitarian relief and economic assistance in relatively secure areas. For all three nations, most forms of economic aid should be tied to their continued observance of political settlements and basic human rights.

- The needs of more than 1 million internal and external refugees must be met—now, in their camps and, as soon as possible, by assisting their return to their homes through resettlement and rural reconstruction programs.

- In addition to mass literacy programs, addressing the critical shortage of skilled personnel must be given first priority among development policies.

- There should be an immediate emphasis on developing and implementing economic policies that are free of state control and the consequent economic distortions that have plagued these and other economies in Africa in the past. Instead of pursuing discredited, statist policies, governments in the region should concentrate on what they can do best to meet the needs of their people: assistance to agriculture and the reconstruction of schools, clinics, and essential transportation routes.

- Regional planning and coordination can enhance not only reconstruction and development efforts by governments, but also the growth of effective private enterprises.

Inevitably, the outlines of strategies for economic reconstruction and development in such countries as war-torn Angola, Mozambique, and Namibia seem like wish lists. In Angola and Mozambique, where the conflicts continue, the road to peace is yet to be clearly charted, and little reliable data are available to make firm estimates on how much reconstruction will cost. However, as we emphasize below, it is important to think about reconstruction *now*, even as wars are still going on, in order to begin certain important tasks and not waste time once peace does come. Measured, country-specific, incremental steps are needed that will enable these countries to increase their aid absorption and program implementation capabilities and also begin to address the needs of their citizens.

# Making Analytical Distinctions

War has ravaged Angola, Mozambique, and Namibia; however, it would be a significant mistake, especially when trying to develop strategies for reconstruction, to treat these countries as a homogenous group. Especially when examining their political situations, it is evident that there are crucial differences among the countries that fundamentally affect not only what is possible in each but even the facts and statistics available to that end.

In the 1990s, the political situation is clearest in Namibia. The Angola–Cuba–South Africa accords signed in 1988 with United States brokerage have been implemented under United Nations supervision with success and have resulted in a multi-party political system and a democratically elected government led by SWAPO. The independence government under President Sam Nujoma includes some members of the opposition parties. The appointment of some whites to the cabinet will serve to build confidence among the white population unsure about SWAPO's economic and political strategy and policies.

Therefore, while the independence government faces a range of political and economic problems as it seeks to build the nation after decades of South African rule rooted in apartheid, armed opposition of the type that the National Union for the Total Independence of Angola (UNITA) and the MNR in Angola and Mozambique is unlikely to be a significant concern of the new government. The post-independence history of Angola and Mozambique will not repeat itself in Namibia in the light of the prevailing spirit of reconciliation and cooperation and the relatively open political system created by the Namibians and guaranteed by the independence Constitution. Pretoria seems to have re-evaluated its policy of destabilization, which has been a threat to peace and security in the region. Therefore, while the economic situation in Namibia may be difficult, the seeds of peace rooted in reconciliation and democracy have been sown; the needs of the country are clear; and it is fairly easy to suggest possible scenarios and options for the government as a basis for policy action.

In Angola, however, there is currently much more uncertainty about the basic political situation. While there have been some recent attempts at negotiation, one cannot be certain at this point if the peace prospects created by South African–Cuban withdrawal can be translated into concrete steps toward national reconciliation and a final negotiated settlement. In addition, as a result of the protracted conflict, relatively little is known about basic conditions inside Angola and thus about the needs of the country once reconstruction begins. However, both the MPLA government and UNITA in opposition have made known their platforms—or at least have made it relatively clear what they are fighting for. While it is uncertain if there is the political will on both sides to move the peace process forward and promote reconciliation, the armed conflict is well defined, as are the basic objectives of each side. The greatest task is to bridge the gap and make peace possible.

In contrast, Mozambique's climate for reconstruction is uncertain because the principles and objectives of the South African–backed MNR rebel movement lack clarity. The MNR has made little information available on its own goals, and the horrifying atrocities perpetrated against the civilian population create an image of nihilistic terrorist bands pillaging the countryside.[6] The uncertainty about what the MNR is and wants obviously poses significant obstacles to the Mozambique government's seeking to negotiate a program of peaceful reconciliation.

However, in 1989, through the mediation of the Catholic Church and the governments of Kenya and Zimbabwe, a leadership group emerging within the MNR indicated a readiness for dialogue and pursued that dialogue in negotiations during the summer of 1990. What remains unclear is the command structure of the leadership and whether or not an agreement with the Mozambican government will be observed by the whole MNR. An additional factor in the equation is the South African government and its destabilization policy, which has been the engine of MNR expansion. The changing climate within South Africa may limit its destabilization of neighboring countries in favor of a policy that engenders peace and development. There may, however, still be significant "private" support for the MNR. At present, South African business and government leaders appear to want to invest in peace and prosperity for Mozambique, while right wing groups continue to pursue destabilization.

Despite the declared determination of President Joaquim Chissano to end the cycle of violence and to build peace in the country, the confusion about the nature of opposition in Mozambique makes it difficult to predict the outcome of the negotiations as well as when some kind of peaceful resolution will be reached—if one is possible at all. On the other hand, this situation could dramatically change due to the strength of the Mozambican government, the international support it enjoys, and the possible termination of Pretoria's materiel supplies to MNR, which could weaken the rebel opposition.

The differences in conditions among the three countries and the varying degrees of uncertainty concerning future arrangements suggest that few policies can be applied uniformly. Accordingly, this essay will both examine those policies and strategies that are applicable to all the countries in the region and go on to detail additional policies in the individual countries.

# Encouraging Political Reconciliation

It is important to examine political reconciliation first because only during peace will significant economic development be possible on a sustainable basis. In all three countries, the possibilities for peace lie in the hands of national leaderships and the oppositions. Just as superpower intervention in the region was ill advised because the conflicts were initially generated by internal conditions and interests, there are powerful limits to what the international community can do to make national reconciliation a reality.

In Namibia, the international community, through the United Nations, made a tremendous contribution by guiding the independence process and laying the foundation for a multi-party democracy. As in Zimbabwe, what happens in terms of representation in Parliament probably will be less important in the long term than whether the government is able to develop lines of communication to all the different groups in society. This will depend on the political will and skill of SWAPO and on the willingness of all Namibians, black and white, to work together.

The challenge facing the independence government and the people of Namibia in general is to enrich the present climate of cooperation. Namibia also needs to strengthen structures, or in many cases build new ones, at local, provincial, and national levels. Western-style democratic institutions that were managed by and for the small racial minority must now be restructured with greatly enhanced capacity to respond to demands of the new, wider, national constituency and electorate far beyond the urban privileged enclaves. Grassroots active participation in wide-ranging political and development issues requires local structures that give human rights, responsibilities, and opportunities for self-reliance fullest expression.

The most important and urgent task for the international community will be to pressure South Africa not to interfere with Namibia and to move as quickly as possible to end its remaining disputes with the new nation. In particular, the status of Walvis Bay must be resolved. Beyond that, there will be a profound ambivalence on the part of the Namibians and the international community concerning the new country's future dependence on South Africa. Certainly one of the fundamental goals of the Namibians is to decrease their dependence on South Africa. However, the leadership in that country is keenly aware of the historical and geopolitical factors that will keep Namibia economically intertwined with South Africa through investment and trade for the foreseeable future.

In Angola, the primary responsibility for making peace possible rests with the parties directly concerned. However, the international community has a crucial role to play in promoting political reconciliation between the government and UNITA. The 1988 Angola–Cuba–South Africa accords were an important step toward this objective. A Cuban withdrawal is already well under way, and the South African government appears to be living up to its commitment to end support for UNITA. The Soviet Union has said it will halt military aid to the MPLA if the United States will cease its arms flows to UNITA. The international community and concerned citizens should press for the "triple zero" formula: no military aid flowing to either side of the Angolan conflict from the United States, the Soviet Union, or other countries. The continuation of U.S. military aid to UNITA not only contributes to the devastation in Angola but also allies the United States with reactionary elements in South Africa seeking to undermine peaceful progress and reconciliation in that country. The "Angolanization" of the conflict could set the stage for successful regional initiatives.

Inevitably, there will be a conflict between trying to end external support for the Angolan government's military efforts and attempting to galvanize the international community to provide more of the aid so urgently required to deal with the economic crisis that the country faces. Clearly the worst possible result of increased foreign aid to the Angolan government would be for those resources to be diverted to its war effort at the expense of development. In the light of the administrative capacities and the legacy of suspicion of the MPLA government on the part of official donors, emphasis should be placed on delivering aid to Angola through non-governmental organizations.

In the case of Mozambique, the role of the international community in promoting some kind of reconciliation is highlighted by the involvement of the leaders of Zimbabwe, Kenya, and Malawi, and the Catholic Church in Mozambique. Portugal, which plays host to so many Mozambican exiles and which could be a key partner for development, may have a positive role in influencing the results of current mediation efforts. Progress in the peace process in Mozambique depends on the willingness of FRELIMO and the MNR to come to some kind of political understanding. Aid to the Mozambican government, especially for the training of troops, continues to be important. But it is essential to cut all aid to MNR in order to strengthen the peace efforts; the MNR has yet to prove that it has a popular base or the control of many inside the country who claim nominal allegiance to it.

As in Angola, the reconstruction process in Mozambique can begin in certain areas before a formal peace is achieved. Indeed, over the last two or three years, security in rural areas of Mozambique has improved remarkably, and Mozambique is beginning reconstruction of its devastated countryside. Between 1988 and 1989, there was a 50 per cent increase in the marketing of commodities such as maize. Between 1986 and 1988, attacks on rural health facilities fell 75 per cent. One study cites the example of the Angonia district of Tete Province, which by late 1987 had only 2,000 of its normal civilian population. Since mid-1988, over 50,000 refugees have returned home to the district, primarily from Malawi.[7]

Beyond political reconciliation and a start at economic reconstruction, all three countries—if they are to have viable political systems—must engage in a great deal of political construction to give nationhood a strong foundation. Political systems that actually promote inclusiveness are absolutely vital for long-term reconstruction in all three countries. Namibia's multi-party democracy clearly promotes popular participation and government accountability. The promise of relatively open political systems may be important in ending the conflicts in Angola and Mozambique. If government opponents feel there is actually some political space in the domestic political systems, as Mozambique is signaling, they may feel less compelled to continue fighting. As in Zimbabwe and Namibia, elections can be the crucial element in a diplomatic settlement. And systems that serve to integrate populations politically are crucial to economic and social integration and growth. The creation of such systems is clearly the responsibility of domestic authorities.

It is evident that the one-party systems that most African countries have established in the last twenty years have not produced political inclusiveness—whatever the theoretical and rhetorical justification offered for their creation. Far from being democratic, most have become authoritarian, intolerant toward political dialogue, complacent, and not accountable to the people. The startling and epoch-making events in Eastern Europe and the Soviet Union since the fall of 1989 suggest that history's verdict on the one-party state is that it is incompatible with a free democratic society and has no future in the long term.

Just as Africans across the continent are coming to recognize this truth, so donors of foreign assistance are becoming frustrated not only by the human rights abuses inherent in one-party states and in military rule, but by the inefficiencies and corruption that come with unchallenged power. Thus even those most sympathetic to the plight of Angola, Mozambique, and Namibia—indeed, *especially* those most sympathetic—should make it clear that the maintenance of generous levels of postwar aid will be dependent on the continued observance both of peacemaking accords and of human rights. This would not represent an effort to dictate future policies so much as a recognition that it would be a waste of precious resources to try to underwrite in the future the failed policies of the past.

Attention to the basic economic as well as political rights of the peoples of the region is important to the future of democracy. For without progress toward economic justice, as well as economic growth, the mass of the people will soon perceive little stake in new democratic institutions. Colonialism left no legacy of democratic habits on which to draw, such as those in much of Eastern Europe. A new democracy cannot be built from the top down. It must be based on economic and social progress in society as a whole: on education; on better health, housing, and water availability; on jobs; and on the enduring hope of further progress. Thus there is a *political* as well as an economic stake in effective economic recovery programs.

## Economic and Social *Construction*

In all three countries, the major task ahead is not the return to the prewar economic life, but national economic and social development for the first time. None of the three countries (except for Mozambique, briefly) has known peace since the outbreak of guerrilla war against colonial rule in the early 1960s. None would wish to reconstruct the colonial structures in place before the wars. In the main, these are countries that have never experienced economic and social development, despite their potentially rich natural and human resources. Therefore, the most critical and urgent problems are the lack of practical and basic human and institutional skills and the need of enhanced capacity for more efficient and effective resource use. Comprehensive macroeconomic and social studies are also vital to put future plans into perspective.

Recovery and economic and social *construction* will involve four basic tasks. Each can be met fully only in a time of peace. But essential beginnings may now be made in ways that can enhance the prospects for peace.

(1) Most pressing is the human nightmare of more than one million refugees whose care and return present a major international challenge.

(2) Training programs should be implemented in all three nations, so that after peace no time is lost in building efficient public and private enterprises. There is grave concern that without such training, the region could fail to absorb effectively even modest quantities of international reconstruction assistance, much less sustain long-term development. And without a professional and committed civil service with effective personnel, local economies will be vulnerable to foreign domination. The training must primarily be (and be seen as) by and for the peoples of the region with the support rather than the direction of foreign donors.

(3) The governments must adopt macro- and microeconomic policies that encourage strong, equitable economic growth based on a vibrant enterprise sector.

(4) Governments should also concentrate on those economic programs that they can implement best—not the state management of economic enterprises but measures to promote private agriculture and to rebuild the transportation and basic services infrastructure.

### Refugees

Angolan refugees in neighboring countries number some 400,000; and there are approximately 1,250,000 Mozambicans in other countries.[8] The cost of resettling the refugee population will be phenomenal. Only with the assistance of the donor community at levels much higher than current efforts can the governments concerned make some impact on a problem of this magnitude. Neighboring countries such as Malawi, Botswana, and Zambia are host to a human tragedy that cannot be managed with their already limited resources. This crisis is an international problem and needs to attract the kind of international aid mobilized in the past for famine victims—for example, for Ethiopia in 1985.

The combination of war and drought put 1.2–2.8 million Angolans at risk of starvation this year, according to the United Nations team sent to propose a plan for emergency food aid. One hundred thousand to two hundred thousand could die before the end of 1990. Last year, thousands starved to death in Angola—although the harvest was better than this year's. In most areas, the war makes relief efforts almost impossible. Roads and even paths are mined. (Angola has the highest rate of amputation in the world.) Relief trucks must travel in armed convoys. When those who are starving come to the towns for food, cholera epidemics occur. Both sides in the conflict will have to allow emergency relief to travel unimpeded through contested areas and to areas controlled by the other; and if mass starvation is to be averted, both sides will have to remove land mines.

In Mozambique, USAID estimates that 5.5 million out of a total population of 15 million are displaced, placed at risk, or refugees in neighboring countries.[9] They are dependent on continuing food aid for survival. Malnutrition in Mozambique affects one-third of all children in the urban areas and about two-thirds in the rural areas. Donor food aid and emergency relief have been generous in Mozambique but are still barely enough to keep people alive. Angola and Mozambique have the highest infant mortality rate in the world.

The human cost of the conflict in Southern Africa is measured not only in lives lost or ruined but also in the destroyed facilities, schools, roads, and bridges as well as transportation systems upon which the vast rural population depends for access to food, medicine, skills training, and other requirements. Rehabilitation thus entails the provision of vitally needed social and other services—not merely the return of refugees to homes destroyed beyond recognition, or the placement of orphans with families they do not know.

### Training and Education

Perhaps the greatest impediment to long-term development in both Angola and Mozambique is the legacy of colonial neglect. According to a UNICEF report, at independence, after over 400 years of Portuguese rule, the illiteracy rate in Mozambique stood at a staggering figure of 93 per cent.[10] The illiteracy rate in Angola was around 85 per cent.[11] In 1988, over 60 per cent of the Mozambican population remained illiterate; the country's percentage of eligible children attending secondary schools is far below the average in Sub-Saharan Africa. In Angola, largely because of the war, the percentage of children attending primary school dropped from 56 per cent in 1980 to 28 per cent in 1986.

Successful national and international coordination on the ground very much depends on the strength, professional skills, loyal commitment, and efficiency of the civil service. The exodus of the Portuguese and other expatriates left Angola and Mozambique virtually without administrative and skilled personnel to maintain the social and physical infrastructure for which its new post-independence bureaucracy had neither training nor experience. The civil conflicts that followed independence exacerbated the manpower crisis and postponed the possibility of early training programs to meet the challenges of development. In Mozambique, fewer than 3 per cent of the civil servants in core economic ministries have university degrees.

The need for training goes beyond the civil administration. All three countries desperately need to increase the skill levels of the population in order to meet the manpower shortage in government, economy, and services. In Mozambique, for example, there is a desperate need for accountants, engineers, and economists. In Namibia, while a significant number of expatriates in commerce and industry will remain, it is clearly desirable that there be a massive increase in the number of Namibians in key areas of government and the economy to enrich and facilitate policymaking and implementation. A Namibian government less dependent on pre-independence white manpower for vital skills will undoubtedly be able to develop a more positive and productive relationship with the white population that remains.

Within a year of President Bush's announcement of a special Peace Corps teacher program for Eastern Europe, the Peace Corps will place over two hundred teachers in Poland, Hungary, and Czechoslovakia. A similar program would be even more appropriate for Namibia, where English will be the language of instruction. As in Eastern Europe, it is in the interest of the United States and other Western nations to reinforce the transition to democracy in Namibia by helping to make education available to the majority. It is important, as soon as possible, to expand the cadre of Namibian teachers at all levels of the educational system.

Namibia might also learn from the example of Zimbabwe, where the numbers in school went from 800,000 at independence to 2.2 million a year later. With the help of outside donors, Zimbabwe within fourteen months constructed a teacher training college where prospective teachers alternated a year of studying with a year of teaching until they earned their degrees.

Educational efforts and agricultural extension are no less important at the grassroots in Angola and Mozambique to facilitate access to information, knowledge, and technical advice on new production techniques, resource mobilization and utilization, marketing, health, nutrition, and environmental management. Such training should also aim to empower people at the local level and to provide women in particular with effective farm and off-farm income-generating skills. Such efforts are needed to widen the options of rural populations not only to survive but also to contribute to growth in freedom.

The cost of needed training and educational programs is high. There can be no "quick fixes" through crash training programs in accountancy or engineering (although such programs are necessary). The pool of secondary school and college graduates is too small to supply all the trainees needed. A massive effort is needed at the primary and secondary school levels. This will be expensive: According to World Bank officials, it will cost some $700 million simply to rebuild schools destroyed by the MNR. But expensive as they are, training and education should be the central priority of all three governments as well as of foreign donors. Indeed, without such programs, the ability of all three nations to absorb and use foreign aid effectively in other sectors will be tightly constrained well into the foreseeable future.

### Creating a Climate for Growth

It is absolutely crucial that African countries have an accountable and stable state to achieve the goals of development. It is also vital that the state do only what it can do well to promote development on a sustainable basis: build and maintain infrastructure, establish a viable legal system, and maintain order. Tax and investment policies that encourage investment are also important if there is to be economic growth.

Conversely, the state should not do what it has proven to be exceptionally poor at throughout Africa and the world: set the prices of goods, allocate foreign exchange, and operate poorly functioning public enterprises. The socialist measures put in place by the governments in Angola and Mozambique increased public-sector participation without developing sufficiently strong management cultures, training local manpower, or providing for autonomous decisionmaking in the running of enterprises.

Therefore, the third priority for all three governments must be the development of a supportive climate for economic growth. While there is still debate on the exact causes of Africa's economic decline over the past twenty years, it is clear that among the most important preconditions for economic growth are effective national macroeconomic policies. Adoption of such policies does not necessarily guarantee growth, but incorrect policies clearly are obstacles to growth.

Angola and Mozambique, despite administrative and structural limitations, have initiated economic recovery programs consistent with the overall objectives of the World Bank. For example, economic liberalization is evident in Mozambican measures to support private sector growth, open up the sectors previously reserved for state monopolies, and reduce the rigidities under which enterprises operate. Both Angola and Mozambique have displayed keen interest in attracting foreign direct investment; the latter is also working to induce greater domestic investment. In Angola, foreign private investment remains dominant in oil and mining. Most of the capital in pre-independence Mozambique was British, South African, and Rhodesian. Given an improved security situation, it is likely that new investors would, with adequate incentives, be attracted to participate in the economic reconstruction program. Indeed, many South African investors are already doing so. Mozambique's Investment Code and its new draft Constitution provide for a market economy and the participation of the private sector in national development. Policymakers realize that foreign investment is simply not enough for economic take-off to desirable levels of sustainable development. Therefore, apart from creating a strong institutional base, the two governments (with Mozambique again in the lead) have initiated measures—including attractive packages of incentives—to stimulate higher productivity and private investment. Both Angola and Mozambique have adopted policies favoring privatization of state monopolies—for example, of many coffee plantations in Angola and government agricultural estates in Mozambique.

Namibia will probably have an easier task in attracting foreign investment because the new government has from the start created confidence and the right environment with policies and incentives favoring economic growth. For instance, Lonrho, a British corporation, recently announced a $150-million investment in a sugar processing plant in northern Namibia.[12] As in the case of Mozambique, there are likely to be many South African investors who will be interested in Namibia's economy.

Long-term reconstruction efforts demand macroeconomic policies designed to align the exchange rate, interest rates, the money supply, and trade regimes with the overall objectives of structural adjustment for economic recovery. Exchange rate policies, for example, should not allow currencies to become overvalued and thereby, as in many other African countries, cause exporting to be an nonviable business proposition. If Namibia opts to stay in the rand zone, then it will not, for the time being, have to worry about exchange rate policies. Namibia inherited an external debt of about $1 billion from the South African administration for which Pretoria must be responsible.

Aid resources must take into account those who have suffered the most from wars and could fare worst from the consequences of reconstruction. If the benefits of peace lag too far behind the end of the conflicts, social and political unrest could seriously threaten nascent democratic processes.

## Agriculture

All three countries must also adopt policies that give strong support to agriculture. In Angola, Mozambique, and Namibia, this must take into account the reality that over 80 per cent of the population is still directly dependent for its livelihood on agriculture. The structure of incentives should, therefore, answer to the special needs not only of the commercial sector but also of the subsistence sector. Yet the history of colonial neglect and post-independence conflict has kept this vital resource outside the mainstream of creative development action. Adequate price incentives and timely access to vital and affordable inputs must all be reinforced by a strong extension service and training of the rural population in requisite skills. This will improve resource and environmental conservation, utilization, and development. Otherwise, the advantages of strong incentives and unfolding opportunities will simply pass the rural population by without the desired improvement in their quality of life.

The differences among the three countries need recognition. In Angola and Mozambique, the Portuguese exodus at independence left the farms and plantations, like factories, schools, hospitals, offices, and city housing without managerial and technical personnel. The commercial farming sector virtually disappeared, and reconstruction strategy will have to focus on attracting new investment to revive it.

Mozambique's economic reforms, aimed at increasing the production and incomes of the small peasant producers who make up 85 per cent of the population, are beginning to have an impact. These reforms have included a currency devaluation of over 95 per cent in two years, removal of price controls on over half of the products affected, significant reduction in products subject to administrative allocation, and reallocation of foreign exchange to agricultural inputs. The results have been an annual growth rate of 4–6 per cent since 1987, arresting the rapid decline after 1982, and the availability of food in urban markets where there was previously none to be found. Mozambique is launching a Priority District Program, targeting 40 of its 130 districts for three years each for reconstruction—restoring basic health, education and water services; repairing transport infrastructure; developing agricultural extension services; and ensuring availability of basic tools, equipment, and seeds. Such efforts to expand and restore health to secure areas are worthy of donor support.

Immediate and large increases in agricultural production could take place in about a quarter of the country if Angola adopted the kinds of economic reforms that Mozambique has implemented: radical devaluation to make the currency worth something to those with produce to sell; the removal of price controls and administrative restrictions on agricultural goods; and the allocation of foreign exchange for agricultural inputs.

In Namibia, the dualism of commercial and subsistence agriculture inherited by the independence government calls for a change of emphasis in state agricultural policy away from aiding solely the large white agrarian sector to bolstering the efforts of the vast small-scale farming community neglected by the apartheid system. As Zimbabwe has demonstrated, there is not a zero-sum game between promoting peasant farmer interests and preserving large-scale commercial agriculture. Zimbabwe has been able to expand government marketing and extension services to peasant areas dramatically while not significantly curtailing the role large farmers have in the production of important food and cash crops. Indeed, the promotion of both can lead to concrete advantages, since large-scale agriculture may be able to produce some types of crops (especially for export) more efficiently than small-scale farmers can. In pre-independence Namibia, economic growth, sectoral diversification, and export drive were determined by South African economic needs and not the development of the country.

How successful countries can be in promoting agriculture will, of course, vary depending on the political and security situation in each country. With peace in Namibia, there is finally an opportunity to develop small-scale agriculture after decades of its neglect by the South African government.

## Transportation

Particularly vital and yet difficult in all three countries is the rehabilitation of the physical infrastructure of railways, roads, bridges, ports and airports, city housing, and office and commercial buildings—with adequate services to support them. Indeed, significant parts of the infrastructure in Angola and Mozambique have effectively ceased to exist. For instance, parts of the Benguela railroad have been severely damaged. However, only in Namibia is a comprehensive program of infrastructure construction and reconstruction now possible. In Mozambique, there are some efforts at infrastructure reconstruction, especially in the Beira Corridor guarded by Zimbabwean troops, in Limpopo, and around Cabora Bassa; but because of the security situation, early efforts at a comprehensive country-wide reconstruction cannot be undertaken. In the long term, policymakers in Mozambique face the monumental task of not only restructuring but also enhancing the existing east-west lines of communication; of adding new south-north corridors; and of tapping the rich resources of the vast hinterland and its population. Similarly, in Angola, the Benguela railway corridor connecting Lobito to Zaire and Zambia, the Luanda-Malange line, and the Namibe-Menongue line all run east-west without north-south connections. The conditions of the existing road and railway systems call for an extensive program of rehabilitation, the cost of which will be billions of U.S. dollars. The major ports of Beira, Maputo, and Nacala in Mozambique, and of Lobito, Luanda, and Namibe in Angola need rehabilitation to match the growing demands of economic reconstruction and future development not only in Angola and Mozambique but also in neighboring countries in the region. The World Bank is just completing a study on how the member countries of the Southern African Development Coordination Conference might even under present conditions improve the efficiency and competitive position of their railroad corridors.

Both Angola and Mozambique have internal air transport potential because of the network of airports built in the defensive colonial war; but these systems need rehabilitation—at enormous cost—to meet peacetime development challenges. The Southern African Development Coordination Conference is undertaking a feasibility study of a regional airline that might serve some of these airports. However, there is a more pressing immediate need for both sides in the Angolan and Mozambican conflicts to reach agreement on provisions assuring access by relief workers to all airstrips to deliver food aid and medical supplies. Namibia's transport sector also requires further development, although it is in comparatively good shape. Today's network of roads and railways was designed to serve the industrial, commercial, and administrative interests of the white enclaves and Pretoria's strategic and logistical needs in the war against SWAPO.

# Regional Initiatives

The Southern African Development Coordination Conference (SADCC) consists of the majority-ruled nations in the region. The group established four principal goals in its "Memorandum of Understanding on the Institutions of the Southern African Development Coordination Conference" signed in Harare on July 20, 1981:

(a) the reduction of economic dependence, particularly (but not only), on the Republic of South Africa;

(b) the forging of links to create a genuine and equitable regional integration;

(c) the mobilization of resources to promote the implementation of national, interstate, and regional policies; and

(d) concerted action to secure international cooperation within the framework of a strategy for economic liberation.

It was soon recognized that these and the following general goals made sense whatever happened in South Africa: the strengthening of national economies, regional integration, improving communications, and facilitating the growth of trade and investment. Indeed, SADCC will be an invaluable mechanism to help integrate a post-apartheid South Africa more deeply into the region at some point in a future more foreseeable than it was a decade ago.

SADCC policies and programs are already benefiting Mozambique and, to a more limited extent, Angola—as they will Namibia, the tenth member of SADCC. Indeed, the accession of Namibia will pose a new challenge to SADCC. The east coast, on which Malawi, Swaziland, Zambia, and Zimbabwe rely for port facilities has received more attention than the western areas of the region. A significant amount of the money donated to SADCC, for example, has been devoted to establishing the Beira Corridor. The import and export trade of Malawi, Zambia, and Zimbabwe depends on shipping east. In any case, projects in the western part of the region could not advance further because of the unsettled political and security situation in Angola and Namibia. Now, Namibia's membership provides SADCC with an opportunity to bring into its planning mechanism projects that have long remained on the drawing board—projects linking Namibia to Angola, Botswana, Zambia, and the rest of the region. Peace and regional integration will strengthen the basis for a formula to develop the Benguela corridor and the contiguous regions of Angola and Namibia in the south and Zaire and Zambia in the north and east. In this context, SADCC can play an important role in helping to rationalize and develop Namibia's communications network to Botswana, Angola, and Zambia. Already, SADCC has given Angola and Namibia the green light to establish the feasibility of reviving and developing the transport network linking the two countries through the Namibe Corridor via Lubango. This would be a major joint reconstruction effort that would aid the development of the rich regions of southern Angola and northern Namibia.

SADCC's first decade has demonstrated the value of coordinating work not only at the government level but also between private sector associations and corporations in the region. The role of the private sector in the national economies and in the region can be expanded through business councils and federated chambers of commerce operating under SADCC's umbrella. Indeed, SADCC's major theme in its second decade is "Enterprise, Skills, and Development." SADCC can also help governments seek foreign private investment while adopting laws and regulations designed to protect local sovereignty and independence.

The primary challenge to SADCC and the region is that resource mobilization by the international community has not yielded the desired results because the capability of the SADCC countries to absorb aid is extremely limited. The causes are to be found in these countries' general economic condition. The poor colonial record on education, the weak institutional base, the shortage of skilled manpower, the weakness and sometimes the absence of functioning administrative systems, and the poor infrastructure, among other factors, all adversely affect the speed at which development projects can get off the ground. There is also a limit to the number of projects that can operate simultaneously. With the support of multilateral and bilateral donors, SADCC's effort to improve the long-term aid absorption capabilities of the countries of Southern Africa will assist those countries still facing conflict. Policies and programs focusing on institutional and human capacity-building and skills training at the community level should receive the highest priority—with emphasis on private sector growth, scientific and technological infusion to aid the grassroots, women and youth training, and economic integration.

A number of proposed or existing Southern African training programs—some focused specifically on the Portuguese-speaking areas of the region—are relevant to this need. SADCC should be aggressive in seeking to rationalize and coordinate these programs. It should also seek to gain access to these programs for qualified applicants from the widest possible political spectrum. If political

allegiances make this impossible, donors should support such training opportunities at institutions outside the region. It would be a
wise investment in the future for the Angolan government to allow
members of UNITA, for example, to receive technical training that
will someday enable them to contribute their skills to a peaceful
Angola.

## Southern Africa and the International Community

There are reasons to be hopeful about international support for
reconstruction projects in the region. First, the areas of serious controversy between the majority-ruled countries in the region and
Western donors are being reduced, particularly with the changed
position of the Western countries on South Africa and its policy of
apartheid. The United States (due to the Congressional override of
President Reagan's veto) and the European Economic Community
imposed a variety of sanctions against Pretoria. Some of the difficulties in relations between the Southern African countries and the
United States in particular were resolved when the United States
brokered the agreement that finally led to Namibian independence
under U.N. supervision. Angola, whose domestic opponents still
receive military aid from the United States, may be a partial exception to this generalization. Finally, Angolan–Cuban–South African
cooperation and the obvious policy coordination between the Soviet
Union and the United States during the Namibian peace process all
but eliminated the Cold War tensions in the region.

Second, ideological divisions—as elsewhere in the world—are
becoming less salient in Southern Africa. The adoption of general
principles of economic development and macroeconomic policies
based on the market economy also will reduce obstacles between
Southern African countries and international donors and prospective investors. Policies abandoned by Eastern Europe and the Soviet
Union do not provide viable options. Indeed, Mozambique has officially renounced its commitment to scientific socialism, and Angola
has announced reforms for economic recovery and development. Private enterprise is not merely encouraged but supported. SWAPO,
despite its original Marxist foundation, has already adopted a mixed
economy approach to Namibia's development that includes limited
state intervention in agriculture or industry and an open-door policy
on investment.

Third, there is the improved possibility—at a point within

years rather than decades—of a post-apartheid South Africa. As South Africa then becomes better integrated within the region, new possibilities will arise for large-scale, innovative international initiatives. An example is the development bank proposed by the President of the Rockefeller Foundation; the bank is designed to redress economic imbalances in South Africa and to attract foreign investment there.[13] (We believe that such a bank should be formed, when feasible, to serve the whole region—as SADCC has already proposed.)

However, even if South Africa makes a relatively easy transition to non-racial rule, there will not be an immediate "peace dividend" for the entire region. If South Africa abolishes apartheid, it will do so because both the domestic and the international costs of the system have simply become too high. A post-apartheid government will be faced with the immediate task of addressing the costs that apartheid imposed, and this task will undoubtedly take decades. In addition, any legitimate post-apartheid government will face demands for large expenditures in the areas of housing, education, and other social services that will require all available free resources. Economic growth in a post-apartheid South Africa will therefore be sporadic and probably will provide very little immediate benefit to the region.

Of the three countries, Namibia would undoubtedly benefit the most by a quick transition from apartheid. The trade links between Namibia and South Africa are strong already, and the Namibia government would have far fewer qualms about becoming more integrated with a black-ruled South Africa. In addition, a quick transition in South Africa will probably make Namibia's relationship with South African multinationals much easier. For Mozambique, the economic benefits of a quick transition to non-racial rule are likely to be far less impressive—if for no other reason than because the Mozambican economy is in such poor shape that it could not quickly take advantage of new opportunities. Economic benefits for Angola would be least significant. Angola, an oil producer, is not really economically integrated into the Southern Africa region. To take advantage of a post-apartheid South Africa, it would have to construct infrastructure and commercial ties from the ground up. Once again, the Angolan economy is in such a bad state that a dramatic increase in economic activity simply is not feasible.

A real "peace dividend" for the region will also depend on governments adopting policies that promote real economic growth. After all, many other African countries have experienced rapid economic decline even though they have been far from South Africa.

The abolishment of apartheid is a necessary but not sufficient condition for prosperity in Southern Africa.

But while there are reasons to hope for generous international assistance to the region, Angola and Mozambique have less cause for optimism than Namibia. Although the requirements of all three countries are great, providing resources for Namibia's needs will be easiest, since the country has a population of only one million. In addition, the drama of Namibia's independence after such a long nationalist struggle against South Africa as well as the prominent role played there by the international community are sure to further attract donors. The planned U.S. aid levels for Namibia—$10 million in FY 1990 and $7.8 million in FY 1991—hardly seem generous. However, West Germany's history as the colonial power there until 1917 and the active German population's significant role in the economy may cause Bonn to feel a special responsibility to fund Namibian development together with other European donors. The Nordic countries have been most generous, pledging a $60-million grant for the first year of Namibia's independence. Overall, donors have already committed over $200 million for the next one to three years.

The needs of Angola (with a population of about 9 million) and of Mozambique (with one of about 15 million) are necessarily much greater on an absolute scale—and neither country can bank on the drama of recent independence to attract donors. It is even more important, therefore, that potential donors cast an especially concerned eye in their direction.

The exact levels of aid required are hard to determine. In Mozambique, even with IMF-projected aid levels of $930 million a year through 1993, there will be a financing gap of $110 million a year after debt rescheduling.[14] According to USAID, "even after a peaceful resolution of the emergency, it will be years before Mozambique can shift from reconstruction to strictly new investment."[15] Over two-thirds of Mozambique's livestock, for example, has been lost in the conflict. According to a recent study, reconstruction in Mozambique will take place under circumstances where over 60 per cent of the entire population live in absolute poverty.[16] Just to support six to seven million rural Mozambicans will require $400 million a year through 1995—at first with food and relief transport and subsequently with household equipment, seeds, tools, and basic infrastructure repair. Already, donor commitments and deliveries are falling far short of the bare minimum needed for rural reconstruction.[17]

It is crucial to note, however, that although increased aid levels are very important, reconstruction in Southern Africa will need much more than external assistance to make it happen. There have been many calls for a "Marshall Plan" for Southern Africa. Yet the preconditions for the success of such a plan are still in the making in the region, particularly in Angola, Mozambique, and Namibia. Western Europe before World War II was already an industrialized region with a trained labor force, efficient administrative structures, and a great deal of private-sector knowledge and support soundly based in scientific and technological research. All that was needed was peace and the capital to rebuild factories and infrastructure. That is why the Marshall Plan was so successful. But in most of Southern Africa, especially in the zones of conflict, workforces must be trained, administrative structures must be created or strengthened, private-sector business knowledge acquired, governance improved, and responsibility instilled for increased levels of aid to be absorbed efficiently and used productively.

Fortunately, no condition is permanent. For forty years it was thought that Eastern European countries could not change, yet in a matter of a few months, popular revolutions overthrew all of these once powerful regimes. Similarly, although Angola and Mozambique now seem to be locked in conflict, prospects for peace look better than ever before. As was the case with Namibia, however, it cannot be predicted when these conflicts will end. It is therefore fitting that the international community begin now to take the important, incremental steps outlined here, so that when peace finally does come, there will be something constructive on which to build. Only in this way will the world begin to address the great human tragedy that has occurred in Southern Africa.

## Notes

[1] United Nations Inter-Agency Task Force, "South African Destabilization: The Economic Cost of Frontline Resistance to Apartheid" (New York: Economic Commission for Africa, 1989), p. 5.

[2] Ibid, p. 5.

[3] Ibid, p. 4.

[4] Jane Perlez, "Mozambique Moving to Democracy," *The New York Times*, Wednesday, August 29, 1990, page A3.

[5] Michael Clough and Jeffrey Herbst, *Beyond Destabilization: South Africa's Changing Regional Strategy* (New York: Council on Foreign Relations, 1989), p. 8.

[6] See Robert Gersony, "Summary of Mozambican Refugee Accounts of Principally Conflict-Related Experience in Mozambique" (Washington, D.C.: U.S. Department of State, April 1988).

[7] R.H. Green, "Mozambique: Into the 1990's," Association of West European Parliaments for Action Against Apartheid, April 1990, p. 3.

[8] U.S. Committee for Refugees, *Peace or Terror: A Crossroad for Southern Africa's Uprooted* (Washington, D.C.: U.S. Committee for Refugees, 1989), pp. 1–2.

[9] U.S. Agency for International Development, *Congressional Presentation, Fiscal Year 1991* (Washington, D.C.: USAID, 1991), Annex, p. 254.

[10] UNICEF, *Children on the Frontline: The Impact of Apartheid, Destabilization and Warfare on Children in Southern Africa*, a 1989 update with a new section on Namibia (Geneva, UNICEF, 1987), p. 19.

[11] Ibid.

[12] "Belt-Tightening and Jobs," *Africa News*, Vol. 33 (April 9, 1990), p. 6.

[13] "Mandela Gets Boost from U.S. Business," *Journal of Commerce*, June 25, 1990, p. 1.

[14] U.S. Agency for International Development, *Congressional Presentation, Fiscal Year 1991*, op. cit., p. 256.

[15] Ibid, p. 254.

[16] Green, "Mozambique: Into the 1990's," op. cit., p. 8.

[17] Ibid., p. 14.

AFTER THE WARS

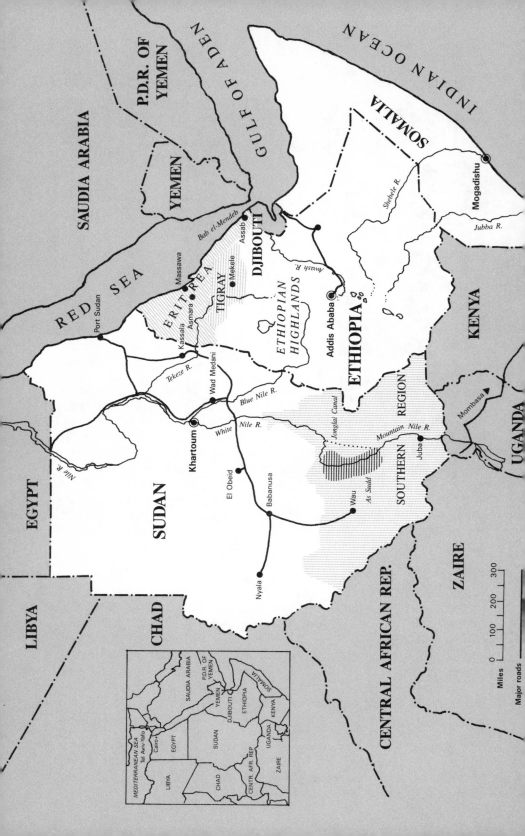

# Chapter 5

# The Horn of Africa

Carol J. Lancaster

One of the most prolonged and complex sets of conflicts in the world is located in one of the globe's poorest regions: the Horn of Africa. Sudan, Ethiopia, and Somalia, the principal countries of the Horn, have each suffered from internal conflicts, often chronic, in which one or more disaffected groups have demanded greater political participation, autonomy, or independence. The governments of Ethiopia, Sudan, and Somalia have frequently supported the challenges of disaffected groups in neighboring countries. Other regional powers have often intervened to arm and support dissident groups or central governments. And the superpowers, too, have supported one or another side in several of these conflicts.

Chronic conflict—together with the low level of economic development, fragile environments, and a series of natural disasters—has turned poverty and economic stress into destitution, displacement, starvation, and death for millions of people. There are at present an estimated 6 million refugees and displaced persons in the Horn. Within the past two years, a quarter of a million people are estimated to have died from starvation in Sudan alone, and uncounted others face periodic threats of starvation. At the time of this writing, a major famine threatens in Sudan. The scope of the human tragedy in the Horn is difficult to comprehend. Millions upon millions of lives truly have followed the old epitaph: "They were born; they suffered; and they died."

Several attempts to negotiate political settlements in Sudan and Ethiopia have been undertaken in recent years, but with little apparent success. No end appears in sight to any of the conflicts. Nevertheless, it is not too soon to begin considering the tasks required to help these countries feed their populations and to promote their economic recovery and development once peace is achieved. This chapter will explore the issues involved in reconstruction in the Horn of Africa, examining the web of conflicts in that region, the costs of those conflicts, the possible paths to peace, and the tasks of reconstruction in the wake of a peace settlement. The analysis will focus mainly on the conflicts in Ethiopia and Sudan, which have been among the most destructive and intractable of any in the world. The conflict in Somalia will also be briefly examined, but the problems of that country—more recent and less rooted in ethnic, religious, or racial cleavages—will not be a major focus of this study.

## The Web of Conflict in the Horn of Africa

Sudan, Ethiopia, and Djibouti all border on the Red Sea. Somalia has a long coastline on the Gulf of Aden and the Indian Ocean. The shape of Somalia—resembling the horn of a rhinoceros—has provided the region with its name. The region's location is a strategic one because of shipping through the Suez Canal, control of the Bab el-Mendeb straits, which are a choke point between Djibouti and Yemen, and proximity to the Middle East and the major sources of world petroleum. Sudan is also strategically located within Africa, bordering on eight African countries (including Egypt and Libya). Ethiopia, one of the longest independent African countries, is the second largest country of Sub-Saharan Africa in population size and potentially one of the most powerful on the continent. Although exceedingly poor, the region has long been of interest to external powers—to the Arabs and Israelis in their search for diplomatic and strategic advantage and to the superpowers in their Cold War competition.

### Ethiopia

The conflict in Ethiopia has been the more protracted of the two major conflicts in the Horn.[1] The principal protagonists today are the Eritrean Peoples' Liberation Front (EPLF), whose demands center on a referendum for the people of Eritrea to decide on the nature of their future ties with Ethiopia, including the option of independence, and the Tigrayan Peoples' Liberation Front (TPLF), which is demanding the replacement of the Mengistu regime with a more democratic government. The EPLF and TPLF now control most of their respective provinces. There are several smaller insurgency movements, the most significant of which is the Oromo Liberation Front.

Eritrea, home to nine major ethnic groups, was colonized by Italy at the end of the 19th century. Britain took over the colony at the beginning of the Second World War after expelling the Italians. After the war, and despite considerable sentiment for independence within Eritrea, the U.N. General Assembly decided in 1952 to federate the province with Ethiopia, a position coinciding with the demands of the Ethiopian Emperor, Haile Selassie. In 1962, the Eritrean Assembly voted for full absorption into Ethiopia, eliminating the autonomy until then enjoyed by the province. This vote, taken under duress, sparked the beginning of the armed resistance by Eritreans to Ethiopian power—a resistance that continues today as the world's longest civil war. In recent years, the EPLF has achieved major military gains against the Ethiopian armed forces. It now controls most of the countryside in Eritrea and many of the towns (including the port of Massawa) but not the port of Assab or the capital city of Asmara and its environs. Although formerly a Marxist-oriented movement, the EPLF now professes support for a mixed economy and a multi-party democracy for Eritrea.

The Tigray Peoples' Liberation Front began operations in 1975, reflecting the discontent among Tigrayans with the Amhara-dominated government in Addis Ababa. (The Amhara had long controlled politics in Ethiopia and had attempted to impose their language, Amharic, as the official language in Tigray, replacing Tigrinya.) The TPLF, aided and advised by the EPLF, has also been a strongly Marxist-oriented movement, favoring an Albanian-style economic and political system. More recently, the TPLF has modified its positions and now supports democracy and free elections. In attempting to build a multi-ethnic movement to challenge the current Ethiopian government, the TPLF has formed an alliance with the predominantly Amharic Ethiopian People's Democratic Movement, which also opposes the government in Addis Ababa. These two groups have set up a joint organization known as the Ethiopian People's Revolutionary Democratic Front (EPRDF). In addition, the Oromo People's Democratic Movement (OPDM) has been established with TPLF support and is now part of the EPRDF.

Since early 1989, the TPLF and its allies have made significant military advances; they now control all of Tigray and Welo provinces, operate in strength in Gonder, Gojam, and northern Shoa, and have probed to within 70 miles of Addis. The development of insurgencies in Ethiopia suggests that these groups, beginning with the EPLF, are pursuing a strategy of "each one teach one" in helping new groups to form and begin armed insurgencies.

Both the EPLF and the TPLF claim that they receive no external financing, acquiring their arms by capturing them from the Ethiopian army. It is possible that this is in part true. But it also appears that the EPLF at least has received outside support from a variety of sources—including, at various times, Arab governments and the Soviet Union. The government in neighboring Sudan has permitted such support to flow through its territory in periods when its relationships with the government in Ethiopia have been tense. Before the Ethiopian revolution, which began in 1974, the Soviets are believed to have supported the Eritrean resistance, as the latter challenged the Western-supported government of Haile Selassie. Soviet support for the Eritreans terminated after the 1977 reversal of superpower alliances in the Horn and the 1978 signing of a Treaty of Friendship and Cooperation between Moscow and the new, Marxist-oriented government in Addis Ababa. The Eritreans are also believed to have received support from a number of the more radical Arab countries, including Iraq and Libya, which have viewed the EPLF as a potential ally along the Red Sea. Saudi Arabia, uncomfortable with the Marxist orientation of the EPLF, is believed not to have aided that movement. The United States has also stated that it has not aided the EPLF, despite the Front's challenge to the Soviet-supported government in Addis Ababa.[2] The TPLF, like the EPLF, has gained from capturing Ethiopian arms and has received some support from the EPLF.

The government of Haile Selassie resisted Eritrean demands for autonomy or independence and waged a low-level counterinsurgency against the Eritrean resistance movements. After the revolution in Addis Ababa in 1974, one of the new leaders, General Aman Andom (an Eritrean) attempted to open negotiations with the Eritrean resistance movements. But the General was killed by Ethiopian government troops sent to arrest him, and a policy of armed repression of the EPLF was resumed. The Ethiopian government, and indeed the Amhara elite generally, including anti-Mengistu critics, have been particularly reluctant to consider any arrangement that might involve independence for Eritrea—fearing that once Eritrea gained its independence, other regions of Ethiopia would also demand independence. The government in Addis Ababa also resists independence for Eritrea because it would then be landlocked—as its only two seaports, Assab and Massawa, are both in Eritrea.

Few African governments have supported Eritrea's demand for independence, since it would contravene one of the articles of the Charter of the Organization of African Unity and the basic tenet of African diplomacy against changing the borders of member states. The Eritreans respond that theirs is an issue not of redrawing borders but of decolonization. They argue that, having been a colony of Italy, they should have received their independence along with the rest of Africa instead of being federated with, and eventually annexed by, the government of Haile Selassie.

Since its alliance with Ethiopia, the Soviet Union has provided the Ethiopian military with equipment worth billions of dollars and several thousand military advisors, facilitating efforts to suppress the Eritrean insurgency. However, the Soviets have recently urged President Mengistu Haile Mariam to seek a political solution to the war with the Eritreans and reportedly have indicated that they will be unable to continue significant military support after 1990. Since establishing diplomatic ties with Addis in 1989, Israel—regarding Ethiopia as a potential strategic partner in a largely Moslem-controlled region—has begun to provide the Ethiopian government with military support and advice.

### Sudan

The conflict in Sudan has almost as long a history as the one in Ethiopia. Sudan is a country of peoples with different ethnic, racial, and religious orientations. Half of the population of 23 million is Arabic-speaking and Moslem and lives mainly in the north of the country. Roughly a quarter of the population lives in the south and includes a variety of ethnic groups of primarily Bantu or Nilotic stock with Christian or traditional religious orientations. Among the southerners, the Dinka people are the most numerous, representing half of the population of southern Sudan. The northerners have long dominated Sudan's politics and economy. Historically, southerners were slaves or low paid workers of northerners.

After Sudanese independence in 1956, the south remained one of the world's most underdeveloped and neglected areas, with few southerners playing a role in national Sudanese politics or serving in senior positions in the Sudanese bureaucracy. Even before independence, southern discontent had turned into armed conflict, with Khartoum's authority in the south first challenged militarily in 1955. A southern insurgency led by the South Sudanese Liberation Movement (SSLM) and its military wing, the Anya Nya, continued until 1972, when a settlement between the SSLM and the government in Khartoum was signed in Addis Ababa. The agreement provided a considerable degree of autonomy for the south, including control over all matters affecting the region except defense, foreign affairs, and overall social and economic planning and policies.

There was peace between the north and the south of Sudan until 1983. In that year, President Gafaar Mohammed Nimeiri imposed Moslem Sharia law throughout the country, alienating the southerners, most of whom are not Moslems. Southern discontent had already been rising as a result of a number of Sudanese government actions. The south had two resources of interest to the north: water and oil. The White Nile flows through the south, and during part of its journey there, spreads out to form a vast swamp called the Sudd, where water evaporation is substantial. With the demand for water for irrigation, industry, and human consumption in northern Sudan and Egypt growing rapidly, the Sudanese government decided—without consulting the south—to construct a large canal through the Sudd to conserve the Nile waters and reduce evaporation. The ambitious and costly Jonglai canal project would benefit Egypt and northern Sudan, but it appeared that by controlling the flow of the Nile through the south, it would destroy the Sudd and damage both fishing and grazing for livestock—the mainstays of the local economy. A second problem involved the discovery of substantial amounts of oil in the south. Southerners, naturally expecting to benefit economically from their petroleum resources, became suspicious of the intentions of Khartoum regarding the proceeds from the oil when it was decided to locate an oil refinery in the north and to construct a pipeline to carry the oil there.

Other 1983 actions by the government in Khartoum that contributed to a resumption of the civil war included President Nimeiri's reorganization of the south, dividing what was one region into three provinces. This was seen by southerners not only as pre-emptory and contrary to the letter and spirit of the Addis Ababa agreement but also as a blatant attempt to weaken them vis-à-vis Khartoum. The same year, it was announced that three garrisons of southern troops would be rotated to the north. The troops, fearing that they would be sent to fight with the Iraqis in the Iran–Iraq war, mutinied. Many of these troops, together with other disaffected southerners, joined the new Sudanese People's Liberation Army (SPLA) and its political wing, the Sudanese People's Liberation Movement (SPLM). The imposition of Sharia law at the instigation of the increasingly influential Islamic fundamentalists in Khartoum came to symbolize to many southerners the efforts by the north to impose its religion, its culture, and its control on the south.

Further contributing to conflict within Sudan has been the recent political repression—especially since the 1989 coup, in which the military deposed an elected president. A deepening economic crisis, involving slowing production, import strangulation, a $12-billion foreign debt, and a series of severe droughts and floods has also worsened living conditions throughout the country.

Talks between the government in Khartoum and the SPLA began to look promising during the first half of 1989, but the military coup in Khartoum in July of that year ended those negotiations. After a cease-fire of several months, fighting resumed in the south, reportedly together with violence by armed Arab militia against southern civilians in the transitional area between the north and the south. (The government in Khartoum now claims that these militias have been disarmed.) At present, the SPLA controls most of the countryside in the south while the government occupies most of the major towns.

It appears that the SPLA has received help from various regional powers, including Libya and Ethiopia, particularly when relations between those governments and the government in Khartoum have become strained. Khartoum has claimed that Israel has also supported the SPLA, and others believe that it has received Cuban support. Persistent complaints out of Khartoum that Ethiopia has been aiding the SPLA have been equally persistently denied by the Ethiopian government. The SPLA, in turn, claims that Khartoum receives large-scale military support from Iraq, and more recently, Libya. If these claims are true, they probably reflect an Iraqi policy of strengthening the Arab and Islamic orientation of Khartoum in a region important in the Arab-Israeli political and military equation. Libyan interests continue to center on challenging Egyptian influence by encouraging Khartoum to distance itself from Cairo.

The United States became a major source of aid for Sudan in the wake of the 1979 Camp David Accords, which the Sudanese government, almost alone among Arab governments, publicly supported. But after the fall of Nimeiri in 1985, and especially in the wake of the 1989 military coup, U.S. support for Sudan has fallen dramatically and is now comprised only of emergency relief. Relations between Khartoum and Washington have chilled due to the influence of Islamic fundamentalism, human rights abuses, gross economic mismanagement, and warming relations between Khartoum and Tripoli. The Soviet Union plays virtually no role in the Sudan conflict.

## Somalia

The third most sizable country of the Horn, Somalia, has not escaped destructive internal conflict, although the troubles in that land have a far shorter history and appear less intractable than those of Sudan or Ethiopia. Somalia is one of the few ethnically homogenous African countries, with virtually its entire population both Somali and Moslem. The population is, however, divided into several large clans. In the past, President Mohamed Siad Barre has effectively co-opted or played off the various clans against one another. In recent years, however, it has been his clan, the Marehans, and in particular his family, that have come to dominate the Somali government. Disaffected Somalis of the other clans, mainly the northern Issaks, formed the Somali National Movement to challenge the existing government for power. There has been widespread fighting in the north of the country and political and military repression with considerable loss of life throughout the country. The Barre government is thought by many to have only a tenuous hold on power and an uncertain future. Its human rights abuses and domestic violence have alienated many of its traditional foreign supporters, including the United States, which has sharply cut back its aid to Somalia.

These stories of protracted conflict raise two questions: what common characteristics do these conflicts share? And how linked are they with one another?

First, the conflicts in the Horn are not primarily ethnic or religious conflicts—although ethnic allegiances and religious affiliations often have played key roles in them. The Eritreans are not a distinct cultural or religious grouping. What they share is a common historical experience and a sense of identity based on that experience. The southern Sudanese, too, are of mixed cultural and religious background, although they share a strong sense of their distinctness from the northern Sudanese. Nor are these primarily conflicts over economic issues—although such issues are by no means irrelevant. Questions of oil and water have certainly exacerbated tensions between the two parts of Sudan, and the economic and security implications of becoming landlocked have undoubtedly increased Ethiopian resistance to Eritrean demands for independence. But at the core of these conflicts are two issues of *power and empowerment:* (1) a sense on the part of insurgent groups and the peoples supporting them of having suffered from sustained social and political injustices; and (2) a fear on the part of the central governments that their authority may be weakened or destroyed and their security impaired if they accede to the demands of the insurgents.

At present, a military solution to these conflicts does not appear possible. The government in Addis Ababa has been unable to suppress the EPLF or the TPLF, and the government in Khartoum has failed to defeat the SPLA. These armed movements have in fact made considerable territorial gains in recent years in their respective regions. The EPRDF may eventually be able to mount a challenge to Mengistu's government sufficient to induce his own military to move against him. But neither can the two principal insurgency movements in these conflicts—the EPLF and the SPLA—gain their objectives by occupying Khartoum or Addis and imposing their policies on the central governments. They are not that powerful.

Despite the unlikelihood that these conflicts can be resolved through military force, repeated attempts at negotiations among warring parties have failed, and there appears to be little prospect of an early political settlement in either of these cases. It is probable that the governments in Khartoum and Addis Ababa have remained intransigent on the basic issues of the conflicts both (a) because they have received sufficient external military and economic support to sustain the conflicts while protecting their key supporters from significant economic costs, and (b) because they have been ruthless enough to eliminate any opposition to their policies within their own governments. The external support enjoyed by all of the parties to these conflicts has probably encouraged intransigence, prolonged the fighting, and discouraged the search for political settlements.

But even with political settlements of these conflicts, peace is not guaranteed. Both of the major insurgent groups—the SPLA and the EPLF—are made up of diverse ethnic groupings. Tensions between the Dinkas, who are predominant in the SPLA, and other southern Sudanese ethnic groups have long been apparent and could become a source of further conflict in southern Sudan. The EPLF is led primarily by Tigrinya-speaking Christians from the highlands, but the region also includes other ethnic groups and a sizable Moslem population located along the coast. Differences between these groups could become a source of tension in a peaceful Eritrea. And tensions between Eritrea and neighboring Tigray are also a possibility after peace is achieved. In all of this sadly troubled region, so inured to violence and conflict, the management of ethnic, religious, racial, economic, and political divisions will continue to be a major challenge even after the current conflicts are resolved.

This analysis suggests an answer to our second question. To what extent are these conflicts linked to one another? Although the conflicts in Ethiopia and Sudan have involved neighboring governments and at times have fed one another, they have arisen from different problems and issues and can be resolved separately. The Eritrean problem can be settled independently of a settlement of the Sudanese conflict and vice versa. It is true that the way one conflict is settled is likely to influence the way other conflicts in the region are resolved. If Eritrea attains independence, for example, this may provoke greater interest in the independence option for southern Sudan. And it is also true that peace in one part of the region will remain fragile as long as conflict continues in another. But these conflicts, complex and difficult as they are, are not so intertwined that they cannot be dealt with separately as opportunities arise. Progress on resolving one need not be delayed by a lack of progress in resolving others.

## The Costs of War

It is practically impossible to put a dollar cost on the destruction of assets resulting from war and production lost during the periods of protracted conflict in the Horn of Africa. Concrete data are scarce, and access for researchers, especially foreigners, is limited. It is, however, possible to describe the impact that these conflicts have had and continue to have on people's lives and the economies of the region.

The economies of Ethiopia and Sudan share a number of characteristics. They are among the world's poorest economies. Ethiopia, with its per capita income of $120, is estimated to be the second poorest country in the world.[3] Sudan has a per capita income of just over $400 per year. In both countries, economic growth has failed to keep up with population growth, and average per capita income is no larger today than in 1965. Both economies are largely agricultural, relying on the export of one or two crops to help finance imports of manufactured goods for consumption, production, and investment. Population growth rates—2.7 per cent a year in Sudan and 3.1 per cent a year in Ethiopia—remain among the world's highest. Life expectancy at birth is between 47 and 50 years. Only a third of Ethiopian and a half of Sudanese children have access to primary education, and only 1 per cent of Ethiopians and 2 per cent of Sudanese have access to university education. Both countries suffer from uncertain rainfall, deforestation, and serious and growing environmental degradation. Their physical infrastructure has never been more than rudimentary, with limited systems of all-weather roads, rail services, and communications facilities. In Sudan, the large distances between cities have made transportation expensive to con-

struct. In Ethiopia, the mountainous terrain has added to the costs
of road and rail construction and maintenance.

These are statistical averages for all of Ethiopia and Sudan.
Similar statistics for provinces or regions of these countries are
rarely available. But anecdotal evidence suggests that in the cases of
Eritrea and southern Sudan, the level of infrastructure, social services, production, and general development is considerably lower
than the national average. One estimate has average life expectancy
in southern Sudan at only 36 years.[4] Although Eritrea had reached
a level of development of its infrastructure, industry, and educational system in advance of that of the rest of Ethiopia, it has almost
certainly lost those advantages with the protracted conflict and
problems of drought and environmental degradation.

Against this brief background on the economies of Sudan and
Ethiopia, we now turn to the details of the costs of war in these countries. We shall examine the costs in terms of human lives, displaced
persons, and refugees; physical and social assets lost or destroyed;
macro-economic problems such as production foregone and high
levels of debt and inflation; and the intangible costs associated with
social problems.

At the time of this writing, there are an estimated 5 million
displaced persons and 1 million refugees in Sudan and Ethiopia.
Most of these people have lost any assets they once owned and are
destitute. Many are in camps, dependent on emergency assistance.
In Sudan, there are roughly 4.5 million displaced persons fleeing
from conflict in the south and searching for food. Most of the displaced have remained in the south, but nearly 2 million have drifted
into Khartoum. In addition, nearly 1 million refugees have fled to
Sudan, mainly from Ethiopia. In Ethiopia, there are an estimated
700,000 refugees from Sudan and Somalia, and 200,000 displaced
persons thought to be mainly from Eritrea and Tigray. (The displaced persons figure is a rough estimate, since reliable data on the
displaced in Eritrea and Tigray are not available.) As in Sudan,
much of the displaced and refugee population in Ethiopia is destitute and must rely on emergency relief programs for shelter, food,
and clothing. Some—especially Ethiopians in eastern Sudan—have
settled in or near refugee camps and have begun to produce their
own food or to work on local farms. Many will probably never return
home.

Foreign governments, international organizations, and private
voluntary agencies have provided large amounts of food and other
supplies to the displaced and refugee populations. But the continuing conflicts in Sudan and Ethiopia have made relief programs difficult to operate. Both central governments and insurgent groups have

at times blocked or attacked shipments of food and relief supplies, interrupted deliveries, and expelled relief workers and agencies. It is estimated that 250,000 Sudanese died in 1988 alone as a result of the combined effects of drought and conflict. Possible deaths from starvation in Sudan in 1990 and 1991 are predicted to be far higher.

The costs of these conflicts are not only to be counted in death and displacement. They have also damaged or destroyed physical assets. Much of the livestock on which many southern Sudanese have depended for their livelihood and for their cultural identity have been stolen, killed, or lost to drought. Houses, schools, clinics, and other public buildings have been abandoned and burned. Roads, both in insurgent areas and in other parts of Sudan and Ethiopia, have been over-stressed and poorly maintained. Some have deteriorated to the point where they may have to be entirely reconstructed.

In Sudan, no progress has been made on constructing the Jonglai canal since 1984, and it appears likely that the large bucket excavator designed especially for constructing the canal is, after three years of idleness, no longer usable. It may have been damaged by insurgents as well, but this is not certain. If it is decided to resume construction of the canal once peace is attained, the replacement of the excavator will be costly. In southern Sudan, the war has disrupted the educational system, with children now missing up to seven years of schooling. Schools above primary level have reportedly been closed in Tigray for some time. Medical services have been interrupted, and diseases previously subject to some control have begun to reappear.

The situation involving social services may not be so desperate in Eritrea. After nearly thirty years of fighting, the Eritreans have constructed educational and health facilities and even factories underground to protect them from attacks from the Ethiopian air force. While such facilities clearly are not available to the entire Eritrean population, they are reported to be well organized and effective and could provide a nucleus for future development.

The deterioration or destruction of assets—physical and human—in regions afflicted by war is only a part of the costs of war. There are also the direct costs of financing a conflict. On this question, there is again little solid information. One estimate has it that it costs the government in Khartoum $1 million a day to finance the war in the south.[5] According to President Mengistu Haile Mariam of Ethiopia, roughly half of his government's revenues and 15 per cent of its gross domestic product, or over $700 million a year, is spent for military purposes mainly related to internal conflicts.[6] Little is known about the direct costs of the war to the insurgent movements. It is remarkable, given these costs, that economic growth in Sudan and Ethiopia has not been even lower than shown by the statistics. The probable explanation of this puzzle is that the costs of these wars are financed largely from abroad.

It is difficult to account for the production lost as a result of the prolonged conflicts in the Horn, but this cost too, is likely to be large. It is reported that Sudan could export as much as 500,000 barrels of oil a day if it were able to extract and transport the oil in the south. At $30–$40 a barrel (the price range during much of the last half of 1990), this would mean an increase in foreign-exchange earnings of around $500 million a year—an amount equal to nearly half the value of Sudanese imports and enough to provide a significant stimulus to the Sudanese economy if used wisely.

Macroeconomic policies in both Sudan and Ethiopia also appear to have inhibited economic development in recent years. The currencies of both countries are overvalued, and Sudan—with a $12-billion external debt—is among the most heavily and hopelessly indebted countries in the world. The Sudanese owe the International Monetary Fund (IMF) $1 billion, which they have not been servicing and probably cannot repay in any conceivable economic scenario for the foreseeable future. Failure to remain current with the IMF can limit a government's access to other sources of concessional and commercial external financing. The Sudanese debt issue will present a major challenge to the international financial community when that government is once again interested in seeking external development financing from developed countries and the international financial institutions. Ethiopian debt has also increased, reaching nearly $3 billion in 1988. However, unlike the Sudanese, the Ethiopians have been servicing their debt[7]—at the cost of compressing imports and slowing economic growth. The debt of these two countries would probably be far smaller and their ability to service it far greater in the absence of prolonged conflicts.

A host of other policy problems—including excessive public spending, overvalued exchange rates, and poor agricultural policies—confronts these two governments before they can move toward economic recovery and growth. These problems are a result of poor economic management rather than conflict, but the conflicts have undoubtedly made them worse.

Finally, there are the intangible social problems resulting from the prolonged hostilities in these countries. Tensions among ethnic, religious, and regional groupings have been heightened by continual conflict, making cooperation among these peoples once peace is achieved particularly challenging. And, more practically, the wide distribution of arms and the habit of resolving problems through the use of arms may feed continuing violence even in a time of peace. On the plus side, many who have observed the Eritreans have commented on their effective organization, their sense of identity and self-reliance, their ability to cooperate, and their incorporation of women into the mainstream of economic and social activities. It may be that almost three decades of fighting will have enhanced their ability to run an effective, efficient, and equitable economy and polity whatever the final shape of a peace settlement.

The costs of the prolonged wars in the Horn of Africa in human, economic, and social terms have been overwhelming. What has made these conflicts especially devastating in human terms has been the poverty of the peoples affected by them together with the periodic natural disasters afflicting the region. For millions of people, the wars have too often turned poverty into destitution and destitution into starvation and death.

## The Paths to Peace

Despite the military stalemates in both Sudan and Ethiopia, there are no overt negotiations under way among the warring parties on settling their disputes. During the past several years, efforts to promote negotiations between the various parties to these wars— efforts by General Olusegun Obasanjo, former Nigerian head of state, and by Francis Deng, a former Sudanese Minister and Ambassador, and later by President Jimmy Carter—thus far have failed. After the annual meeting of the Organization of African Unity (OAU) in 1990, the foreign ministers of the governments of the region met to discuss these conflicts under the auspices of the Intergovernmental Committee on Drought and Desertification (IGAAD) and issued a statement favoring a regional approach to addressing the conflicts. It is not clear what follow-up may occur in the wake of this meeting.

The positions of the warring parties remain far apart. In Sudan, the SPLA demands secure autonomy for the south, a voice in the government in Khartoum, the elimination of Sharia law (and by implication, the separation of church and state in Sudan), and a measure of control over the south's oil and water resources. The major obstacle to a settlement appears to be the application of Sharia law, which is still strongly supported by Islamic fundamentalists in Khartoum. (The fundamentalists have at times suggested that southern Sudan could be separated from an Islamicized and Arabized Sudan, becoming an independent state. The SPLA does not support independence for the south.)

In Ethiopia, under the auspices of the United Nations, the EPLF demands a referendum in which independence would be an option. It seems likely that after nearly three decades of war, a majority of Eritreans would vote for independence. However, the government in Addis Ababa remains strongly opposed to independence for Eritrea. These may be opening positions in the negotiations that must eventually come. It is not clear whether an arrangement involving Eritrean autonomy within Ethiopia could be worked out to the satisfaction of the Eritreans—or whether an arrangement involving Eritrean independence with guarantees of Ethiopian access to ports on the Red Sea could be worked out in a way acceptable to Ethiopia.

In both Sudan and Ethiopia, an agreement among warring factions on some form of autonomy would seem preferable. It would avoid the creation of yet more mini-states of doubtful economic viability in Africa. (Eritrea has a population of roughly 3 million. Southern Sudan has a population of approximately 5 million.) Such an agreement would also avoid setting precedents that could encourage insurgencies in other parts of this ethnically divided continent. And it would reduce the potential for conflict arising from the existence of a large number of independent states with potentially diverse ideologies, foreign policies, and foreign backers in an already unstable region.

The challenges of making autonomy work would not, however, be easy ones. Autonomy would imply a degree of political decentralization, national democracy, and political compromise rare anywhere, but particularly in countries of the Horn of Africa. Continuing economic problems will exacerbate rather than ease these challenges. Healthy growth provides governments with increasing economic pies to divide among competing interests. It is likely to be a long time before either of these countries is able to achieve the 5–10 per cent growth rates that would ease social and political tensions generated by the inevitable competition for resources among different ethnic groups, regions, and classes. The difficulties of making autonomy work suggest that external powers, in their efforts to encourage negotiated settlements, should not dismiss the independence option out of hand.

These speculations bring us to the question of what external powers can do to encourage meaningful negotiations in each of these conflicts. John Prendergast, one of the most prolific writers on the conflicts in the Horn of Africa, has urged governments to cut their non-emergency aid to warring parties as a means of pressuring them toward negotiations and the implementation of a peace agreement.[8] Some have urged a joint U.S.–Soviet initiative to bring about negotiations in Ethiopia, hoping that success there would encourage negotiations in Sudan. Others have suggested that the creation of a sizable regional aid fund, to be distributed after peace has been achieved, might increase the incentives for the warring parties to negotiate. Apart from the promise by President Bush and President Gorbachev at their Washington summit of U.S.–U.S.S.R. cooperation on providing emergency relief to Ethiopia, no action has been taken on this or other proposals and none seems imminent.

However, events elsewhere in the world may result in a reduction in external support and involvement in these conflicts. The warming of relations between the United States and the Soviet Union has reduced the incentives for these governments to intervene in disputes in the Horn as part of their geo-strategic competition. A worsening economic situation at home has also resulted in a decrease of Soviet economic support to the government in Addis Ababa. The Iraqi occupation of Kuwait is likely to reduce or eliminate one source of external financing for the government in Khartoum and may reduce both the involvement and support of other Middle Eastern powers in the Horn as they focus their attention on their own regional conflict. To the degree that external financing has been an important element in the continuing resistance by warring parties to a political settlement of conflicts in the Horn, the time may be approaching when these parties may take a greater interest in serious negotiations. Such a possibility makes consideration of the tasks of reconstruction all the more compelling.

## The Tasks of Reconstruction

The first question to address is whether or not reconstruction can begin before peace is achieved in this troubled region. Should the rebuilding of schools and clinics, the rehabilitation of roads, and other critical tasks of reconstruction begin *now*—or must these wait until war is ended? The continuation of active fighting in Ethiopia and Sudan suggests that efforts to begin reconstruction now may be a waste of effort and resources. Lulls in fighting that would permit such activities are typically followed by renewed fighting and destruction. Governments and insurgent groups have been reluctant to permit relief shipments through their territories and have at times targeted their attacks at foreign relief workers. Reconstruction projects and those working on them would be even more obvious targets, particularly by the side not benefiting from the projects.

What could usefully be undertaken now are special programs of education for young people from the war-torn areas outside their countries. Whatever the shape of the final peace arrangements, educated nationals will be needed to manage economies and governments and to promote development. Special programs of scholarships could begin immediately. Studies might best be undertaken in African institutions to reduce the tendency of educated refugees to settle permanently abroad.

The tasks of reconstruction in the Horn of Africa, once peace arrives, are essentially three:

- Continuing relief for refugees and displaced persons (and others threatened by natural disasters) until these individuals can return to their homes and produce enough to feed themselves;
- Reconstruction of the assets lost in war; and
- The creation of conditions that will support future development in the region—including public investment in infrastructure and economic and social services, the strengthening of public institutions, and the adoption of macroeconomic policies.

The large number of displaced persons and refugees suggests that returning them to their homes will have to be gradual, and that relief to them will have to continue for a considerable period after peace settlements. Those returning home will need not only food but also seeds, agricultural and household implements, and possibly livestock to enable them to reestablish themselves as farmers.

In addition to a continuing need for relief, several reconstruction efforts should begin immediately after peace is achieved. Particularly important is the opening of schools to ensure that children are no longer deprived of even primary education. Ideally, schools should be able to provide children with at least one nutritious meal a day to reduce the widespread problem of malnutrition (particularly prevalent in southern Sudan). The reestablishment and expansion of health services (including veterinary services), seldom adequate even in the best of times, is also important if people and livestock are to be productive. Finally, transport systems need to be rebuilt and maintained if the poorer areas are to hope for anything more than a subsistence existence. Planning for the reconstruction and expansion of transport networks should include not only the obvious international concerns of the warring parties for secure trade routes but also concerns expressed by Africans generally about encouraging the maximum feasible regional trade and integration within and among African countries.

These are the tasks basic to moving people from dependence on relief to subsistence production. To move them beyond subsistence, another set of tasks will be important. Priority problems in moving from reconstruction to recovery and development include the following: tackling the external debt burden in both Sudan and Ethiopia; expanding infrastructure; reforming economic policies to promote recovery and development; establishing or strengthening agricultural research, training, and extension services; addressing the severe problems of environmental degradation; and the related problem of introducing sources of energy that slow deforestation. Longer-term opportunities include the development of water and mineral resources in the region, the creation of a tourism industry, and the promotion of industrial development.

The debt problem of Sudan must be dealt with in the period immediately after a settlement if that country is to obtain access to substantial international financing. The Sudanese debt of $12 billion is by any stretch of the imagination unserviceable. Private and public bilateral creditors will have to write off or substantially write down the debt. This will not be so difficult with the precedents set by the Brady Plan and other private debt-reduction schemes and by most industrialized countries in reducing or canceling public debts owed them, but the size of the Sudanese debt and the desperate shape of the economy will require particularly generous approaches. What will be most challenging is the Sudanese debt to the International Monetary Fund (IMF). The IMF does not reschedule or cancel debts owed it. Its programs for dealing with repayment problems (through loans from the concessional Enhanced Structural Adjustment Facility to in effect refinance harder IMF credits in its regular Stand-by programs) will not work for Sudan due to the large size of the Sudanese debt to the Fund. It may be that, in the case of Sudan, IMF policies governing the repayment of its credits will simply have to be suspended for an indefinite period. This is a problem that will require creative solutions by IMF staff and the governments of member countries. It is not too early to begin thinking about this.

The debt of Ethiopia is large, but thus far the Ethiopian government *has* serviced it. The World Bank foresees that this may become more difficult in the future. Ethiopia's debt can be managed through existing mechanisms involving rescheduling and possibly cancellation. In the cases of Ethiopia and Sudan, debt cancellation should be conditional both on sound economic policy management and on governments abiding by whatever agreements they have negotiated with insurgent movements. This suggests that debts should be reduced or canceled as they come due rather than all at once and that decisions on debt cancellation should be taken periodically after reviews of conditions in debtor countries by creditor governments and institutions.

In both Sudan and Ethiopia, macroeconomic policies will need to be reformed, including overvalued exchange rates; overextended bureaucracies; wage, price, and credit controls; agricultural policies (particularly in Ethiopia, with its villagization and government marketing agencies[9]); and trade policies. In short, both countries will face the challenges of structural adjustment—challenges made particularly difficult by their poverty as well as the social tensions and sensitivities likely to prevail even after the destructive conflicts have been resolved. It may make political sense to tackle only the most pressing adjustment problems, such as exchange rates or agricultural policies, until a modicum of recovery is apparent in these two countries.

In all of the warring regions, agriculture is the mainstay of economic life for the vast majority of the people. Agricultural recovery and growth will be critical to the economic future of these regions. A particular problem has been that of food production. Most agriculture is rainfed, and farmers rely on very rudimentary techniques, including unimproved seeds, hand tools, and occasionally oxen for plowing. Irrigation and fertilizer are scarce and tend to be concentrated in the modern, often export-oriented agriculture sectors—for example, in Sudan's large Gezira project. Agricultural yields in many of these regions are reported to be falling in the face of rapid population growth and the pressure of humans and animals on fragile land. Moreover, the application of inappropriate agricultural technologies—including mechanized deep plowing in parts of eastern Sudan—has "mined the soil" for a rapid but brief increase in export crop production and constitutes another source of environmental degradation.

Policies to expand exports in these countries must be shaped with an eye to avoiding further environmental degradation. It is imperative that the decline in agricultural yields be reversed. This will require much-improved agricultural extension services and an effective agricultural research system. And if these problems are to be resolved and an agricultural surplus marketed, the transport system of these countries must be strengthened. It has been estimated by the World Bank and others that 80 per cent of Ethiopia's population still lives at least a half day's walk from a road. Addressing the cluster of issues involving agricultural productivity and environmental protection must be among the top priorities for development throughout the region.

Part of the environmental problem derives from the destruction of forests and trees to meet the needs of poor peasants for fuelwood and other essential uses of wood. Effective substitutes for wood and conservation measures must also be among the top priorities in addressing the longer-term development challenges of this region.

It is worth considering the economic implications of independence for Eritrea and possibly southern Sudan. The population of Eritrea is estimated to be around 3 million people. The Eritrean economy relies mainly on agriculture and livestock. Rainfall is erratic, and the land appears to be suffering from environmental degradation stemming from population pressure and successive droughts. It is thought that Eritrea has some minerals, including copper and possibly off-shore gas and oil. Despite optimistic assessments by Eritreans of the economic potential of their region, it seems likely that an independent Eritrea would be one more African mini-state struggling to achieve minimal development. The market of independent Eritrea would be both extremely small and likely to be able to support only small-scale manufacturing. Eritreans would be denied the opportunity to migrate to less populous regions—an option that would exist for them as part of Ethiopia.

An independent southern Sudan would confront the problems of being land-locked but would have more economic possibilities than Eritrea. Southern Sudan's relatively small population of around 5 million makes for a very small domestic market, but the region does have three important assets: good agricultural land, oil, and water. Markets for its oil and water already exist if these commodities can be effectively marketed, but the exploitation of agriculture will require improved research, extension, training, and credit services. For transport routes, which will be of continuing importance, two possibilities will exist: reestablishing long distance transport through Sudan to Port Sudan, and opening up transport through Kenya to the port of Mombasa. (The all-weather road from Mombasa to Juba in southern Sudan is completed up to the Sudanese border.) The southern Sudan–Mombasa road is important for political as well as economic reasons. It would provide southern Sudan with an alternative transport route to the sea and reduce its reliance on transport through northern Sudan. Not surprisingly, northern politicans have resisted and southerners have supported the construction of this road. It is important that the road be completed as a confidence-building measure for the south and as a means of reducing any temptations on the part of the north to exploit southern transport dependence. Both routes are likely to be expensive to use—especially the one to Port Sudan. Despite these problems, strengthening the transport networks of the entire region is important both to facilitate trade and development for all states and to encourage national and regional integration.

There is no doubt that substantial amounts of external assistance will be needed over an extended period of time for either Ethiopia or Sudan to address the economic tasks of reconstruction. Given the history of poverty and insecurity in the area, talk of the private sector playing a significant role in development in the near term appears unrealistic. An extensive informal sector is likely to continue to function. But as in other countries, it will not be strong enough to become an engine of recovery or growth.

Although it is difficult to estimate the magnitude of needed assistance, it could well reach several billion dollars a year for each country if the major priorities of relief and reconstruction are to be addressed. This is at least double the amount of aid to Sudan and Ethiopia in 1988, when each country received roughly $1 billion excluding emergency relief. In the best of circumstances, the needs for relief, rehabilitation, and significant development assistance are likely to extend over a decade at least.

It is worth considering for a moment the arrangements for delivering postwar assistance. Relief aid and aid for localized projects like reopened schools and health clinics are best channeled through private voluntary organizations—especially local ones, where these are effective. For example, the Eritrean Reconstruction Association (ERA) and the Relief Society of Tigray (REST) are widely recognized to be reliable and effective and should be used to the extent possible. Foreign private voluntary organizations have also been active throughout the war-torn regions and should be used to channel reconstruction assistance. Government-to-government aid and aid from international financial institutions, including socialist and Middle Eastern governments, will also be necessary if import constraints are to be eased and if major development projects like the construction of all-weather roads are to be undertaken. Aid in support of structural adjustment and debt relief should be conditioned on the maintenance of peace as well as effective economic management. Conditioning aid on recipient-government behavior requires coordination among donor governments and institutions. Such coordination will be particularly important in the Horn, where the temptation may continue for external powers to use their assistance to promote their national political objectives without regard for local consequences. With the apparent end of the Cold War, superpower intervention is likely to diminish, but regional opportunism plus the "spill-over" of Middle Eastern conflicts into the region will continue to threaten division and destabilization.

Of the devastating, prolonged wars discussed in this volume, the conflicts in the Horn of Africa are the most complex and the most destructive of human life. They also appear to be the furthest from resolution. But some of the elements encouraging continued fighting in the Horn appear to be changing, and the possibility of negotiations on political settlements in the foreseeable future cannot be ruled out. It is time for the generations in this troubled region that have been unfamiliar with either peace or prosperity—and for the rest of the world concerned about their future—to begin considering how that future can be shaped into one of hope rather than of suffering and despair.

## Notes

[1] For background and up-to-date analysis of the situation in Eritrea, Tigray, and Ethiopia, see the testimony of Edmond Keller, Professor at the University of Southern California, before a joint hearing of the Africa Sub-Committee of the House Foreign Affairs Committee and the Hunger Committee's International Task Force, U.S. House of Representatives, February 28, 1990.

[2] The United States has divided interests regarding the EPLF. The Front has been challenging Soviet-supported Marxist government with a record of widespread human rights abuses, making it a logical recipient of U.S. support—particularly during the period of the "Reagan Doctrine." But the EPLF's aims appear to include independence for Eritrea. With independence would come Eritrean control of the Red Sea coast and the ports of Assab and Massawa. The Eritreans have received Arab support, and in the past there has been talk among the Arabs that, with independence for Eritrea, the Red Sea would be an "Arab lake." With the strategic importance of the Red Sea to shipping and Western and Israeli trade, the notion of Arab control of the Red Sea must be seen in Washington and Tel Aviv as contrary to U.S. and Israeli interests. This may be a misreading of the policies and orientation of an independent Eritrean government, which, like the EPLF today, is likely to contain a majority of Christians. At any rate, the United States claims not to have supported the Eritreans and continues to oppose independence for Eritrea. Officials of the EPLF also deny that they have received U.S. support.

[3] World Bank, *World Development Report 1990: Poverty* (Washington, D.C.: World Bank, 1990). Data are drawn from this document.

[4] See William House, "Population, Poverty and Underdevelopment in the Southern Sudan" in *Journal of Modern African Studies*, Vol. 27, No. 2 (1989), p. 203, for this and other details on the economic status of the southern region of the Sudan.

[5] From Francis Deng, cited in John Prendergast, "Facilitating Famine and Civil War in the Sudan," *Transafrica Forum*, Vol. 6, Nos. 3 and 4 (1989), p. 19.

[6] Christopher Clapham, op. cit. from the Central Report to the 9th Regular Plenum of the Central Committee of the Workers Party of Ethiopia, Addis Ababa, November 1988.

[7] In a recent analysis of the Ethiopian economy, the World Bank reported that the ratio of debt service payments to exports was 44 per cent, one of the highest in the world.

[8] John Prendergast, op. cit., p. 24.

[9] President Mengistu announced in 1990 that he was implementing reforms that would in effect constitute an abandonment of Marxism and of villagization and would move Ethiopia toward a mixed economy. See, for example, *Africa Confidential* (May 1990), pp. 6–7.

# About the Overseas Development Council

The Overseas Development Council is a private non-profit organization established in 1969 for the purpose of increasing American understanding of the economic and social problems confronting the developing countries and of how their development progress is related to U.S. interests. Toward this end, the Council functions as a center for policy research and analysis, a forum for the exchange of ideas, and a resource for public education. The Council's current program of work encompasses four major issue areas: trade and industrial policy, international finance and investment, development strategies and development cooperation, and U.S. foreign policy and the developing countries. ODC's work is used by policymakers in the Executive Branch and the Congress, journalists, and those concerned about U.S.-Third World relations in corporate and bank management, international and non-governmental organizations, universities, and educational and action groups focusing on specific development issues. ODC's program is funded by foundations, corporations, and private individuals; its policies are determined by a governing Board and Council. In selecting issues and shaping its work program, ODC is also assisted by a standing Program Advisory Committee.

John W. Sewell is President of ODC. Victor H. Palmieri is Chairman of the ODC Board and Council, and Wayne Fredericks, Stephen J. Friedman, and Ruth J. Hinerfeld are Vice Chairmen.

Overseas Development Council
1717 Massachusetts Ave., N.W.
Washington, D.C. 20036
Tel. (202) 234-8701

# ODC Program Advisory Committee

**Chairman:**
**John P. Lewis**
*Woodrow Wilson School of Public
and International Affairs
Princeton University*

**Nancy Birdsall**
*The World Bank*

**Colin I. Bradford, Jr.**
*OECD Development Centre*

**Lawrence Brainard**
*Bankers Trust Company*

**Shahid Javed Burki**
*The World Bank*

**Mayra Buvinic**
*International Center for
Research on Women*

**Lincoln Chen**
*School of Public Health
Harvard University*

**Stanley Fischer**
*The World Bank*

**Albert Fishlow**
*University of California at Berkeley*

**James Galbraith**
*Lyndon B. Johnson School
of Public Affairs
University of Texas at Austin*

**Denis Goulet**
*University of Notre Dame*

**Davidson R. Gwatkin**
*International Health Policy Program
The World Bank*

**Catherine Gwin**
*The Rockefeller Foundation*

**Edward K. Hamilton**
*Hamilton, Rabinovitz, and
Alschuler, Inc.*

**Chandra Hardy**
*Washington, D.C.*

**G. K. Helleiner**
*University of Toronto*

**Albert Hirschman**
*Institute for Advanced Study
Princeton, New Jersey*

**Gary Horlick**
*O'Melveny and Myers*

**Michael Horowitz**
*Institute for Development Anthropology
and State University of New York
at Binghamton*

**Gary Hufbauer**
*School of Foreign Service
Georgetown University*

**Tony Killick**
*Overseas Development Institute*

**Paul R. Krugman**
*Massachusetts Institute
of Technology*

**John Mellor**
*International Food Policy
Research Institute*

**Theodore H. Moran**
*Landegger Program
School of Foreign Service
Georgetown University*

**Henry Nau**
*Elliott School of International
Affairs
The George Washington University*

**Maureen O'Neill**
*North-South Institute*

**Kenneth A. Oye**
*Swarthmore College*

**Dwight H. Perkins**
*Harvard Institute for
International Development*

**Gustav Ranis**
*Economic Growth Center
Yale University*

**Jeffrey Sachs**
*Harvard University*

**Ronald K. Shelp**
*New York City Partnership, Inc. &
New York Chamber of Commerce & Industry*

**Robert Solomon**
*The Brookings Institution*

**Lance Taylor**
*Massachusetts Institute of
Technology*

**Judith Tendler**
*Massachusetts Institute of
Technology*

**Norman Uphoff**
*Center for International Studies
Cornell University*

# The Series Editors

*After the Wars: Reconstruction in Aghanistan, Indochina, Central America, Southern Africa, and The Horn of Africa* is the sixteenth volume in the Overseas Development Council's policy book series, U.S.–Third World Policy Perspectives. The co-editors of the series, often collaborating with guest editors contributing to the series, are Valeriana Kallab and Richard E. Feinberg.

**Richard E. Feinberg** is Executive Vice President and Director of Studies of the Overseas Development Council. Before joining ODC in 1983, he served as the Latin American specialist on the Policy Planning Staff of the Department of State from 1977 to 1979, prior to which he worked as an international economist in the Treasury Department and with the House Banking Committee. Dr. Feinberg has published numerous articles and books on U.S. foreign policy, Latin American politics, and international economics in this series as well as *The Intemperate Zone: The Third World Challenge to U.S. Foreign Policy;* (as editor) *Central America: International Dimensions of the Crisis;* and *Subsidizing Success: The Export-Import Bank in the U.S. Economy.*

**Valeriana Kallab** is Vice President and Director of Publications of the Overseas Development Council. She has been responsible for ODC's published output since 1972. Before joining ODC, she was a research editor and a writer on international economic issues at the Carnegie Endowment for International Peace in New York. She was co-editor (with John P. Lewis) of *Development Strategies Reconsidered* and *U.S. Foreign Policy and the Third World: Agenda 1983;* and (with Guy Erb) of *Beyond Dependency: The Third World Speaks Out.*

# The Guest Editor and Authors

**Anthony Lake,** Guest Editor of this study, is Five College Professor of International Relations at Mount Holyoke College. From 1977–1981, he was Director of Policy Planning at the U.S. Department of State, and before that, a member of the National Security Council staff. He has also been director of the International Voluntary Services and of projects at the Carnegie Endowment for International Peace and the Council on Foreign Relations. Between 1963 and 1965, he served on the U.S. embassy staff in Hue and Saigon, Vietnam. His most recent book is *Somoza Falling.*

**Selig S. Harrison,** a Senior Associate of the Carnegie Endowment for International Peace, is the author of *In Afghanistan's Shadow* and four other books on Asian affairs. He has covered Pakistan, India, and Afghanistan as a foreign correspondent for *The Washington Post* and other publications for more than thirty years and has served as Senior Fellow In Charge of Asian Studies at The Brookings Institution; as a Professorial Lecturer in Asian Studies at The Johns Hopkins School of Advanced International Studies; and as a Senior Fellow at the East-West Center in Honolulu.

**Nayan Chanda,** Editor of the *Asian Wall Street Journal Weekly,* has published over nine hundred articles on Asian politics and development during his many years at the *Far Eastern Economic Review.* He has also contributed chapters to many books, including *Conflict Resolution in Kampuchea, Postwar Indochina: Old Enemies and New Allies,* and the forthcoming *Foreign Policies of Southeast Asia.* Until recently, he was a Senior Associate at the Carnegie Endowment for International Peace.

**Benjamin L. Crosby,** an ODC MacArthur Scholar in Residence in 1989-90, was previously Chief of Mission of the Central American Institute of Management (INCAE) in Ecuador and is a Professor at the Center for Political Economy at INCAE in San José, Costa Rica. His publications include (with Marc Lindenberg) *Managing Development: The Political Dimension,* and "Fragmentación y Realineamiento: Respuesta Política a la Crisis Centroamericana," in Forrest Colburn, ed., *Centroamerica: Estraategias para el Desarrollo.*

**Mark C. Chona**—an ODC MacArthur Scholar in Residence in 1989-90—was for many years political advisor to President Kaunda of Zambia. He is presently chairman of his own Zambian company, Sumika Investments Ltd., with interests in farming, banking, freight, and insurance. He serves as a director on a number of Zambian and international boards in industry and finance as well as on those of charitable organizations. He is also a council member of Copperbelt University in Zambia and a consultant engaged in the promotion of private investment and joint ventures in Africa. His is actively involved in the programs of a number of international organizations concerned with development and security issues in Africa.

**Jeffrey I. Herbst** is an Assistant Professor of Politics and International Affairs at Princeton University's Woodrow Wilson School of Public and International Affairs. He was a Fulbright Research Assistant at the University of Zimbabwe and recently conducted research in Ghana on the politics of economic reform. He is the author of *State Politics in Zimbabwe,* as well as several articles on politics in Southern Africa and on the dynamics of economic reform throughout the continent.

**Carol J. Lancaster** is an Assistant Professor in the School of Foreign Service of Georgetown University and a Visiting Fellow at the Institute for International Economics. She has formerly worked at the Office of Management and Budget and has served on the Policy Planning Staff of the Department of State and as a Deputy Assistant Secretary of State in the Bureau of African Affairs (1980–81). She was also a Congressional Fellow (1976–77). She has published in *Foreign Policy, Washington Quarterly,* and other journals and books. She co-edited *African Debt and Financing* (1986) and is currently writing a book on *Foreign Aid, Diplomacy and Development in Africa* for the Twentieth Century Fund.

# FROM CONFRONTATION TO COOPERATION? U.S. AND SOVIET AID TO DEVELOPING COUNTRIES

*Richard E. Feinberg, Ratchik M. Avakov, and contributors*

The waning of the Cold War opens up opportunities for the two superpowers to transform their relations with the Third World. The Soviet Union and the United States now both face the difficult political challenge of clearly defining and reaching domestic consensus on the purposes and priorities of their bilateral assistance programs. In this context of major rethinking, when new ideas are most welcome, this book makes a groundbreaking and valuable contribution in offering specific proposals for joint U.S.-U.S.S.R. cooperation with developing countries in the form of "triparite projects."

The study was prepared in 1988–90 by a group of American and Soviet development analysts under the joint auspices of the Overseas Development Council and the Institute of World Economy and International Relations (IMEMO) of the U.S.S.R. Academy of Sciences. The paired American and Soviet chapters—on development assistance themes selected as *perestroika* and *glasnost* were evolving in the Soviet Union—provide informative and interesting background for the new opportunities for tripartite cooperation outlined in the chapter by Arefieva and Bowles.

## Contents:

**Richard E. Feinberg** is executive Vice President and Director of Studies of the Overseas Development Council.

**Ratchik M. Avakov** Head of the Department of External and Political Relations of Developing Countries at the Institute of World Economy and International Relations (IMEMO) in Moscow.

U.S.-Third World Policy Perspectives, No. 15
December 1990, 256 pp.

ISBN: 0-88738-879-5 (cloth) $15.95
ISBN: 0-88738-391-2 (paper) $24.95

# ECONOMIC REFORM IN THREE GIANTS: U.S. FOREIGN POLICY AND THE USSR, CHINA, AND INDIA

*Richard E. Feinberg, John Echeverri-Gent, Friedemann Müller, and contributors*

Three of the largest and strategically most important nations in the world—the Soviet Union, China, and India—are currently in the throes of historic change. The reforms in the giants are transforming global economic and geopolitical relations. The United States must reexamine central tenets of its foreign policy if it is to seize the opportunities presented by these changes.

This pathbreaking study analyzes economic reform in the giants and its implications for U.S. foreign policy. It assesses the impact of the reforms on the livelihood of the nearly half the world's population living in their societies. Each of the giants is opening up its economy to foreign trade and investment. What consequences will this new outward orientation have for international trade, and how should U.S. policy respond to these developments? Each giant is attempting to catch up to global technological frontiers by absorbing foreign technologies; in what areas might cooperation enhance American interests, and in what areas must the U.S. protect its competitive and strategic assets? What role can key international economic institutions like the GATT, the IMF, and the World Bank play to help integrate the giants into the international economy?

Economic reform in the giants has important consequences for their political systems. What measures can and should the United States take to encourage political liberalization? How will the reforms affect the foreign policies of the giants, and what impact will this have on U.S. geopolitical interests?

The contributors suggest how U.S. foreign policy should anticipate these new circumstances in ways that enhance international cooperation and security.

---

**Richard E. Feinberg, John Echeverri-Gent, and Friedemann Müller—** Overview: Economic Reform in the Giants and U.S. Policy

**Friedemann Müller**—Economic Reform in the USSR

**Rensselaer W. Lee III**—Economic Reform in China

**John Echeverri-Gent**—Economic Reform in India

**John Echeverri-Gent, Friedemann Müller, and Rensselaer W. Lee III—** The Politics of Economic Reform in the Giants

**Richard P. Suttmeier**—Technology Transfer to the Giants: Opportunities and Challenges

**Elena Borisovna Arefieva**—The Geopolitical Consequences of Reform

---

**Richard E. Feinberg** is vice president of the Overseas Development Council and co-editor of the U.S.-Third World Policy Perspectives series. From 1977 to 1979, Feinberg was Latin American specialist on the policy planning staff of the U.S. Department of State.

**John Echeverri-Gent** is a visiting fellow at the Overseas Development Council and an assistant professor at the University of Virginia. His publications are in the fields of comparative public policy and the political economy of development in India.

**Friedemann Müller** is a visiting fellow at the Overseas Development Council and a senior research associate at Stiftung Wissenschaft und Politik, Ebenhausen, West Germany. His publications on the Soviet and Eastern European economies have focused on economic reform, energy policy, and East-West trade.

U.S.-Third World Policy Perspectives, No. 14
Winter 1989, 256 pp.

$24.95 (cloth)
$15.95 (paper)

# PULLING TOGETHER: THE INTERNATIONAL MONETARY FUND IN A MULTIPOLAR WORLD

*Catherine Gwin, Richard E. Feinberg, and contributors*

Side-stepped by the developed countries, entangled in unsuccessful programs in many Latin American and African nations, whipsawed by heavy but inconsistent pressure from commercial banks and creditor countries, and without effective leadership from its major shareholders, the IMF is losing its bearings. It needs a sharp course correction and a strong mandate from its member countries to adjust its policies on each of five criticial issues: global macroeconomic management, Third World debt, the resuscitation of development in the poorest countries, the integration of socialist nations into the global economy, and relations with its sister institution, the World Bank. In addition, the IMF needs to bolster its own bureaucratic, intellectual, and financial capacities.

In an economically interdependent but politically centrifugal world, a strong central institution is needed to help countries arrive at collective responses to complex global economic problems. But only if its member states are willing to delegate more authority to the IMF can it help pull together a multipolar world.

## Contents:
**Richard E. Feinberg and Catherine Gwin**—Overview: Reforming the Fund
**Jacques J. Polak**—Strengthening the Role of the IMF
  in the International Monetary System
**Peter B. Kenen**—The Use of IMF Credit
**Jeffrey D. Sachs**—Strengthening IMF Programs
  in Highly Indebted Countries
**Guillermo Ortiz**—The IMF and the Debt Strategy
**Louis M. Goreux**—The Fund and the Low-Income Countries

**Catherine Gwin,** guest co-editor of this volume, is currently the Special Program Advisor at the Rockefeller Foundation. In recent years, she has worked as a consultant on international economic and political affairs for The Ford Foundation, The Rockefeller Foundation, The Asia Society, and the United Nations. In the late 1970s and the early 1980s, she was a Senior Fellow at the Council on Foreign Relations and at the Carnegie Endowment for International Peace, where she directed the Study Group on international financial cooperation and developing-country debt. During the Carter administration, she served on the staff of the International Development Cooperation Agency (IDCA). Dr. Gwin has taught at the School of International Affairs at Columbia University and has written frequently on international development cooperation, the World Bank, and the International Monetary Fund.

**Richard E. Feinberg** is Executive Vice President and Director of Studies of the Overseas Development Council. Before joining ODC in 1983, he served as the Latin American specialist on the Policy Planning Staff of the Department of State from 1977 to 1979, prior to which he worked as an international economist in the Treasury Department and with the House Banking Committee. He has published numerous articles and books on U.S. foreign policy, Latin American politics, and international economics, including *The Intemperate Zone: The Third World Challenge to U.S. Foreign Policy*; and (as editor) *Central America: International Dimensions of the Crisis* and *Subsidizing Success: The Export-Import Bank in the U.S. Economy*.

U.S.-Third World Policy Perspectives, No. 13
1989, 188 pp.

ISBN: 0-88738-313-0 (cloth) $24.95
ISBN: 0-88738-819-1 (paper) $15.95

# ENVIRONMENT AND THE POOR: DEVELOPMENT STRATEGIES FOR A COMMON AGENDA

*H. Jeffrey Leonard and contributors*

Few aspects of development are as complex and urgent as the need to reconcile anti-poverty and pro-environmental goals. Do both of these important goals—poverty alleviation and environmental sustainability—come in the same package? Or are there necessary trade-offs and must painful choices be made?

A basic premise of this volume is that environmental degradation and intractable poverty are often especially pronounced in particular ecological and social settings across the developing world. These twin crises of development and the environment can and must be addressed jointly. But they require differentiated strategies for the kinds of physical environments in which poor people live. This study explores these concerns in relation to irrigated areas, arid zones, moist tropical forests, hillside areas, urban centers, and unique ecological settings.

The overview chapter highlights recent efforts to advance land and natural resource management, and some of the real and perceived conflicts between alleviating poverty and protecting the environment in the design and implementation of development policy. The chapters that follow offer economic investment and natural resource management options for reducing poverty and maintaining ecological balance for six different areas of the developing world.

Contents:

**H. Jeffrey Leonard,** guest editor of this volume, is the vice president of the World Wildlife Fund and The Conservation Foundation and Director of the Fairfield Osborn Center for Economic Development. Dr. Leonard has been at The Foundation since 1976. He is the author of several recent books, including *Pollution and the Struggle for the World Product, Natural Resources and Economic Development in Central America,* and *Are Environmental Regulations Driving U.S. Industries Overseas?* He is also editor of *Divesting Nature's Capital: The Political Economy of Environmental Abuse in the Third World* and *Business and Environment: Toward a Common Ground.*

U.S.-Third World Policy Perspectives, No. 11
1989, 256 pp.

ISBN: 0-88738-282-7 (cloth) $24.95
ISBN: 0-88738-786-1 (paper) $15.95

# FRAGILE COALITIONS:
# THE POLITICS OF ECONOMIC ADJUSTMENT

*Joan M. Nelson and contributors*

The global economic crisis of the 1980s forced most developing nations into a simultaneous quest for short-run economic stabilization and longer-run structural reforms. Effective adjustment is at least as much a political as an economic challenge. But political dimensions of adjustment have been much less carefully analyzed than have the economic issues.

Governments in developing countries must balance pressures from external agencies seeking more rapid adjustment in return for financial support, and the demands of domestic political groups often opposing such reforms. How do internal pressures shape external bargaining? and conversely, how does external influence shape domestic political maneuvering? Growing emphasis on "adjustment with a human face" poses additional questions: Do increased equity and political acceptability go hand in hand? or do more pro-poor measures add to the political difficulties of adjustment? The capacity of the state itself to implement adjustment measures varies widely among nations. How can external agencies take such differences more fully into account? The hopeful trend toward democratic openings in many countries raises further, crucial issues: What special political risks and opportunities confront governments struggling simultaneously with adjustment and democratization?

The contributors to this volume explore these issues and their policy implications for the United States and for the international organizations that seek to promote adjustment efforts.

**Contents:**

**Joan M. Nelson** has been a visiting fellow at the Overseas Development Council since 1982; since mid-1986, she has directed a collegial research program on the politics of economic adjustment. She has been a consultant for the World Bank, the Agency for International Development, and for the International Monetary Fund, as well as a staff member of USAID. In the 1970s and early 1980s, she taught at the Massachusetts Institute of Technology, the Johns Hopkins University School of Advanced International Studies, and Princeton University's Woodrow Wilson School. She has published books and articles on development assistance and policy dialogue, political participation, migration and urban politics in developing nations, and the politics of economic stabilization and reform.

U.S.-Third World Policy Perspectives, No. 12
1989, 186 pp.

ISBN: 0-88738-283-5 (cloth) $24.95
ISBN: 0-88738-787-X (paper) $15.95

# BETWEEN TWO WORLDS:
# THE WORLD BANK'S NEXT DECADE
*Richard E. Feinberg and contributors*

In the midst of the global debt and adjustment crises, the World Bank has been challenged to become the leading agency in North-South finance and development. The many dimensions of this challenge—which must be comprehensively addressed by the Bank's new president assuming office in mid-1986—are the subject of this important volume.

As mediator between international capital markets and developing countries, the World Bank will be searching for ways to renew the flow of private credit and investment to Latin America and Africa. And as the world's premier development agency, the Bank can help formulate growth strategies appropriate to the 1990s.

The Bank's ability to design and implement a comprehensive response to these global needs is threatened by competing objectives and uncertain priorities. Can the Bank design programs attractive to private investors that also serve the very poor? Can it emphasize efficiency while transferring technologies that maximize labor absorption? Can it more aggressively condition loans on policy reforms without attracting the criticism that has accompanied IMF programs?

The contributors to this volume assess the role that the World Bank can play in the period ahead. They argue for new financial and policy initiatives and for new conceptual approaches to development, as well as for a restructuring of the Bank, as it takes on new, systemic responsibilities in the next decade.

**Contents:**

**Richard E. Feinberg**—Overview: The Future of the World Bank
**Gerald K. Helleiner**—The Changing Content of Conditionality
**Joan M. Nelson**—The Diplomacy of the Policy-Based Lending:
  Leverage or Dialogue?
**Sheldon Annis**—The Shifting Ground of Poverty Lending
**Howard Pack**—Employment Generation Through Changing Technology
**John F. H. Purcell and Michelle B. Miller**—The World Bank and Private International
  Capital
**Charles R. Blitzer**—Financing the IBRD and IDA

**Richard E. Feinberg** is Executive Vice President and Director of Studies of the Overseas Development Council. From 1977 to 1979, Feinberg was Latin American specialist on the policy planning staff of the U.S. Department of State. He has also served as an international economist in the U.S. Treasury Department and with the House Banking Committee. He is currently also adjunct professor of international finance at the Georgetown University School of Foreign Service. Feinberg is the author of numerous books as well as journal and newspaper articles on U.S. foreign policy, Latin American politics, and international economics.

ISBN: 0-88738-123-5 (cloth)                    $19.95
ISBN: 0-88738-665-2 (paper)                    $12.95
**June 1986**                                  208 pp.

# STRENGTHENING THE POOR: WHAT HAVE WE LEARNED?

*John P. Lewis and contributors*

**"bound to influence policymakers and make a major contribution to renewed efforts to reduce poverty"**
—B. T. G. Chidzero, Minister of Finance, Economic Planning, and Development, Government of Zimbabwe

**"deserves wide readership within the broader development community"**
—Barber B. Conable, President, The World Bank

The issue of poverty alleviation—of strengthening the poor—is now being brought back toward the top of the development policy agenda.

The current refocusing on poverty is not just a matter of turning back the clock. Anti-poverty initiatives for the 1990s must respond to a developing world and a policy environment that in many ways differs dramatically from that of the 1970s and even the 1980s. Much has been accomplished during and since the last thrust of anti-poverty policy. The poor themselves have in some cases become more vocal, organized, and effective in pressing their own priorities. A great deal of policy experience has accrued. And national governments, donor agencies, and non-governmental organizations now employ a much wider range of tools for poverty alleviation.

*Strengthening the Poor* provides a timely assessment of these changes and experience. In an overview essay, John Lewis draws important policy lessons both from poverty alleviation's period of high salience in the 1970s and from its time of lowered attention in the adjustment-accentuating 1980s. An impressive cluster of U.S. and developing-country authors react to these propositions from diverse points of view.

---

**Contents:**

---

U.S.-Third World Policy Perspectives, No. 10
1988, 256 pp.

ISBN: 0-88738-267-3 (cloth) $19.95
ISBN: 0-88738-768-3 (paper) $12.95

# GROWTH, EXPORTS, AND JOBS IN A CHANGING WORLD ECONOMY: AGENDA 1988

*John W. Sewell, Stuart K. Tucker, and contributors*

"particularly timely, as the Administration and Congress face critical decisions on the trade bill, the budget, and other issues affecting the economic future of the U.S. and countries around the globe"
—Frank C. Carlucci, Secretary of Defense

*Agenda 1988,* the eleventh of ODC's well-known assessments of U.S. policy toward the developing countries, contributes uniquely to the ongoing debate on U.S. jobs and trade competition with other nations.

The administration that takes office in 1989 faces a situation without precedent in the post-1945 period. Like many developing countries, the United States has to balance its trade accounts, service its foreign debts, and rebuild its industrial base. The challenge is twofold.

The immediate task is to restore the international economic position of the United States by taking the lead in devising measures to support renewed *global* growth, especially rapid growth in the developing countries.

Meanwhile, however, the world is on the threshold of a Third Industrial Revolution. Rapid technological advances are radically changing the familiar economic relationships between developed and developing countries. The kinds of policies needed to adjust to these technology-driven changes— policies on education, training, research and development—generally have longer lead times than the immediate measures needed to stimulate global growth. In the next four years, the United States must therefore proceed on *both* fronts at the same time.

**John W. Sewell**—Overview: The Dual Challenge: Managing the Economic Crisis and Technological Change
**Manuel Castells and Laura D'Andrea Tyson**—High-Technology Choices Ahead: Restructuring Interdependence
**Jonathan D. Aronson**—The Service Industries: Growth, Trade, and Development Prospects
**Robert L. Paarlberg**—U.S. Agriculture and the Developing World: Opportunities for Joint Gains
**Raymond F. Mikesell**—The Changing Demand for Industrial Raw Materials
**Ray Marshall**—Jobs: The Shifting Structure of Global Employment
**Stuart K. Tucker**—Statistical Annexes: U.S.-Third World Interdependence, 1988

**John W. Sewell** has been president of the Overseas Development Council since January, 1980. From 1977 to 1979, as the Council's executive vice president, he directed ODC's programs of research and public education. Prior to joining the Council in 1971, Mr. Sewell directed the communications program of the Brookings Institution. He also served in the Foreign Service of the United States. A contributor to past *Agenda* assessments, he is co-author of *Rich Country Interests and Third World Development* and *The Ties That Bind: U.S. Interests in Third World Development.* He is a frequent author and lecturer on U.S. relations with the developing countries.

**Stuart K. Tucker** is a fellow at the Overseas Development Council. Prior to joining ODC in 1984, he was a research consultant for the Inter-American Development Bank. He has written on U.S. international trade policy, including the linkage between the debt crisis and U.S. exports and jobs. He also prepared the Statistical Annexes in ODC's *Agenda 1985-86.*

U.S.-Third World Policy Perspectives, No. 9
1988, 286 pp.

ISBN: 088738-196-0 (cloth) $19.95
ISBN: 0-88738-718-7 (paper) $12.95

# THE UNITED STATES AND MEXICO: FACE TO FACE WITH NEW TECHNOLOGY

*Cathryn L. Thorup and contributors*

Rapid technological advance is fast changing economic and political relations between industrial and advanced developing countries. The new technologies encompass innovations in automation and robotization, the substitution of synthetic for natural materials, advances in communications and information technology, and changes in social organization. These advances are transforming production, trade, and investment in manufactures, commodities, and services—with major repercussions on jobs, wages, and politics in many countries.

This study explores what adjustment to this worldwide transformation means close to home—for people and policies in Mexico and the United States, and for relations between the two nations.

The authors come from both sides of the border—bringing together varied experience and expertise from government, business, and academic institutions. They highlight the interplay of economic, political, social, and cultural forces in the process of technological change. Among the themes they explore are the relationships between technological advance and employment, immigration, foreign debt, and protectionism. From their analysis of the objectives and policies of both countries emerge insights into the politics of technology change—the policy constraints faced in each country, the limits of political will, and the changing horizons of domestic interest groups.

The study draws together specific recommendations on improving the efficiency of bilateral economic interaction, reducing the adjustment costs of technological change, and avoiding diplomatic tensions between the two nations.

---

Contents:

---

**Cathryn L. Thorup** is the director of the U.S.-Mexico Project of the Overseas Development Council. Prior to joining ODC in 1980, she spent six years in Mexico, studying and working as a journalist for the Mexican news magazine *Razones*. She has written extensively on U.S. policymaking toward Mexico, conflict management in U.S.-Mexican relations, regional security, and Mexican economic and political reform. Ms. Thorup is a member of the Board of Directors of the Consortium for U.S. Research Programs for Mexico (PROFMEX).

---

ISBN:0-88738-663-6 (paper)
October 1987

$12.95
No. 8, 238 pp.

# INVESTING IN DEVELOPMENT: NEW ROLES FOR PRIVATE CAPITAL?

*Theodore H. Moran and contributors*

The tone of the debate about foreign direct investment in Third World development has changed dramatically since the 1970s. There are expectations in both North and South that multinational corporations can play a key role in restoring growth, replacing aid, providing capital to relieve the burden on commercial bank lending, and (together with the private sectors in the local economies) lead to an era of healthier and more balanced growth.

To what extent are these expectations justified? This volume provides a reassessment of the impact of multinational corporate operations on Third World development. It covers not only direct equity investment in natural resources and manufacturing, but non-equity arrangements extending to agriculture and other sectors as well. It examines whether the efforts of less developed countries to attract and control multinational corporations have constituted a serious "distortion" of trade that threatens jobs in the home nations. It analyzes the link between international companies and the "umbrella" of World Bank co-financing as a mechanism to reduce risk. Finally, it attempts to estimate how much of the "gap" in commercial bank lending might plausibly be filled by direct corporate investment over the next decade.

In each case, it draws policy conclusions for host governments, for home governments (focused particularly on the United States), for multilateral institutions such as the World Bank and the agencies of the United Nations, and for the multinational firms themselves.

## Contents

**Theodore H. Moran** is director of Georgetown University's Landegger Program in International Business Diplomacy as well as professor and member of the Executive Council of the Georgetown University School of Business Administration. A former member of the Policy Planning Staff of the Department of State with responsibilities including investment issues, Dr. Moran has since 1971 been a consultant to corporations, governments, and multilateral agencies on investment strategy, international negotiations, and political risk assessment. His publications include many articles and five major books on the issues explored in this new volume. He is a member of the ODC Program Advisory Committee.

ISBN: 0-88738-044-3 (cloth)                          **$19.95**
ISBN: 0-88738-644-X (paper)                          **$12.95**

# DEVELOPMENT STRATEGIES RECONSIDERED

## *John P. Lewis and Valeriana Kallab, editors*

**"First-rate, comprehensive analysis—presented in a manner that makes it extremely valuable to policy makers."**
—Robert R. Nathan
Robert Nathan Associates

Important differences of opinion are emerging about the national strategies best suited for advancing economic growth and equity in the difficult global adjustment climate of the late 1980s.

Proponents of the "new orthodoxy"—the perspective headquartered at the World Bank and favored by the Reagan administration as well as by a number of other bilateral donor governments—are "carrying forward with redoubled vigor the liberalizing, pro-market strains of the thinking of the 1960s and 1970s. They are very mindful of the limits of government." And they are "emphatic in advocating export-oriented growth to virtually all comers."

Other prominent experts question whether a standardized prescription of export-led growth can meet the needs of big low-income countries in the latter 1980s as well as it did those of small and medium-size middle-income countries in the 1960s and 1970s. They are concerned about the special needs of low-income Africa. And they see a great deal of unfinished business under the heading of poverty and equity.

In this volume, policy syntheses are proposed to reconcile the goals of growth, equity, and adjustment; to strike fresh balances between agricultural and industrial promotion and between capital and other inputs; and to reflect the interplay of democracy and development.

## Contents:

**John P. Lewis**—Overview —Development Promotion: A Time for Regrouping
**Irma Adelman**—A Poverty-Focused Approach to Development Policy
**John W. Mellor**—Agriculture on the Road to Industrialization
**Jagdish N. Bhagwati**—Rethinking Trade Strategy
**Leopoldo Solis and Aurelio Montemayor**—A Mexican View of the Choice Between Inward and Outward Orientation
**Colin I. Bradford, Jr.**—East Asian "Models": Myths and Lessons
**Alex Duncan**—Aid Effectiveness in Raising Adaptive Capacity in the Low-Income Countries
**Atul Kohli**—Democracy and Development

---

**John P. Lewis** is Professor of Economics and International Affairs at Princeton University's Woodrow Wilson School of Public and International Affairs. He is simultaneously senior advisor to the Overseas Development Council and chairman of its Program Advisory Committee. From 1979 to 1981, Dr. Lewis was chairman of the OECD's Development Assistance Committee (DAC). From 1982 to 1985, he was chairman of the three-year World Bank/IMF Task Force on Concessional Flows. He has served as a member of the U.N. Committee for Development Planning. For many years, he has alternated between academia and government posts (as Member of the Council of Economic Advisors, 1963-64, and Director of the USAID Mission to India, 1964-69), with collateral periods of association with The Brookings Institution, The Ford Foundation, and the World Bank.

**Valeriana Kallab** is vice president and director of publications of the Overseas Development Council and series co-editor of the ODC's U.S.-Third World Policy Perspectives series. She has been responsible for ODC's published output since 1972. Before joining ODC, she was a research editor and writer on international economic issues at the Carnegie Endowment for International Peace in New York.

---

U.S.-Third World Policy Perspectives, No. 5
1986, 208 pp.

ISBN: 0-88738-044-1 (cloth) $19.95
ISBN: 0-87855-991-4 (paper) $12.95

# HARD BARGAINING AHEAD: U.S. TRADE POLICY AND DEVELOPING COUNTRIES

*Ernest H. Preeg and contributors*

U.S.-Third World trade relations are at a critical juncture. Trade conflicts are exploding as subsidies, import quotas, and "voluntary" export restraints have become commonplace. The United States is struggling with record trade and budget deficits. Developing countries, faced with unprecedented debt problems, continue to restrain imports and stimulate exports.

For both national policies and future multilateral negotiations, the current state of the North-South trade relationship presents a profound dilemma. Existing problems of debt and unemployment cannot be solved without growth in world trade. While many developing countries would prefer an export-oriented development strategy, access to industrialized-country markets will be in serious doubt if adjustment policies are not implemented. Consequently, there is an urgent need for more clearly defined mutual objectives and a strengthened policy framework for trade between the industrialized and the developing countries.

In this volume, distinguished practitioners and academics identify specific policy objectives for the United States on issues that will be prominent in the new round of GATT negotiations.

**Contents:**

**Ernest H. Preeg,** a career foreign service officer and recent visiting fellow at the Overseas Development Council, has had long experience in trade policy and North-South economic relations. He was a member of the U.S. delegation to the GATT Kennedy Round of negotiations and later wrote a history and analysis of those negotiations, *Traders and Diplomats* (The Brookings Institution, 1969). Prior to serving as American ambassador to Haiti (1981-82), he was deputy chief of mission in Lima, Peru (1977-80), and deputy secretary of state for international finance and development (1976-77).

ISBN: 0-88738-043-3 (cloth)
ISBN: 0-87855-987-6 (paper)
**1985**

**$19.95**
**$12.95**
**220 pp.**

# UNCERTAIN FUTURE: COMMERCIAL BANKS AND THE THIRD WORLD

*Richard E. Feinberg and Valeriana Kallab, editors*

> "useful short papers by people of differing backgrounds who make quite different kinds of suggestions about how banks, governments and international bodies ought to behave in the face of the continuing debt difficulties"
> —*Foreign Affairs*

> "the very best available to academia and the general public . . . on the criteria of reader interest, clarity of writing, quality of the research, and on that extra something special that sets a work apart from others of similar content"
> —James A. Cox, Editor
> *The Midwest Book Review*

The future of international commercial lending to the Third World has become highly uncertain just when the stakes seem greatest for the banks themselves, the developing countries, and the international financial system. Having become the main channel for the transfer of capital from the North to the South in the 1970s, how will the banks respond in the period ahead, when financing will be urgently needed?

The debt crisis that burst onto the world stage in 1982 is a long-term problem. New bank lending to many developing countries has slowed to a trickle. The combination of high interest rates and the retrenchment in bank lending is draining many developing countries of badly needed development finance. While major outright defaults now seem improbable, heightened conflict between creditors and debtors is possible unless bold actions are taken soon.

New approaches must take into account the interests of both the banks and developing-country borrowers. No single solution can by itself resolve the crisis. A battery of measures is needed—reforms in macroeconomic management, in the policies of the multilateral financial institutions, in bank lending practices as well as information gathering and analysis, and in regulation.

Contents:

**Richard E. Feinberg**—Overview: Restoring Confidence in International Credit Markets
**Lawrence J. Brainard**—More Lending to the Third World? A Banker's View
**Karin Lissakers**—Bank Regulation and International Debt
**Christine A. Bogdanowicz-Bindert and Paul M. Sacks**—The Role of Information: Closing the Barn Door?
**George J. Clark**—Foreign Banks in the Domestic Markets of Developing Countries
**Catherine Gwin**—The IMF and the World Bank: Measures to Improve the System
**Benjamin J. Cohen**—High Finance, High Politics

ISBN: 0-88738-041-7 (cloth)
ISBN: 0-87855-989-2 (paper)
**1984**

**$19.95**
**$12.95**
**144 pp.**

# ADJUSTMENT CRISIS IN THE THIRD WORLD

*Richard E. Feinberg and Valeriana Kallab, editors*

> "major contribution to the literature on the adjustment crisis"
> —B. T. G. Chidzero
> Minister of Finance, Economic Planning
> and Development Government of Zimbabwe

> "The adjustment crisis book has really stirred up some excitement here"
> —Peter P. Waller
> German Development Institute (Berlin)

> "good collection of papers"
> —*Foreign Affairs*

Just how the debt and adjustment crisis of Third World countries is handled, by them and by international agencies and banks, can make a big difference in the pace and quality of *global* recovery.

Stagnating international trade, sharp swings in the prices of key commodities, worsened terms of trade, high interest rates, and reduced access to commercial bank credits have slowed and even reversed growth in many Third World countries. Together, these trends make "adjustment" of both demand and supply a central problem confronting policy makers in most countries in the mid-1980s. Countries must bring expenditures into line with shrinking resources in the short run, but they also need to alter prices and take other longer-range steps to expand the resource base in the future—to stimulate investment, production, and employment. Already low living standards make this an especially formidable agenda in most Third World nations.

What can be done to forestall the more conflictive phase of the debt crisis that now looms ahead? How can developing countries achieve adjustment *with growth?* The contributors to this volume share the belief that more constructive change is possible and necessary.

Contents:

ISBN: 0-88738-040-9 (cloth)
ISBN: 0-87855-988-4 (paper)
1984

$19.95
$12.95
220 pp.